Not So Golden After All

The Rise and Fall of California

Not So Golden After All

The Rise and Fall of California

Larry N. Gerston

CRC Press
Taylor & Francis Group
Boca Raton   London   New York

CRC Press is an imprint of the
Taylor & Francis Group, an **Informa** business

CRC Press
Taylor & Francis Group
6000 Broken Sound Parkway NW, Suite 300
Boca Raton, FL 33487-2742

© 2012 by Taylor & Francis Group, LLC
CRC Press is an imprint of Taylor & Francis Group, an Informa business

No claim to original U.S. Government works

International Standard Book Number: 978-1-4398-8012-8 (Hardback)

Visit the Taylor & Francis Web site at
http://www.taylorandfrancis.com

and the CRC Press Web site at
http://www.crcpress.com

For Gia Gabriella Gerston

California's future lies in your hands and those of your fellow toddlers.

Contents

SECTION IV   Restoring the Dream

Preface

What makes California tick—or not? How do we account for the many contradictions that intersect in one special place? *Not So Golden After All: The Rise and Fall of California* attempts to tell the story of the dream, decay, and desperate hope to restore the sheen of this once glistening paradise.

Some love it, some loathe it, and many are in awe of it. Say what you will, but California is a land of mystery, magic, and most recently, malfunction. This is the place where outcomes rarely live up to expectations, while the unanticipated occurs with uncanny regularity. Opportunity and obstacles are the tension points in a political environment dominated by rigid extremes. If you're looking for "normal," look elsewhere. If you're looking for a rich, yet discordant collision of culture, economy, and politics that links the Pacific Rim with the rest of the nation and the world, you belong in California. No other state is simultaneously so compelling and yet appalling.

All these attributes combine to make California exotic and attractive—but much more so for the casual voyeur than the resident trying to climb a ladder with endless rungs. In fact, the real California is a place where people commonly have two jobs just to keep a step ahead of financial calamity, where kids drop out of school at rates well beyond the national average, where congested roads chew up huge portions of the workday (and one's car!), where farmers and environmentalists battle over valuable drops of water, where big business roils against excessive taxation while actually benefitting from creative tax breaks, where countless special interests protect themselves and no one else, and where today's immigrants serve as the doormats for yesterday's immigrants-turned-citizens.

All this occurs in an environment where the differences between those who have and those who don't seemingly grow before your very eyes. Year after year, state policymakers struggle to cobble together budgets that are underfunded and overcommitted. As they endeavor to find the balance, our elected officials strip away major chunks of the state's safety net, whether in the form of support for K–12 public education, higher education, the increasingly tattered infrastructure, or services for the old, the young, and the infirm. In fact, California has become the poster child for shortsighted governance.

Some people say that the state's many challenges make California ungovernable, and that its best days are long gone in a region with an economy equal to the eighth-largest nation in the world. Still others fervently cling to the hope that the best is yet to come in a place where, historically, anything seemed possible and, more times than not, seemed to come true. Yet out of this debate, one fact is certain: California rarely lives up to its potential and repeatedly beats down its believers. It is the land of unfulfilled dreams and diminished returns.

Not answered in this riddle is the question of whether the people and politics weigh down this unusual piece of real estate or whether the political system and its poorly organized government promote a fractured polity. We know this much—that with so many powerful groups taking their bite out of the state's political process, politics in the state are as dismembered as everything else. A large part of the problem is that California suffers from a 21st-century society operating within the framework of a 19th-century political system.

All of which takes us to *Not So Golden After All: The Rise and Fall of California,* an effort designed to describe California's ascendance and decline. Step by step, the book discusses the many historical developments that led California to its present dysfunctional condition and what, if anything, can be done to change course.

Can this state be saved? Can Californians collectively find a way to recapture some of the state's glorious past? Only if Californians are prepared to sacrifice in ways that most people have eschewed in recent years.

Acknowledgments

Several people offered their wisdom and guidance along the road to this book. Particularly valuable assistance came from Scott Budman, business and technology reporter at NBC, Bay Area; Terry Christensen, professor of political science at San Jose State University; Peter Detwiler, consultant to the California State Senate Committee on Local Government; Kevin Starr, California State Librarian Emeritus and professor of history at the University of Southern California; and Robert Stern, former counsel to the Fair Political Practices Commission.

At Taylor & Francis, thanks go to all the people involved in the editing/production process. Special thanks to Lara Zoble, associate editor, who believed in this project and shepherded it through the process from beginning to end. Also, I extend appreciation to Katherine Younce, project coordinator; Elise Weinger, cover designer; Mimi Williams, manager, production and editing; Stephany Wilken, copywriting manager; Bill Pacheco, copywriter, Pam Morrell, typesetter, and Chris Manion, senior marketing manager.

Finally, my deepest gratitude goes to Elisa Gerston, spouse and in-house editor-in-chief, who painstakingly went over every word of every draft in hopes of saving her husband from countless examples of questionable writing.

The Author

Larry Gerston is a professor of political science at San Jose State University and the political analyst at NBC11 (the Bay Area NBC station). He has written ten other books in addition to *Not So Golden After All: The Rise and Fall of California*, including *Politics in the Golden State, Recall!*, and *California Politics and Government* (all with Terry Christensen).

In addition to his larger works, Gerston has penned more than 100 op-ed columns in newspapers including the *San Jose Mercury News, San Francisco Chronicle*, and *Los Angeles Times*. Frequently interviewed for his political insight, he has appeared on *NBC Nightly News*, BBC, NPR, and CNN's *Inside Politics*.

Section I

The Setting

1

California Dreaming — Not!

Toto, I don't think we're in Kansas anymore!

—Dorothy, in *The Wizard of Oz*

With that startling revelation, Dorothy and her dog, Toto, began their magical, yet uncertain journey to Emerald City in *The Wizard of Oz*. Catapulted in a dream from placid, drab Kansas to colorful, exotic Munchkinland courtesy of a mighty tornado, the story's protagonist discovers an entirely new world. From her adventure, of course, Dorothy concludes that "home" is a lot more than she had given credit. That stark comparison and endless challenges leading up to the conclusion keep the movie audience on the edge of their seats for the rest of the story—but it's just that, a story.

California is neither dustbowl Kansas nor bizarre Munchkinland. If anything, it's a tad closer to the unpredictable and mysterious Emerald City, the over-the-top venue where Dorothy meets the almighty Wizard who seems to manipulate everything and everyone from behind the infamous green curtain while, in reality, owning only the empty power of illusion. But that's where the comparison ends. Conditions in California are often orchestrated inexplicably in ways that few people ever truly comprehend, giving a not so kind political affirmation to legendary economist Adam Smith's invisible hand.

But the greatest significance of *The Wizard of Oz* comparison lies in the extent to which the dream many call California is so far removed from reality. Like the disconnect between Dorothy's daily routine and her fantasy world, California is anything but what most people think, especially voyeur non-Californians who rely on television commercials and romance novels as their sources of truth and inspiration. In fact, in many ways the state is a big tease: It offers enormous potential for a few and deep disappointment for many others.

Even the origin of California's name has a sense of allure. "California" first appeared in a Spanish romance novel written by Garci Rodriguez de Montalvo in 1510. In the book, California is described as an imaginary island, an earthly paradise somewhere east of Asia. When Spanish explorers discovered the southwest coast and inland areas of the North American continent later in the 16th century, they attached "California" as the name of the land mass. It made sense because they could reach this new "island" only by ship. For many, few attributes about California have made sense since.

Rather than pure allure, California is a place of extremes, unfulfilled hopes, and unsolved mysteries. Just when you think you have the place and its people figured out, Californians do something totally out of character. Just when you anticipate that the economy will soar, a major company moves out, an exotic insect invasion upsets the state's delicate agricultural equilibrium, or Mother Nature wreaks havoc with drought or a devastating earthquake that rips apart the dilapidated infrastructure.

So, why is it so difficult to wrap your arms around California? Maybe it's because there is no one overriding characteristic that defines the place. Maybe it's because California is a poorly stitched sociological quilt of equally poorly fitting pieces. Maybe it's because California's awkward collection of earthquake faults, topographical extremes, clashing cultures, and weather excesses symbolize a state perpetually strained at the edges, with occasionally powerful forces pushing it to the brink of total political meltdown. Whatever the reasons, California doesn't easily fit any one particular description. It's all of the above and more, and at the same time so much less.

The discordant linkages between the social, economic, and political strands of California are almost too many to mention, but here are a few contemporary examples of the contradictions that dominate the state:

- We embrace cutting-edge science like nanotechnology, cleantech, and stem cell research, yet rank dead last of the 50 states in the availability of classroom personal computers.
- We rely on illegal immigrants to perform countless vocational tasks on the bottom rungs of the economic latter, yet refuse to grant them driver's licenses to get to their jobs.

- We pride ourselves for being stewards of the environment, yet operate more emissions-polluting automobiles per capita than any state or country in the world.
- We're the eighth-largest economy in the world, yet can't manage to balance a state budget without transparent gimmicks that fool virtually no one.
- In a state where water may be its most precious resource, farmers tend to plant the most water-intensive crops.
- In terms of per capita income, California ranks 10th of the 50 states; in terms of per capita philanthropic commitments, California ranks 42nd.
- In the same election, we spurn gay marriage as an affront to social values while establishing new protective housing standards for chickens awaiting slaughter.

Welcome to California. Have a good look around, but don't get too comfortable with what you see, for the directions we take tomorrow may be very different from where we go today. The only continuity is California's profound lack of continuity. You can never quite get your arms around the behemoth, but don't get in its way. Endless combinations of frivolousness and gravitas produce unpredictable yet explosive outcomes. It's in this setting where a few of us thrive, while most of us struggle to get by.

Behemoth. Perhaps that's as good a description as any other of what devotees have long called the "Golden State." Like a beast, California is both large and powerful, but often unmanageable and out of control. It's so unwieldy that on more than 200 occasions since the state's formation in 1850, there have been serious movements to break up the nation's third-largest state land mass into smaller, more governable political units.[1] Of course, such an outcome would never gain the constitutionally required congressional approval. After all, why would anyone in his or her right mind cede more national representation to an area of the country that is so dysfunctional?

But along with its strength and largesse, California is incredibly fragile. The state's complex foundation is so weak that it's always on the verge of falling apart because of its many fissures. We may never be able to fully control the beast, but we can try to better understand it. That's our task here.

What does the fabric of the state have to do with California's politics? Everything. With little tradition or continuity, California often drifts—and sometimes swerves—in strange directions. Few long-time family dynasties, historical themes, or political customs keep the state on a steady course. Fads overpower the treasures of tradition. More often than not, politics seem an awkward blend of protecting the status quo and promoting powerful interests at the expense of the rest of society. Forces representing the common good tend to come in a distant third in this horse race, leaving gridlock as the true winner to the delight of the prevailing forces.

All this takes a toll on the state's political environment and its people, even if they don't always appreciate the cost. The policymaking process in Sacramento is so dysfunctional that legislators and the governor often shunt aside the most significant public policy decisions to the voters in the form of cumbersome ballot propositions, leaving a confused and uninformed public seemingly in charge. Why, many critics demand of the legislature, are you asking *us* to do the things that we elect *you* to do? Elected officials often mumble in response their desire to let the "people" speak their minds as they run from responsibility.

In the end, however, more times than not the voters are manipulated by powerful interest groups who, although officially outside of the policymaking process, play huge roles in election outcomes through campaign contributions and management. Like the puppeteer and his marionette, interest groups and their lobbyists often pull the strings more skillfully than the Wizard of Oz ever dreamed. The bottom line is that what you think you see in California politics is far from what you actually get. No wonder so many Californians scratch their heads in disgust. No wonder so many give up. No wonder so many are leaving the state.

THE TURNSTILE SOCIETY

The old joke is that you're officially a native Californian as soon as you have unpacked your U-Haul that has brought your possessions from another state or country. Like many attempts at humor, there's a good bit of truth to the line. The movement of people is a key element of the state's DNA and helps to define California's ever-changing economy, social mores, and political culture. Percentage-wise, fewer Californians are born in California than the populations of almost any other state. That fact alone helps us understand the state's lack of core and rag-tag appreciation of history. Everyone has a different memory set framed, in part, by their pre-California experiences that brought them here.

Comings and Goings

California is also a two-way magnet for other states. A large number of residents come from other states in hopes of getting a fresh start free of snow and absent from rust belt economy woes. They view the state's abundant sunshine and available land as their guiding light to begin anew. The numbers are dramatic. U.S. Census Bureau statistics show that between 1995 and 2000, nearly 1.5 million people moved to California from other states, second only to the 1.9 million who moved to Florida. Unlike the retiree-oriented Florida influx, however, the new Californians came to join the labor force—or at least hoped to. Little did they realize that the state's unemployment figures routinely exceed the national average, especially in recent years.

Those who do attain success in California often do so at a steep price. While the state may be spacious, its land is extremely expensive, rendering the possibility of home ownership only a dream for many and little more. According to 2010 U.S. Census Bureau data, of the 50 states, California ranks 49th in homeownership; 55 percent of the state's residents own homes, compared to 67 percent across the nation. The inability to buy a home—or hold on to it while attempting to ride out a miserable economy—is an early source of disappointment, especially for the newcomer. In 2010, while 21.5 percent of the nation's homes were worth less than what buyers owned, in California 33 percent of all residential properties were "underwater."[2] During the same year, California ranked third in the nation in home foreclosures, with one of every 25 families forced to leave their homes.[3] That's upheaval almost beyond belief.

There are other obstacles. The high cost of living and limited employment prospects present stark realities, especially to California transplants who came here expecting unbridled opportunity. It has been so difficult in recent years that waves of Californians have begun to move elsewhere. Between 2000 and 2009, California grew by 3 million people, most of whom were born here. The data is most interesting in terms of who came and left. The state had a net gain of 300,000 arrivals, but the numbers show tremendous volatility with respect to composition. About 1.8 million people arrived from other countries; meanwhile, 1.5 million Californians left for other states, eclipsed only by New York, which lost 1.7 million residents to other states. For those who departed, the allure of the "Golden State" delivered "fool's gold" and little else.

These massive turnstile-like movements generate a unique transient quality for the state. No other part of the country exhibits such dramatic population gyrations both in and out at the same time. As a result, developing a relationship with your neighbor in California is almost self-defeating because the person with whom you share a fence today may well move far away tomorrow.

It's not much different in the workplace, where people motor individually to and from their jobs, totally removed from the kind of interaction that might occur on a train or subway. Roots are shallow in this state and friendships are brief. It's very difficult for people to connect socially and therefore politically. Sure, a few cities—historically San Francisco and belatedly Los Angeles—have addressed mass transit, but the long distances between homes and work don't make such transportation economically viable. Here the intersection between individualism and alienation creates an unusual social phenomenon described by Robert Putnam as "social disconnectedness."[4] As a result, few people are wed to long-term commitments, whether in the form of rebuilding the state's teetering infrastructure or contributing to philanthropic causes. After all, why get involved if you have little history or even less of a future? Such are the political obstacles in a state constructed of weak social fabric. They result is a weave so loose that few threads ever form any fiber. We all pay the price in the form of a society with little agreement and less direction.

Uneven Opportunities and Consequences

A glance at immigration patterns shows the extent to which California has become an incredibly diverse society with equally complex issues. It's a mini United Nations of sorts with challenges similar to those experienced in that august body. Many pay a steep price. Consider the public schools, essential building blocks for any society. Today, more than 50 languages are spoken in California schools—this, in a state where the voters through a ballot initiative declared that students must learn in English only.[5] This policy invites disaster given that more than 35 percent of all students speak a primary language other than English, compared with 13 percent nationwide. As many as 60 percent of non-English speaking students are not fluent in English by the 12th grade, assuming they stay in school—and that's a big assumption.

The result? School dropout rates for those without English as their native language tower above those who are fluent in English, with the losses approaching 40 percent.[6] Not surprisingly, race figures in as well. Latinos and African Americans leave high school before graduation at twice the rate of non-Hispanic whites. At the other end of the spectrum, Asian Americans drop out at about half the rate of non-Hispanic whites, or about 10 percent.

For most minorities, however, the promise of California is denied before adulthood. Without any education foundation or communications capabilities, they are quickly marginalized to second-class status, regardless of any constitutional guarantees. And so it goes, the "haves" climbing up the ladder and most of the "have nots" never moving from the bottom.

Incomes vary widely as well. An analysis by the Public Policy Institute of California shows Latinos—the fastest growing group in the state—earning about 80 percent of the incomes generated by whites. African Americans incur the same percentage disadvantage. And that's the *good* news. Among immigrants, Latinos earn only 43 percent of the money garnered by whites. Sure, income disparities decrease with the next generation, but they remain well beneath the money earned by whites for decades.[7]

These patterns foreshadow ugly consequences in adulthood. Fewer life chances translate into more problems, especially when people can't get by. For these individuals, criminal activity becomes an alternative, and many end up in prison for their transgressions. According to the National Institute on Corrections, California has an incarceration rate 3 percent above the national average and a probation rate 37 percent lower than the national average.[8] That means more people staying in prison longer than elsewhere. About 10 percent of the state budget is spent on incarceration, compared to 6.7 percent nationwide; that lessens the ability of the state to spend scarce resources on other important programs.

Predictably, our prison population reflects state education and income patterns. Three of every four incarcerated men are nonwhite, with Latinos and African Americans constituting the largest blocks at 38 and 29 percent, respectively. Among incarcerated women, 28 percent are Latinas and 29 percent are African Americans. The bottom line: The paths of Californians vary greatly, depending in large part upon their race and ethnicity. Clearly, the state provides anything but a level playing field. Yet, many fail to see that all of us pay the price one way or another.

UPSIDE DOWN STATE

Along with the scrambled make-up of the state's population, California's physical composition is equally complex. Few elements seem to go well with any other, leading people to force-fit physical conditions similarly to the way that a metal screw is jammed into a piece of wood. It holds sometimes, but not very well, leaving one always wondering if the connection will fall apart. Many of our problems would be under control if our leaders could agree on ways to protect people and land, but most of us have been in too much of a hurry to gobble up the most desirable opportunities now and let future generations deal with any consequences. In California, the present has caught up to the future and the picture isn't pretty.

The Land

We can begin with the land, which from an agricultural perspective, is arguably among the best in the nation. Whether near the coast, hugging the foothills, or along the 450-mile-long Great Central Valley boasting one fifth of the state's total acreage, rich California soil and relatively mild weather have created a near perfect environment for agriculture. California is the nation's largest agricultural state, yielding twice as much farm products annually as number two Texas and number three Iowa combined. Collectively, California agriculture accounts for $40 billion annually—not exactly small potatoes. But, agricultural land and people don't always go well together, especially when people place cities and manufacturing sites in some of the most fertile areas of the state.

And that's the problem. Lack of planning and the high financial value of homes relative to farms have rendered useless a huge chunk of valuable land once used for agriculture, and the pattern shows no sign of abating. One recent study shows that between 1990 and 2004 alone, nearly half the farmland transformed into urban use was high-quality farmland; that is, the most fertile in the state.[9] You might think that's not a problem, given the state's 101 million acres, a vastness larger than any other state except Alaska and Texas, but it is.

Of all the land in California, only about 9 percent is rich enough to grow just about anything, and that land is disappearing from agricultural use faster than the rest. The biggest losses by far have occurred in the San

Joaquin Valley, which historically has accounted for more than half of the state's agricultural production. In addition, valuable ranch land in the southern part of the state has disappeared, too, and in big chunks. For example, in 2003 the 12,000-acre Newhall Ranch in a then-remote northern corner of Los Angeles County was converted to a suburb containing as many as 20,000 homes.[10] And with that came the need for more roads, water connections, power lines, schools, and all of the other elements required to support a new development far from anywhere. Urban sprawl has become suburban sprawl, which itself has metastasized into rural sprawl. This largely uncontrolled horizontal movement has become a death knell to California's agricultural future.

Water

No commodity is more valuable to California than water. Once the province of agriculture, water increasingly has become the source of huge battles between urban and rural interests. More than 100 years of soaring population growth have only added to the problem in a state where drought is a perennial threat. Agriculture uses about 80 percent of California's developed water supply, leaving precious little for the cities and industries dependent upon water. Most of the time, the distribution works out but during those winters when enough rain fails to fall, political battles and fallout take center stage. As a way of assuring enough water, farmers have demanded a larger share of the supply that flows into rivers and streams. That might not be a problem except for the fact that California's vulnerable fishing industry depends upon enough water to protect spawning salmon and sturgeon, which have been declared endangered species.

The strong environmental community has also weighed in on agricultural water use in terms of quantity and quality. Repeatedly, environmentalists have warned of disastrous outcomes for many of the species that lack adequate supplies, and the courts have agreed.[11] Environmentalists have also stood up to farmers on their use of pesticides as threats to the food chain and human consumption—yet another indicator of the ongoing struggle between groups of different values in California politics.

Then there's the difficulty of moving water, most of which must travel hundreds of miles from the wet north to the arid, populated south. Movement is coaxed through the protection of 1,600 miles of levees that provide flood control in the Great Central Valley as well as the safety of hundreds of thousands of nearby residents, $47 billion worth of property, major highways, aqueducts, and pumping stations in the Sacramento-San Joaquin Delta. But the levees are more than 100 years old and have been in great disrepair for decades. Shortly after New Orleans was deluged from broken levees destroyed by Hurricane Katrina, a state report described California's dilapidated levee system as a "ticking time bomb."[12] That was in 2005, and little has been done in the decade since because of the $2 billion price tag—$2 billion that California simply doesn't have. Between an inadequate supply and a perpetually endangered supply, Californians have serious water problems.

Jobs

California emerged from World War II as an employment factory. The massive naval shipyards and airplane manufacturing plants that provided so much of the nation's firepower during the war were transformed into missile and satellite enterprises. Supported by generous federal contracts for aircraft, ships, tanks, and a variety of machinery designed for war, the state thrived. Historian Kevin Starr notes that during the 1950s the U.S. Department of Defense awarded one fourth of all contracts to companies in California.[13] During the same period, California's share of the national population grew from 7 percent to 9 percent. No wonder the state unemployment varied between 3 and 4 percent. Times couldn't have been better in what could be described legitimately as the "Golden State," and from the standpoint of jobs, they never were again.

The federal government remained California's employment angel during the Cold War. The threat of conflict with the then-Soviet Union and the shipment of billions of dollars of arms to allies kept manufacturing in high gear. It almost didn't matter that the once prominent automobile industry slowly slipped away as American companies consolidated most of their factories in Detroit for what would be their last stand a couple of decades later. After all, in California there was always a job, first in the defense plants, then the massive automobile and airplane production facilities, next in aerospace engineering and production, and eventually the booming electronics industry. During those years, the state seemed to be one huge evolving job factory. The middle class was thriving.

The end of the Cold War in the early 1990s not only changed international relations, but also hit the state's economy hard. Never again would

California's unemployment rate be below the national average. According to the U.S. Bureau of Labor Statistics, California's unemployment rate mirrored the national average between 1981 and 1990. Between 1990 and 2010, the state's unemployment rate persisted at 1.8 percent above the national average. Yes, Hollywood and Silicon Valley have taken up some of the slack, but much movie making now takes place in other states and other countries. Meanwhile, Silicon Valley may have become the land of innovation, but the bulk of its creations by California-based companies are produced offshore by cheap labor.

These days the federal government is a banker for California rather than an investor. Like many other states, California has not had enough funds to cover its unemployment benefits in a time of great recession, so the state has borrowed heavily from the feds to the tune of nearly $10 billion. State leaders have been hoping that a revived economy would ease the pain of repayment. But the upsurge has yet to come and beginning January 2011, California faced an annual interest charge of $362 million on its federal loan—nearly three times more than the next closest state in hock to the feds.[14] One more bill for a state unable to pay the bills already on the table.

BROKE AND FALLING FURTHER BEHIND BY THE DAY

Balancing budgets is a tough task these days at all levels of government. Still, the national government has one advantage over the states: it can run deficits year after year and just add the tab to the national debt. Not so in states, including California, where budgets must be balanced one way or another each year. The problem is that for years, the state has been "balancing" the budget through creative financing. The temptation, of course, is to assign blame to the legislature and governor, who for decades have used various gimmicks to match revenues with expenditures. But most of their sleight of hand work has centered on moving funds from one pot to another and taking away from local governments funds that the state agreed to provide for various services.

The most egregious behavior has occurred by the voters who have a penchant for approving bonds through ballot propositions. Bonds allow the state to build infrastructure projects now, with the idea of paying them off over 30 or 40 years. That payment, including interest, comes from the state budget general fund. The categories have included traditional areas such as school buildings, water storage facilities, prisons, and low-cost housing programs. To these the voters have added support for a $3 billion stem cell research program in 2004 and a $10 billion down payment for a $43 billion high-speed rail system in 2008, which has since been revised to $98.5 billion.

There's nothing wrong with bonds per se, it's just the extent to which Californians rely upon them. Increasingly, the voters are using bonds to compensate for inadequate state budgets. But bonds take a heavy toll. In 2010, the state treasurer estimated that the state was paying interest on nearly $90 billion worth of bonds, amounting to 6.7 percent of the budget. Worse yet, the treasurer estimated that by mid-decade, interest on state bonds would be 10 percent of the budget. The state now ranks second only to New York in per capita bond indebtedness of $2,362.[15] The result: California now has the lowest bond rating in the nation, a reflection of the lenders' assessments of the state's ability to redeem its loans. That, in turn, has resulted in the highest interest rates paid by any state bonds. The impulse to buy now and pay later—often *much* later—has cost Californians dearly and will continue to do so for generations to come.

COUNTLESS PIECES OF AN UNFINISHED PUZZLE

Fifty years ago, California was a national trendsetter with its infrastructure. Outstanding public education, modern highway systems, and reasonably priced housing adorned the state to the envy of the rest of the nation. The state smelled "new," looked clean, and operated smoothly. It wasn't Nirvana, but for many it was the next best thing. Year 'round sunshine in California assured the nation of bountiful supplies of fresh fruits and vegetables that could be found nowhere else in such flavor and quantities. "But most of all," Peter Schrag observes, "to judge from the prevailing imagery, it was the home of millions of well-educated young families (all white, needless to say) with good jobs at major defense plants, aerospace facilities, and electronics companies."[16] It was the place where everyone wanted to come. Millions did. And as the numbers multiplied, the state lost its way. Today, California is almost totally disconnected from its past.

Public Education

Sadly, there is little "education" in California's public education system. Instead, most students are kept in place in overcrowded, dilapidated facilities known to some as classrooms. Of course, there are the few wealthy communities whose residents are prepared to spend thousands of extra dollars annually in property taxes. But for the great majority, state funding, the primary source of support, has shriveled to the point where California ranks 48th of the 50 states in per capita spending. In terms of other industrialized states, California commits to public education about two-thirds of the dollars they do. That statistic is a window into the state's bleak future.

It's hard to imagine that the news regarding public education could be any worse, but it is. With respect to the student–teacher ratio, arguably the single most important factor in providing quality education, California ranks 50th in the nation. Ditto for the number of computers per classroom—this in the state that had more to do with the invention of computers than anywhere else. Ditto for per capita number of books in libraries. Of those students entering the ninth grade, between 25 and 30 percent drop out before graduation; for these souls, there is no reason to wait for the "quality education" they will never encounter. Bottom line: A poorly educated state means a poorly trained, uncompetitive workforce. And that inadequacy yields disappointing results all the way up the state's public education food chain. Among those who enter the state's workhorse four-year higher education institution, California State University (CSU), nearly half must take remedial English or math upon admission to the university.

Funding plagues all levels of public education from K–12 through the elite University of California (UC), the state's research and advanced degree institution. Between 1990 and 2010, average state funding per UC student dropped by 54 percent when adjusted for inflation.[17] In fact, as of 2011, UC students now pay a larger share of their education than the state does. Matters have become so grim that as of fall 2011, UC began turning away between 20,000 and 30,000 fully qualified applicants simply because of a lack of funds. CSU also reduced admissions by 40,000 students simply because of the lack of resources to instruct them.[18] Yet, at the same time that higher education officials contracted the number of admissions, they accepted more students from out of state.[19] Why? Because non-Californians pay three times the tuition as do in-state residents, and those funds are badly needed because of massive reductions in state assistance. However, at what cost?

Between dramatically increased fees and a lack of space, California's high school graduates are seeking and gaining admissions in universities outside the state. Will they return to California after graduation, or will they settle down where they obtain their education? We don't know, but we do know that according to research by the Public Policy Institute of California, current trends project that 35 percent of the state's working adults will have bachelor's degrees, short of the 41 percent required to perform college degree–related jobs.[20] Clearly, the paltry supply of California college graduates is not keeping up with the state's needs, but how can it, given the financial obstacles?

Highways and Byways

It stands to reason that the state with the most people would have the most motor vehicles. Given the nature of the state's perpetual fiscal condition, it shouldn't be surprising that the roads used by our vehicles are among the worst in the nation. Using safety, congestion, and data from the Federal Highway Administration, *Reader's Digest* in 2008 ranked California 48th, with only Hawaii and Louisiana trailing behind. Another study has the greater Los Angeles area and San Francisco-Oakland as the first and eighth most congested cities in the United States. Perhaps the most comprehensive study has come from the Reason Foundation, which finds California's rural and urban roads each ranked 48th of the 50 states. Why not? California ranks 47th in per capita highway expenditures.[21]

Getting any major project off the ground and completed more often than not transforms a reasonable idea into an impossible feat. Reconstruction of the San Francisco-Oakland Bay Bridge stands out as a telling case in point. The bridge carries 270,000 vehicles each day between Oakland and San Francisco, and was a casualty in the 1989 Loma Prieta earthquake, a 15-second temblor that registered a powerful 6.9 on the Richter scale. Occurring at the height of the afternoon rush hour, the quake caused substantial damage and loss of human life throughout the San Francisco Bay area. The top portion of the double-decked bridge collapsed on the bottom portion, leading to the deaths of 42 people. It took 11 years just to rebuild the freeway portions leading to the bridge. As for the bridge itself, the new permanent span was not scheduled for completion until 2013—24 years after the quake! Engineering disputes, conflicting environmental reports, and a final tab of $6.3 billion—far exceeding the original estimate of $780 million—combined to cause the delay of repairs to this vital transportation artery. Adding insult to injury was the fact that most of the construction (think jobs!) was done in China because of lower materials and labor costs. Gridlock in California manifests in many ways.

Environmental Stewardship—A Plus and Model for Other Improvements

There is a bit of light in California's otherwise dark tunnel—environmental management. As mentioned earlier, ever since the 1969 Santa Barbara oil spill, residents and elected officials alike have been nearly united in opposing offshore oil drilling. But it's the topography that has been particularly unkind to California. It almost seems that the state was carved out to store pollutants. In addition to the 450-mile-long Central Valley, hills and mountains surround major areas throughout the state, leaving dangerous pollutants no way out. It's not simply a matter of ugly air; California's smog has a history of causing major respiratory problems affecting millions of people. Long known as the state with five of the seven most polluted areas in the nation, California's elected officials have struggled to improve the state's air quality, sometimes under pressure of the federal government.

With respect to comprehensive initiatives, passage of the Global Warming Solutions Act 2006 (sometimes known as AB 32) has made the state a leader in the effort to reduce greenhouse emissions. Enactment was not easy, given the opposition of the petroleum industry and major users of energy. Yet, early signs suggest that the new law has the potential for changing the state's energy equation. Between 2007 and 2010, a state initiative led to installation of 924 megawatts of solar energy panels, enough to power 185,000 homes.[22] The law mandated statewide reductions in greenhouse emissions by 15 percent to 1990 levels by 2020. Seizing this platform, in 2010, the state Air Resources Board mandated that public utilities derive at least 33 percent of their energy from renewable sources by 2020, the same percentage as required in the nation.[23] These are noble efforts, but much more has to be done.

One environmental initiative is the 665-mile-long "bullet train," a vehicle that planners expect to run at speeds of 200 miles per hour between the Bay Area and Southern California. Proponents claim that the project will take the place of 12 lanes of Interstate 5, the state's major highway corridor. Californians passed a $10 billion bond in 2008 to launch the project but, as discussed previously, the effort requires more than $98.5 billion altogether. The Feds have chipped in a bit more than $3 billion to help fund the first portion between Modesto and Bakersfield. Exactly where the remainder will be found is one of those great California mysteries. And let's face it—Modesto and Bakersfield are not the state's population centers, their local charms notwithstanding.

In other instances, governments have responded at the local and regional levels. Los Angeles' Alameda Corridor, a sunken track that moves freight 20 miles from Los Angeles and Long Beach ports to the city, has made a sizable dent in reducing local air pollution. Now trains make the trip in 30 minutes instead of four hours, and drivers don't wait with pollutant-emitting vehicles at train crossings. Similar successes have occurred elsewhere. Since 2000, northern California has relied upon the San Francisco Bay Area Water Transit Authority, which has operated ferries between San Francisco and nearby communities. Traffic has grown from 104,000 passengers in 2000 to 1.4 million in 2009 on vessels that pollute at much lower levels than automobiles do.[24]

Whatever else may be said about California, the state has moved boldly on environmental issues. Yet, these efforts stand in stark contrast to the state's management of other policy areas.

WEAKENED POLITICAL CAPACITY

Perhaps some of California's many problems might be solved if the state had the capability to do so, but Californians and the occupants of the state's political institutions have foundered over the years. Fifty years ago, the state's leaders were pragmatic in responding to emergent problems, usually finding common ground in the process. Those were the years of a California with seemingly unlimited potential.

These days, the state suffers greatly from political gridlock. Elected officials are not willing to take bold steps in a state with a population increasingly hostile to the workings of government. Between recent laws, term limits, and intrusive interest groups in a polarized political environment, elected officials find it difficult to find common ground.

Then there's the public. In some ways, it's hard to blame the public for the state's failings; in other ways, the public bears much of the responsibility. It's hard to blame the public because so many are losing their way. A bad economy, a changing demographic composition, and disaffection of large numbers with the political process are among the many factors that have led many Californians to hunker down and withdraw from participation in the state's many issues. On the other hand, that very retreat has left policymaking in the hands of a few elected officials, who have become increasingly reluctant to deal with pressing issues that the majority are too willing to ignore. Frustrated, the public has been too willing to take the easy way out by passing ballot propositions that handcuff the ability of policymakers to act or by refusing to pass new taxes that would allow California to bloom yet again.

This ugly combination explains today's politics in California—one increasingly that underscores despair over hope, yesterday's memories over today's fears. Consequently, California finds itself today in a kind of political "no man's land." At the same time that residents are frustrated over the state's direction, they are equally reluctant to do anything about it.

THE LOST LUSTER—WHERE HAS IT GONE AND HOW DO WE GET IT BACK?

The picture we see of California today is remarkably different from the vision of the first few generations of settlers. It's a state spiraling downward to mediocrity and less, with no urgency among most of the leaders and public alike to do much about it. Hopes and dreams have been buried under conditions that become more burdensome every day. Californians know it. A Field Poll conducted in 2010 found that only 39 percent of a statewide sample agreed that California is "one of the best places to live," compared with 78 percent who shared that sentiment in 1985.[25]

The blame game is in full swing, with everyone pointing a finger at everyone else. Worse yet, as grim as it is today, the picture is only likely to become uglier in the years to come unless Californians get a reality grip on their state's condition and act on it. We're not simply talking about a new law or constitutional amendment; we're talking about wholesale overhaul of the way Californians live their lives.

So, what should we do first? The question is simple enough, but we already know that the problems are complex. Before we write any prescriptions for a cure, we must have an accurate assessment on the condition of the patient. That will be the task of the coming chapters—to understand fully the totality of California circumstances, how and why the state has lost its golden sheen, and just as fully explain the long-term consequences. Only then, can we propose and work toward solutions; only then can we prepare ourselves for the hard work that lies ahead.

ENDNOTES

1. California Counties Talk of Cutting Ties to State," *The New York Times*, July 13, 2011, p. A18.
2. See "Fewer U.S. Homeowners Underwater as California Home Prices Rise," *Bloomberg Businessweek*, August 9, 2010, http://www.businessweek.com/news/2010-08-09/fewer-u-s-homeowners-underwater-as-california-home-prices-rise.html, and "California Has 2.3M 'Underwater' Homes, *San Francisco Business Times*, August 26, 2010, http://www.bizjournals.com/sanfrancisco/stories/2010/08/23/daily52.html.
3. "Top Ten Foreclosure States of 2010," RealtyTrac, http://www.huliq.com/10178/top-ten-foreclosure-states-2010.
4. Robert Putnam, *Bowling Alone* (Cambridge, MA: Harvard University Press, 2000).
5. California's Proposition 227, passed by the voters in 1998, requires that immigrant students be taught primarily in English.
6. "English Isn't Language of Many in State," *San Francisco Chronicle*, September 23, 2008, pp. A1, A13.
7. Deborah Reed and Jennifer Cheng, "Racial and Ethnic Wage Gaps in the California Labor Market," Public Policy Institute of California, San Francisco, CA, 2003, p. 45.
8. www.nicic.gov/Features/StateStats/?State=CA.
9. American Farmland Trust, "Paving Paradise," 2007.
10. "Supervisors OK Newhall Ranch," *Los Angeles Times*, May 28, 2003, pp. A1, A17.
11. See "Diversion in Delta a Threat to Salmon, Judge Rules," *San Francisco Chronicle*, July 19, 2008, pp. A1, A6.
12. Quoted in "Central Valley Vulnerable to Flooding," *San Francisco Chronicle*, September 9, 2005, p. A18.
13. Kevin Starr, *Golden Dreams: California in an Age of Abundance, 1950-1963* (New York: Oxford University Press, 2009), p. 219.
14. "Interest Adds Up to a $1.3 Billion Bill for States," *The New York Times*, January 15, 2011, pp. A1, A3.
15. See Bill Lockyer, State of California Debt Affordability Report, Sacramento, CA, October 2010, and "Rising Debt a Threat to State General Fund," *San Francisco Chronicle*, November 24, 2009, p. C3.
16. Peter Schrag, *Paradise Lost: California's Experience, America's Future* (Berkeley: University of California Press, 1999), p. 30.

17. "University of California Plans to Slash Spending," *The Wall Street Journal*, May 18, 2010, p. A4.

18. See "Yudolf Warns of a More Exclusive UC," *San Francisco Chronicle*, January 21, 2011, pp. A1, A10, and "CSU Prepares 20% Fee Hike," *San Jose Mercury News*, July 17, 2009, pp. A1, A15.

19. "Non-Californians Get More UC Seats," *Los Angeles Times*, July 1, 2011, pp. AA 1, 5.

20. Hans Johnson, "California Workforce: Planning for a Better Future," Public Policy Institute of California, San Francisco, CA, January 2011.

21. Reason Foundation, "19th Annual Highway Report," http://reason.org/studies/show/19th-annual-highway-report-californ.

22. "State's Use of Solar Power Takes Off," *San Jose Mercury News*, July 6, 2011, pp. D1, 2.

23. California Air Resources Board, "California's Clean Energy Future: Implementation Plan," Sacramento, CA, September 2010, p. 20.

24. Draft, Final Transition Plan, Water Emergency Transportation Authority, June 18, 2009, http://www.watertransit.org/files/TransitionPlan/TP0618909.pdf.

25. "Quality of Life Plunges in State," *San Francisco Chronicle*, March 18, 2011, pp. C1, C7.

2

The Canary in the Mine

Whatever starts in California unfortunately has the inclination to spread.

—Former President Jimmy Carter

Maybe he had a chip on his shoulder. After all, California voted for Republican Gerald Ford in Carter's 1976 presidential victory and for Republican Ronald Reagan in Carter's 1980 failed effort to gain re-election. Still, Jimmy Carter's observation is not without merit, although not always in the negative manner that he implies.

California is a trendsetter, not consistently, but so much of the time that it pays for any serious futurist to closely study the state's inclinations— whether in politics, economics, fashion, or culture—as harbingers of what's to follow down the road. No, the state doesn't have a monopoly on innovation, creativity, or bizarre behavior, but you would be hard-pressed to find another as influential in so many respects so much of the time. The dreamers, the inventors, the iconoclasts, and yes, the many misfits of all stripes dwell in California in proportions significantly greater than you will find almost anywhere. At times, the combination of forces can be uproarious, at other times intimidating, and still at other times almost comical, but rarely without interest.

As a congested intersection of competing ideas and values, California is often the beta site for all kinds of themes, products, and applications. Folks take risks here. Tens of thousands of 19th-century entrepreneurs jeopardized their lives when they crossed thousands of miles of unwelcome territory to become part of the Gold Rush in 1848. Millions voted to drain the system of tax dollars in 1978, setting the stage for a nationwide tax revolt as well as virtual bankruptcy in the years to come. And when the federal government cracked down on activities ranging from marijuana use to stem cell research, the state's voters pretty much said "up yours" by passing ballot propositions that directly contradicted federal rules. People don't merely "talk" in California, they "do," although what they do is not always in their or the state's best interests.

Not only people, but also ideas have come into their own. Endless inventions have thrived here, from industrialist Henry Kaiser's modern shipbuilding breakthrough method during World War II to 15-year-old Blake Ross who co-developed the Firefox Browser. According to the U.S. Patent Office, California dwarfs all other states in securing new patents. In 2009, a typical year, 20,646 patents were awarded to Californians, more than three times the number handed out to Texas, the next closest state. Dreams and crusades that might be ridiculed or dismissed in other places as capricious whiffs of fancy often capture a following here, enabling the state to become a kind of giant incubator.

We don't want to overstate the case. Not every aspiration has come true, not every invention has changed the world, and not every new idea has spawned instant millionaires; in fact, many have turned out to be incredible disasters financially and otherwise. Howard Hughes, the eccentric inventor/entrepreneur/industrialist, designed the Spruce Goose, a giant flying boat made mostly of wood (birch, to be precise) to transport hundreds of troops at a time during World War II. As late as 1947, two years after the war's end, the plane still had not flown and precipitated a congressional investigation over massive cost overruns. An embarrassed Hughes was hauled before a congressional committee to explain the failure funded by tens of millions of federal dollars. Ultimately, Hughes took the plane on a single flight lasting about a mile, just to prove it was viable.[1] Moral victory, maybe, but failure otherwise.

And it's not as if everyone has benefitted from the state's successes; in fact, quite to the contrary. Poverty, both inner-city and rural, is a staple of this otherwise wealthy state, leaving millions with no hope of ever crawling out of an ever-deepening abyss that separates them from the others. An anti-tax mentality among the "haves" and threatened middle class has produced generation after generation of elected officials unwilling to support collection of sufficient revenues to assist the underclass. It may not have started out this way, but California has become an "I've got mine, you're on your own" state. Whatever the value of the anti-tax, small government-is-the-best-government "Tea Party" in national politics, such ideas took root in California decades before.

Still, there is something about the ever-changing collective DNA of California that has produced—and continues to produce—a strange combination of risk-taking, bullishness, and individualism. If you're not tough enough to stick it out here, you're not likely to garner a lot of sympathy because most others are trying to operationalize their own dreams or struggling to hold on until they can. Hollywood endings and Disneyland fantasy notwithstanding, there's little room in California for sideline voyeurism or passivity. Either you make it or you're left behind. In one of the nation's wealthiest states, there are an awful lot of pained casualties.

It's not that the aforementioned tendencies don't exist elsewhere, because they do. But California's uniqueness lies in the abundance—some would say excess—of these characteristics and the synergies that emerge from their interaction. Like a rich stew recipe, all of these ingredients fold into the state's political culture to impact California politics, often with unpredictable outcomes and sometimes with unfortunate results. If there ever were a state where the parts diminished the whole, it would be California. Indeed, the state's legacy may be that it is rarely able to get enough players on the same page.

The remainder of this chapter concentrates on some of the many themes that have germinated in California, occasionally scorned and other times emulated elsewhere. It's a state that succumbs to clashes over values, resources, and our very quality of life. Some of these battles pass quickly, but others become wellsprings of national debates. It's also a state that has led the way in dividing the "haves" from "have nots," virtually placing the term "middle class" on the economic equivalent of the endangered species list. Still, this is a state with a unique cultural chemistry that inspires visionaries to take risks and cobble together iconoclastic combinations. Finally, California is a state with endless political battles, some of which are temporarily patched and others of which persist in endless, furious conflict. Coping with so many issues leaves California almost kaleidoscope-like in nature. What you see on the public policy agenda one minute no doubt will change the next time you blink; it's that fast and that confusing—even to insiders. Still, there's value in parsing the state's issues and underlying themes.

All this reminds us of the simple, yet predictive warning system used by early coal miners to guard against lethal methane carbon dioxide accumulations as they toiled deep underground under precarious circumstances. Like the canary in those poorly ventilated mines that warned of trouble, the trends in California tell us much about not only the state's political issues today but also the likely condition of the nation tomorrow.

THE LAND OF MOVEMENTS AND TRENDS

Earthquakes aren't the only elements that send large portions of California into disarray from time to time. The state also experiences tremors on a regular basis in the form of unique lifestyles among California's very heterogeneous population. Both tremors are often unpredictable, but there are differences between the natural and human-caused jolts. Whereas the locations of earthquakes can be identified readily and assessed after the fact, unusual "outside the box" behavior not only distinguishes various groups but also occasionally sparks confrontations between their values and the traditional values of mainstream society. Sometimes, the differences are so great that they lead to government intervention in the form of legislation, court decisions, or other political actors. Regardless, these movements all contribute to the framework of California's political system.

Two influences that have permeated California at the extremes are the exotic nonconformist lifestyles and fervent evangelism. Whether by literature, song, exhortations to action, or mass demonstrations, the participants in these social phenomena have influenced the state's political make-up and public policies.

Nonconformist Lifestyles

Maybe it's the consistently good weather, or maybe it's the fascination with nearly year-round sun, or maybe it's the proximity to a deceptively taunting coastline whose waters are anything but "pacific." Whatever the causes or reasons, seemingly every generation large numbers of Californians explore alternative lifestyles. This in itself might not be worthy of discussion except that these lifestyles become the templates for similar comportment elsewhere. Like so many other examples, California sets the trend in nonconformist behavior.

Bohemians

Some of the earliest social rebels in the state were known simply as "Bohemians." Originally coined in Europe, the term refers to people who commonly favor nontraditional lifestyles that incorporate idealism, a profound rejection of materialism, and a contempt of affluence.[2] Historically, musicians, writers or artists, and their followers have adopted this routine in disproportionate numbers. Gays and individuals sympathetic to communism rounded out the cast.[3] Such people were—and still are—known for leading unconventional lives, often flowing from one community to another with few permanent ties. Their unique views notwithstanding, these social rebels have often contributed rich ideas to the conventional world and have been prominent in the development of California politics.

Much of California's Bohemian flavor bubbled to the surface after World War II. The fusion of jazz, drugs, and unconventional—sometimes radical—literature blended into a counterculture that challenged the status quo. San Francisco was "ground zero" for the movement, nurtured by the proximity of a strong anti-establishment sentiment festering at the University of California, Berkeley just across the bay. Other anti-status quo centers flourished as well, most notably in Hollywood and Venice, a unique colony of muscle builders, poets, and social dropouts just south of Santa Monica.

In California, Bohemian behavior pushed political conservatives into a consternated reactive mode. While people with unconventional morals, left-wing political values, and vocations off the beaten path created an exotic interaction, the combination was too much for the establishment. So threatened were the traditionalists by the strands of Bohemia that the voters in Los Angeles recalled Mayor Frank Shaw in 1938 for his inability to maintain moral order.[4] Political tolerance was in short supply then as it often is now.

California wasn't the only home for Bohemians. Some clusters also thrived in New York's Lower East Side, Boston, and a handful of other urban locations throughout the nation, mostly near universities. Still, San Francisco generated the most consistent energy of what longtime *San Francisco Chronicle* columnist Herb Caen came to describe in the late

1950s as "beatniks." The term fused the word "beat" associated with jazz and Sputnik, the 184-pound Soviet Union satellite that added a new level of intensity to the Cold War.

Hippies

Within a few years, many of those participating in the anti-establishment movement became better known as "Hippies." The term referenced the idea that adherents were "hip," a jazz and drug term suggesting that they were aware or "in the know." Others referred to these devotees as "flower children" for their commitment to nonviolence in their opposition to establishment policies. Sometimes, excesses of drugs pushed Hippies to the edge, leading to confrontations with authorities over their lifestyles.

Hippies abhorred the status quo; they balked at "the system." Marriage, 9-to-5 workdays, suburban living, and other traits associated with "the Establishment" were dismissed in favor of "free love," individual craftsmanship, bartering, and a "live for the moment" mentality that eschewed both the past and the future.[5] Why? Because the past and future represented tired bookends of the social order, and for Hippies, the social order was a fraud propped up by a political system that promoted elitism and class warfare.

Still, despite their disdain for politics and the Establishment, Hippies themselves became political during the 1960s, if for no other reason because of their growing opposition to the war in Vietnam and the violence associated with the conflict. Perhaps the high point of the movement came in 1967, when more than 100,000 people descended on San Francisco for a "Summer of Love" that focused on peace, love, drugs, and ending the war.[6] Declarations of harmony and bliss notwithstanding, the epoch was marked by great tension between city officials, residents, and visitors.

Despite its professed opposition to "the system," the Bohemian/Hippie movement ultimately played a prominent role in California politics. Over time, the anti-establishment culture became the energy source for public opposition to the Vietnam War, which was fought by draftees.[7] That opposition (and the reaction to it) helped to deny re-election to incumbent Democratic Governor Pat Brown in 1966, paving the way for Republican Ronald Reagan. The counterculture also opened California to other long-repressed themes such as gay rights, sexual freedom, and civil rights, issues that became important discussion points in California and national politics for decades to come. Candidates seeking office were forced to take positions on these and other counterculture themes, controversial legislation sometimes emerged, and the public often "settled" the debate over such issues through approving or denying state ballot propositions.

It's not that social questions didn't concern Californians before the Hippie movement; rather, by the 1970s and 1980s these issues were elevated to the state's political agenda on a regular basis. Perhaps, more significantly, many remain in place to this day, helping to underscore the transcending nature of California culture and politics as well as the ongoing struggle between "the Establishment" and everyone else, whoever that might be at the time.

Evangelism

People often say that it's wise never to discuss religion and politics in a social setting; to do otherwise may auger ugly conflict. That may be true in some quarters, but religion and politics have a long, intertwined history in California. Here evangelism has been critical to framing much of the state's political agenda and the role of government. Its roots extend as far back as the Catholic missions that accompanied Spanish explorers who worked their way up the California coast in the 1700s. Only the issues have changed. In the early days of Spanish settlement, missionaries sought to convert Native Americans to the Catholic religion and European ways. Today, evangelists proselytize about gay marriage, a woman's control over her body, creationism, alcohol and drugs, and the proper place of religion in the public school classroom.

No religious group has a lock on evangelism, but the concept of promoting the gospel as the only way to live has been invoked mostly by fundamentalist Christians. Using the church as a conservative social incubator, preachers often have exhorted their flocks to extend fervent, unbending religious themes to the public policy arena either by pressuring legislators or through the ballot proposition process. We often think of these proselytizers as religious soldiers of the American South, but many have flourished in California, producing large congregations of followers in the process.

Aimee Semple McPherson

One of the earliest California evangelists to advocate political change from the pulpit was Sister Aimee Semple McPherson. Canadian-born, this

Pentecostal faith healer held tent revivals throughout the United States before settling in as the pastor at the 5,300 seat Foursquare Gospel Church in Los Angeles in 1923. In 1924, McPherson and her followers raised enough money to build a radio station, only the third in Los Angeles at the time, from which she broadcast nightly sermons. She became "a power in Los Angeles and a national figure, often called the 'world's greatest evangelist.'"[8]

During much of the Roaring Twenties, McPherson preached about morality, Prohibition, anti-communism, creationism, and the importance of America as a devoutly Christian nation. She was anti-immigrant and particularly opposed to teaching evolution in the classroom, and pounded home her themes through her weekly radio program. Over the next decade, her flock grew thanks to the continuous migration of Pentecostals and other "Dust Bowl" transplants from the southwest.[9]

As her stature and influence swelled, McPherson increased her involvement in the political realm. In the 1934 Governor's race, she campaigned for Republican Frank Merriam, who opposed Democrat and socialist Upton Sinclair. Merriam won, and McPherson's power seemed to grow only more.

Ultimately, Aimee McPherson was deposed by scandal stemming from an affair and allegations of skimming donations. But for a time, her religious teachings were accepted by hundreds of thousands and had a profound impact on the lives of Californians and the political system in California.[10] Even at her funeral in 1944, more than 50,000 mourners paid their respects in her open casket at the Foursquare Gospel Church. Whatever the merits, McPherson touched people.

Robert Schuller

As California grew, evangelists found better ways to penetrate their potential audiences. Robert Schuller was among the first to blend the ministry with California's indispensable source of transportation, the automobile. As a recently ordained minister of the Reformed Church in America, in 1955 he established his first church in a drive-in movie theater in Orange County. There, Schuller preached to families in automobiles that filled the 300 parking slots.

Schuller ministered about the positive aspects of life. No matter how bad things might seem today, they would be better tomorrow. Although he was officially nonpartisan, Schuller drew conservative politicians to his church on a regular basis. His television shows frequently drew upon patriotic themes and morality, although they were less overtly political than were many others, according to one study.[11] He gave the invocation at the 1988 Republican national convention and was said to be close to President George H.W. Bush.

As his flock grew, Schuller changed locations, added more buildings, and then changed locations again. Ultimately, his congregation grew so large that Schuler oversaw construction of the Chrystal Cathedral, a golden-coated edifice with 10,000 glass windows that served 9,500 parishioners, at a cost of $20 million. From that location, he launched the Hour of Power in 1970, a weekly television program that at one point was viewed by 20 million people in 156 countries, including an estimated 200,000 weekly viewers in California.

But Schuller, like McPherson, also fell upon hard times. Stories began appearing about the vast sums of money spent by his organization to support core employees,[12] and his "look on the sunny side" approach lost appeal in a state beset with problems. In 2010, he announced his retirement as senior minister, turning over everyday responsibilities to his daughter who also was a minister. Shortly thereafter, the Chrystal Cathedral ministry announced bankruptcy.[13]

Rick Warren

Only a few miles from Schuller's Crystal Cathedral sits Saddleback Church, a fundamentalist congregation under the province of California-born Pastor Rick Warren. With more than 22,000 members, this religious institution is now the largest in California and one of the largest in the nation.[14]

Like Schuller, Warren considers himself a healer in the traditional sense of the term. In that context, he tries to bring people of different views together in the hope of finding common ground through Christ's teachings. Warren has been a force in state and national politics, although he would say otherwise. During the 2008 presidential campaign, he persuaded candidates Barack Obama and John McCain to visit his church for a "Civil Forum on the Presidency," a testament to Warren's clout and the extent to which he was willing to insert himself into the political process. Two thousand parishioners watched the candidates answer ethical and social questions relating to Christianity, while another 2,400 viewed the exchange from venues outside the church.

Baptist Rick Warren has taken on numerous social issues. He has repeatedly expressed opposition to abortion, gay marriage, and stem cell research. Warren found himself in a good deal of controversy in 2008, when he announced his public support for Proposition 8, a ballot issue that defined marriage as an arrangement between a man and a woman. In a video message to his congregation, Warren said, "I urge you to support Proposition 8."[15] The week after the election, he claimed that he had never endorsed the measure when he appeared on the "Larry King Live" television show, although videotapes of his endorsement clearly showed otherwise. The turnabout caused a ruckus among some of Warren's conservative followers. Still, he was asked by then President-elect Barack Obama to give the invocation at his inauguration.

Other Participants

While the three individuals cited previously have been particularly noteworthy in the religious movement, they are by no means alone. Over the years, other players have inserted themselves into the political process, often in concert with particular issues. The Catholic Church, for example, has taken strong positions on abortion, gay marriage, and immigrant rights, especially as they relate to farm laborers.[16] Regarding gay marriage, prominent members of the Mormon Church and several thousand Mormon families may have contributed as much as $17 million to promote passage of Proposition 8 in 2008, an amount equivalent to about three-fourths of the entire "Yes on 8" campaign.[17] On the other side of the gay rights issue, several ministers of the United Methodist Church openly opposed the ballot proposition in 2008, putting their jobs at risk.[18] Whether short term or long term, the clergy often has weighed in on California issues, and their flocks have often heeded their calls. From questions on the "right to die" to the "rights" of the unborn, these controversies have spilled into the state's public policymaking arenas.

THE GROWING CHASM BETWEEN THE HAVES AND THE HAVE NOTS

American jurisprudence and tradition may define equal opportunity as a cornerstone of our value system, but the concept often is "missing in action" in California. Worse yet, over time, the gap between the "haves" and the "have nots" has evolved into a major chasm. Income patterns, the public education system, and the deterioration of social welfare programs all point to a disturbing pattern that is gradually eliminating the middle class, once the backbone of this state. Instead of increasing parity, the new configuration shows a few thriving on the backs of the many.

Income and Taxation Patterns

It goes without saying that different people earn different amounts of money, almost everywhere. Age, gender, race, education, vocation, and even sheer drive are among the many socio-economic factors that shape income patterns. Of course, some of these influences are self-selected choices, others are personal conditions well beyond our control, and still others are structured situations that exclude particular people from some routes to potential economic success. Observers may disagree which elements are accidents of history and which are forced upon us, but distinct differences in income patterns remain nonetheless.

Personal Income and Poverty

Income patterns among various groups in California vary widely. Perhaps more significantly, the spread is becoming larger over time. Not only has the income disparity grown more in California than elsewhere, but also the state's income-generating ability has fallen well below the national average. The differences have been building for some time. Census data show that while national per capita income grew 49.7 percent between 1990 and 2000, per capita income growth in California was 38.4 percent. This is another sign that California's present doesn't match its golden past.

The Census data show striking differences in income earning capabilities by race. Whereas per capita Latino incomes grew in California by 37.3 percent during the decade, per capita white incomes soared by 66.6 percent. Here, too, the patterns were more divergent than those at the national level were.[19] These differences have continued into the 21st century. In 2006, whites had median personal incomes of $35,000, significantly higher than Asians ($27,862) and African Americans ($26,000), and nearly double the median incomes of Latinos ($19,000).[20]

Although some Californians are very wealthy, the poverty rate is higher in the state than the rest of the nation. At the end of 2008, 14.6 percent of the population was below the poverty line established by the Census Bureau, 1.4 percent higher than the national rate. The number of families in poverty living with children exceeded 20 percent, again above the U.S. average.[21] It's a fair statement to say that the Great Recession was more painful to California than the rest of the nation.

In recent years, income gains in California have gone overwhelmingly to the wealthy, leaving everyone else behind. Data compiled by the California Franchise Tax Board, the state's major tax collection agency, shows that between 1995 and 2007, incomes of the bottom fifth of the state's taxpayers increased by 7.7 percent. During the same period, incomes of the top fifth increased by 64.1 percent. It gets worse at the extremes. Among the top 1 percent of the state's taxpayers, incomes soared a staggering 117.3 percent. How significant are the incomes of those at the top? This relatively small group accounted for 25 percent of all the money earned in California.[22]

It might be tempting to assume that perhaps the surge in personal income differences has come from temporary influxes in the state's economy, maybe something like the selective impacts of the dot com boom in the first part of the 21st century. Unfortunately, that's not the case. Statistics compiled over the 30-year period extending from 1969 to 1998 show that income inequality increased greatly in California and the nation, but the rate was significantly faster in California than the rest of the nation.[23] In other words, the growing separation has become an endemic feature of California, rather than a one-time oddity.

Taxation Disparities

The chasm continues with respect to taxation. At issue is not only the question of income earning potential, but also the taxes people pay from their respective income levels. Percentagewise, individuals who earn the most don't necessarily pay the most taxes in terms of percentages of total income, while those near the bottom pay a disproportionate share of their incomes in taxes. According to 2007 data compiled by the Institute of Taxation & Economic Policy, total taxes—income, sales, and property— paid by the bottom 20 percent of California's residents who earned less than $22,000 amounted to 10.2 percent of total income. Total taxes paid by the top 1 percent who earned $600,000 or more were 9.8 percent. With respect to the 4 percent earning $216,000 to $600,000, the tax bite was even less—9.2 percent. And among the next 15 percent, those earning $99,000 to $216,000, the tax obligation was only 8.8 percent of income.[24] Conclusion: The more you earn, the smaller the percentage of taxes you pay. What a system!

The situation is no better with California corporations. To begin with, the state legislature has reduced the tax rate for California businesses several times in the past 30 years. In 1982, the corporate tax rate was 9.6 percent. Today, the tax rate stands at 8.84 percent. This reduction has meant billions of dollars annually in lost revenues to the state. Whereas in 1978 corporation taxes accounted for 15.4 percent of all general fund revenues, in 2010 this same source accounted for 10.7 percent of all general fund revenues. This shift has come at a huge cost to the state. According to data compiled by the nonpartisan California Budget Project, if corporations paid taxes at the same rate today as in 1981, the state would be taking in an extra $8.4 billion annually.[25] That amount in itself would go a long way toward overcoming what state economic experts refer to as California's annual "structural deficit," which amounts to about $20 billion.[26]

Income and Taxation Patterns in Perspective

These data are compelling. Simply put, to the extent that California bleeds from inadequate revenues, the origin of that hemorrhage lies with a taxation system that is "progressive" in name only. California gives a "pass" to the wealthiest individuals and powerful corporations, while sticking it to those with the fewest resources and the least ability to pay. At the same time, California has shifted much of the tax burden from corporations to individuals. All of this occurs in an environment where the few are pulling away from the many at lightning speed. It's nothing less than a double whammy, much of which has gone undetected because of the incremental way these patterns have developed. All the while, the state hungers for revenues.

Public Education

Mention the words "public education" in California and you will encounter anything from a rolling of the eyes to a barrage of expletives not for mention in mixed company. No one is happy about the system or the product. Taxpayer groups grumble that they're not getting their money's worth, teachers grouse that they are overworked and underpaid, and public education administrators feel caught between the confluence of unions, parent groups, and impossible-to-meet state standards. But the biggest disappointment exists with the poor education experienced by California's children, which, in most cases, is robbing them of their futures and the state of their under-developed talent.

K–12 Public Education

As a general proposition, American public education today is in deep, deep trouble from Kindergarten through university graduate school. It's bad enough that the United States has sunk below so many others in the international effort to educate children. Recent studies show the American student science scores placing 15th among the 30 most industrialized nations, and tied for a paltry 24th in math.[27] But the problem is exacerbated in California, where the state hovers near the bottom in per pupil spending, at the bottom in classroom sizes, and near the bottom in test scores when measured against other states.[28] Reductions in per pupil spending speak volumes about the education product. According to the state Legislative Analyst, in 2010–2011, California spent $7,358 per pupil, down from $8,464 in 2007–2008; that's a decrease of 13 percent.

It wasn't always this way. Once upon a time, public education was the crown jewel in California. K–12 instruction ranked among the best in the nation, as demonstrated through government financial commitment and student performance on national tests. During the 1959–1960 school year, the state ranked 10th in per capita funding, well above the national average. At the post-secondary level, the state provided education opportunities through three sources: (1) the largest community college system in the nation, (2) a four-year university system focusing largely on undergraduate instruction, and (3) a four-year research system with emphases on both undergraduate and post-graduate academic programs and research. The opportunities were welcome, as half of all high school graduates went on to institutions of higher learning.[29] Other than incidental fees, higher education was free of cost—that's right, free.[30] In terms of public education, this was a golden period for California.

Much has changed at all levels of public education. Nowadays, sizable test score gaps exist among ethnic groups, with whites achieving much higher scores than Latinos and African Americans. It's yet another indicator of the "haves" and "have nots" dilemma playing out in California. On the one hand, about one-fourth of all ninth-grade students never graduate, resulting in a virtual vocational death sentence. Some groups are more doomed than others are. Among Asians, only 10 percent drop out; with respect to whites, the figure is 15 percent. Among Latinos, now a majority of students in the public schools, 30 percent drop out, a percentage exceeded only by Native Americans at 31 percent and African Americans at 42 percent.[31]

On the other hand, some students fare just fine, thank you. According to the College Board, a nonprofit dedicated to helping students gain access to higher education, 22 percent of all California high school students in 2010 passed at least one Advanced Placement test, good enough for the state to rank sixth among the 50 states. In other words, some students are succeeding in spite of an education deck stacked against them. But there's a catch: They live disproportionately in white, more affluent communities usually in the suburbs.

There is one more major factor that helps to explain uneven student performance, and that's language. According to the California Department of Education, in 2010 about 6,190,000 students attended California public schools, 50 percent of whom were Latino. Other ethnic groups were represented in smaller amounts—whites accounted for 27 percent. During that same year, 1,242,000 of the Latino students spoke Spanish as their first language. Moreover, students from other countries spoke 57 other languages as their language. That's not necessarily a problem if students have the opportunity to learn English, but in 1998 Californians passed a ballot proposition that restricts bilingual education to one year. The problem is that it typically takes someone between 5 and 7 years to become fully immersed in a second language.[32] Thus, in the most formative years of their lives, non-English speaking students lose the opportunity to compete. No wonder the dropout rates are so different; students with primary languages other than English start out behind and few catch up.

Not only do we see changing ethnic composition of California's schools, but also we see increased segregation as part of the change. Increasingly, Latino and African American students find themselves in schools with others of their races. Moreover, the change has happened over the span of two generations. In the early 1970s, most Latinos attended public schools where at least half the student population was white. By the turn of the century, whites were only 22 percent of public school students in the schools attended by Latinos. As researcher Belinda Reyes notes, "Even though the state is becoming more diverse, people still live in segregated communities with limited interaction."[33] "Diversity" in name only doesn't necessarily contribute to a better society.

Year after year, California has short-changed its students, to the point where nothing less than a major overhaul can right all the wrongs. Some of the loss has come from per pupil state funding that has gone down precipitously over many years; in a revenue challenged environment, state policymakers have chosen to cut spending rather than increase taxes. Matters became so bad in 2010 that the legislature reduced the required number of attendance days to 175. Only four states—Idaho, Michigan, Missouri, and North Dakota—require less. The rest of the problem is due to the vast differences between communities and their capabilities to raise funds. Wealthier cities like Palo Alto and Beverly Hills routinely pass large parcel taxes to supplement state funds; poorer areas do not have the same tax base and voter willingness. Because of this ongoing neglect, California has a huge mountain to climb in order to make students competitive with others in the nation and the world.

The cost to repair the funding deficit is now staggering. According to a 2007 report commissioned by state leaders, it would take an additional $1.5 trillion more annually to bring all students up to speed—about 25 times the amount the state has been committing to public education.[34] Why so much? Because the state has systematically neglected the needs of its kids for decades. Of course, spending that kind of money is never going to happen, but it would be nice to see the state's public policymakers point the school finance arrow in a direction other than down.

Higher Education

California's colleges and universities have suffered, too. The problems here have been twofold—budgetary and political. The budget issues stem from the draconian cuts made by the state legislature and governor to the tune of $47 billion between 2008 and 2012. The political problems stem from the fact that unlike most items in the state budget, there are no formal formulaic requirements for funding the state's public universities. Unlike K–12 public education, there are no built-in constitutional guarantees for higher education. Without that protection, the two major university systems have been vulnerable to funding reductions at levels much deeper than have been other recipients of state funding.

The state's economic woes have cost the universities dearly. Because of the budget cuts, the University of California (UC) and California State University (CSU) systems have been forced to raise tuition. Undergraduate tuition at UC skyrocketed from $3,429 in 2001–2002 to $12,192 in 2011–2012, an increase of 256 percent. In 2011, for the first time, total student tuition of $2.8 billion actually accounted for more UC revenue than state support, which amounted to $2.4 billion—raising serious questions of whether UC had become a "private" university.[35] At CSU, tuition rose at an even higher astronomical rate, from $1,428 in 2001–2002 to $5,472 in 2011–2012, or 283 percent. These numbers don't include several hundred dollars more each year in "incidental fees." Both systems have used some of the increases to provide additional student aid, leaving middle class students too "wealthy" for eligibility and too poor to afford an education without massive borrowing.

In addition to massive tuition increases, the two university systems have laid off faculty and support staff to help make ends meet. With fewer classes available, they have reduced the numbers of available slots for student admissions by 60,000 students, forcing many to leave the state in search of an education.[36] At the same time, they have increased acceptances of out of state applicants who are charged significantly higher tuition, leaving even fewer slots for in-state residents.[37] Talk about a double whammy!

All this comes at a great cost to California's future. A statewide survey by the Public Policy Institute of California in 2007 found that 64 percent believed that college educations are imperative for individuals to succeed compared with 50 percent nationwide. More disconcerting, 53 percent agreed that affording college was now a "big problem."[38] And these opinions were registered before the whopping tuition increases of 2009, 2010, and 2011. The situation is far worse today.

In the days of the "Master Plan for Higher Education," the parents of Baby Boomers just assumed their kids would go to college and the state's voters enthusiastically approved bonds to build them. So, the legislature enacted the Master Plan, which guaranteed the top 12.5 percent of all high school graduates admission to UC and the top 33.3 percent admission to CSU. Any others could attend the state's community colleges. As noted previously, these institutions would be virtually free of cost, other than books, incidental fees, and supplies. Of course, we know what has happened since.

Meanwhile, with large numbers of undergraduates denied admission or going elsewhere for their university education, their collective absence is threatening to leave California without enough educated workers. Recall the PPIC survey discussed in Chapter 1: By 2025, the various jobs available in the state will require 41 percent of the workforce to be college graduates. Yet, California's graduates amount to only 34 percent of the workforce.[39] With jobs going begging, you wonder when the companies in need of labor will relocate to the states with the educated workers.

Social Welfare Programs

It's no secret that California's residents have a wide variety of life experiences. Some succeed quite nicely, thank you. Many spend their lives making a go of it as members of that amorphous group known as the "middle class." Then there are those who are old, infirmed, or mentally unstable. Most of the members of this loosely constructed aggregation share only one trait—they are without the properties necessary to make it in society. They depend upon government for their survival.

In California, historically, those with few resources could always count on a generous safety net to pull them through hard times. And for good reason. As recently as the turn of the century, California was considered one of the most attentive states in the union on matters related to healthcare and welfare.[40] No more. While the nation may have suffered the Great Recession between 2008 and 2011, California was decimated by a near-Great Depression. State funding for all programs has been ratcheted down considerably, but those without the means to fend for themselves have suffered the most. Many of these programs have matching federal funds, but in recent years the state's public policymakers have concluded that even with those sources of financial assistance, in some cases the state has had to eliminate the programs or pare them down in order to avoid raising the necessary matching revenues. Just a decade earlier, a statewide poll found a large majority favoring increased taxes to avoid social services cuts,[41] but those days are gone.

In recent years, public opinion on social welfare issues has been conspicuously ambivalent, if not downright contradictory on the topic. For example, one recent statewide poll showed strong support for spending reductions over tax increases, yet opposed cuts in 10 of 12 program areas including programs focusing on mental health, childcare, and the disabled.[42] Meanwhile, those social program recipients on the margins have few capabilities to make their case. Given a relatively equivocal political environment, the state's elected officials repeatedly have taken the easy way out. Besides, the dispossessed don't vote nearly in proportion to everyone else!

Healthcare

Several state programs are designed to provide a safety net for those incapable of providing for themselves. Medi-Cal, California's version of the federal/state Medicaid program, supports the managed healthcare needs of nearly seven million poor Californians who can't afford health insurance. That comes to nearly one-fifth of the state's population who are elderly, disabled, or pregnant. The seven million recipients also account for about 14 percent of all Medicaid recipients throughout the nation, even though California has only 12.5 percent of the nation's population.

Nearly one out of four children also is covered by Medi-Cal, at a rate much higher than the national average. These numbers have grown substantially over the past decade as the state's economy has tumbled and people lost their jobs. Even so, the quality of children's healthcare is among the worst in the nation, 49th of the 50 states according to a recent study by the Commonwealth Fund in areas such as access, prevention, and treatment.[43]

Funding for Medi-Cal is split on a 50/50 basis between the state and federal government. Under the program, the state contracts with physicians and hospitals to treat Medi-Cal recipients. The problem is that over the past decade, state legislators have reduced the payments structure, leading to nearly half of all physicians to decline to participate in the program.[44] Another problem has to do with the renewal process for those enrolled in Medi-Cal, particularly children. Studies show that as many as three-quarters of those eligible are dropped during the renewal period for a variety of reasons, many of which are preventable. Because of clumsy administration, medical costs go up due to the gap in medical care. The bureaucratic process associated with renewal is expensive—more than $100 million annually, according to one study.[45]

California's share of Medi-Cal has been running at about $6 billion annually. Some co-payments come from program beneficiaries. Depending upon their income levels, Medi-Cal recipients must pay for a portion of their insurance. The program is available to people who earn no more than 133 percent of the poverty line annually, or about $14,400 for a single person. Still, Governors Gray Davis and Arnold Schwarzenegger tried to cut Medi-Cal costs by reducing payments and eligibility. In some cases, they have succeeded; in others, their efforts have been blocked by the courts.

The most recent cuts to Medi-Cal occurred in 2010, when the legislature and Governor Schwarzenegger made drastic reductions in Medi-Cal payment categories, including elimination of payments for adult dental services, podiatry visits, and chiropractic services. In 2011, Democratic Governor Jerry Brown proposed an additional $1.7 billion in cuts by reducing state payments to doctors, limiting the number of visits by patients to no more than ten per year, limiting the number of prescriptions, and requiring all Medi-Cal enrollees to pay $5 co-pays for physician's visits. The legislature agreed, further reducing the state's obligation to those most in need.

The bottom line is whereas California once led the nation in providing a strong healthcare safety net for the poor, it now leads the nation in reduced assistance. Those who need care the most have the least help at their disposal.

Welfare

With the state's perennial budget shortfall, California public policymakers have also taken a long look at welfare, temporary state safety net payments to individuals out of the workforce. Most welfare recipients are single mothers who are attempting to shift from childcare responsibilities to the workforce; it's a difficult task at best, given the lack of quality job training programs and the paucity of programs to care for children.

California's CalWORKS program is the state's primary welfare program. It operates in concert with the Temporary Assistance to Needy Families Program (TANF) enacted by Congress in 1996. Under TANF, the federal government pays about half of the state's welfare cost, with the proviso that no one can accept welfare money for more than 60 months over the course of their life.

California has been among the most active states in finding ways to successfully move people from welfare to work with its CalWORKS program, while assuring recipients enough financial security during the transition. As recently as 2006, the state ranked 14th in benefits at $981 per month for a family of three.[46] Since then, each year the state has drastically scaled back support. In 2011, the maximum CalWORKS monthly grant (regardless of family size) stood at $694, the same as it was in 1989. The most anyone could receive amounted to 39 percent of the poverty line established by the U.S. Census Bureau. Still, Governor Jerry Brown proposed another 13 percent cut and a 48-month participation limit instead of the current 60 months. The legislature balked at the totality of Brown's proposal, but cut funds by 5 percent while maintaining the 60-month limit.[47]

What Safety Net?

Whether public education, healthcare, welfare, or just about any other form of social service, California has dropped the ball on serving basic needs and assisting those most in need. Time after time during the past decade, state policymakers have faced a simple choice: find the necessary revenues or reduce programs and social services. Given the antagonistic voices of powerful interests and the whimpers of the weak, policymakers have taken the easy way out. Meanwhile, those who need help the most have found themselves with fewer commitments from the state. California's once supportive safety net has been reduced to a very small safety pin.

MAGNET FOR VISIONARIES

California may be a harsh environment for some, but something about the state continues to draw the curious and creative alike. It's not only a place where people come "to remake yourself," to quote Peter Schrag,[48] it's also a place where people overcome the status quo, inertia, and other kinds of obstacles to make something new. Because of so many challenges, it's not a place for everyone, and those who either fall behind or start behind to begin with, rarely have much of a chance.

But for some dreamers, entrepreneurs, or innovators, things seem to happen here that don't occur as easily elsewhere. In the old days, large lots of available land allowed for the creation of unique developments; these days, large amounts of venture capital facilitate another generation of dreams—"start-ups," small businesses that win early financial support from investors. And all along, researchers at a collection of top notch private and public universities have provided special expertise for all kinds of scientific experiments, some of which have become extraordinary contributions to society and the economy. Are these experiences found elsewhere? Absolutely, but as with so many other attributes of California, they occur in greater numbers here and seem to produce stunning changes in the state's economic, cultural, and even physical environments that often reshape the nation. This speaks to the magnetism of California—a state that draws people to live out their dreams, even if many never convert those dreams into reality.

Dreams and Dollars

In many respects, nature has been an ally to California's dreamers. Aside from a swath of desert in the southeast corner and the towering Sierra Nevada Mountains that separate the state from the east, California has an incredibly mild weather environment devoid of extremes. Most residents experience two seasons, fall and summer—truly a climatological mystery to those who live elsewhere and suffer everything from blinding snow to oppressive humidity. Not only does the weather make California a pleasant place to live, it provides a reliable outdoor work environment and hospitable destination for vacationers—a perfect mix for the state's entertainment sector.

Making Movies

In retrospect, it seems only natural that the movie industry would be born in California. Particularly in southern California, weather, talent, and technological innovation combined early in the 20th century to anoint the area the movie capital of the world. Carey McWilliams explains the convergence as almost inevitable. In a sense, it was the Hollywood version of real estate's favorite mantra—location, location, location: "[W]ithin a two hundred-mile radius of Los Angeles was to be found every variety of natural scenery from the Sahara Desert to the Khyber Pass. There was also available in Los Angeles an abundant supply of cheap labor."[49] A compelling combination.

By the 1930s, major motion picture studios on large tracts of land posing as small cities in and near Hollywood collectively were the epicenter of the movie industry. They included Paramount, Warner Brothers, Fox,

Universal, MGM, and later United Artists. The timing couldn't have been better, given the nation's need to escape the pain of the Great Depression. Even if the journey lasted only two hours, movies became the new foundations for fantasy.

Of course, some aspects of the industry were born out of state and even before the 20th century—Edison's projector in 1879 and Eastman's movie film in 1889 are two prominent aspects of the industry that were developed in New Jersey and New York. But while these and other inventions may have been conceived elsewhere, they were put to use in California with lighting, creative sets, and eventually sound, followed by color, and then again by superior animation. Most movie historians point to D.W. Griffith's controversial *Birth of a Nation* as the starting point for modern movies. The 3-hour silent movie was made in Los Angeles in 1915.[50]

Today, California still dominates the movie industry and its related elements, with most of the activity in the Los Angeles area. Data supplied by the Motion Picture Association of America for the 2008 calendar year shows that of the 713,000 jobs in movies and television across the nation, nearly 210,000 were in California, a number representing 29 percent of the entire industry workforce. In terms of income, jobs associated with movies and television brought in $16.7 billion during the same year, or more than one-third of all the dollars earned throughout the nation.[51] These figures relate solely to direct industry employment. When supporting industries such as catering, set moving companies, equipment rentals, location accommodations, advertising, and other elements are added to the mix, the multiplier effect is staggering. One recent study estimates the entertainment industry multiplier effect at between 1.7 and 3.6 times the number of dollars directly generated, or in the range of $28.4 billion to $60.1 billion annually in income revenues.[52] Simply put, movies and television are a major sector of California's economy.

In recent years, Hollywood magic has tapped into the high-tech creativity of Silicon Valley, sending the industry to new heights. Pixar Animation and Industrial Light and Magic have been among the leaders in establishing new standards for visual effects projection and animation. While globalization has led to the export of jobs in some aspects of the entertainment industry, California's innovation magnet has kept hundreds of thousands here—ground zero for "Lights, Camera, Action!" Never mind that the overwhelming percentage of those who come here to make it don't, it's still a place of dreams.

Disneyland and Others

Walt Disney was one of those dreamers who brought his fantasy to California and converted it into a spectacular reality beyond even his own imagination. An artist by training, a creative photographer, and a believer in story-telling through film, Disney and his brother Roy worked their way to California from Kansas in 1923, where they cobbled together and sold a series of cartoon shorts. Walt Disney's experience is a rags-to-riches story, but his gestation period was long and painful. For years, he barely scratched out a living. Then, in 1928 Disney broke through with his cartoon short *Steamboat Willie*, featuring a scrawny-looking rodent known as Mickey Mouse.[53] Over the next 25 years, the Disney team slowly blossomed, first creating feature-length cartoons and ultimately motion pictures with real people instead of celluloid characters.

In his own way, Disney matched the entertainment successes of the better-funded and better-known movie studios. Where he differed, however, was in his creation of a theme park, an accomplishment that transformed motion pictures and cartoon stories into personal "hands-on" experiences. This was his genius, a participant connection that added to California's folklore as a fantasy state for residents and visitors alike—a fantasy that most of us will never have other than through the portals of temporary escape into the theme park's environment.

Disneyland quickly became the entertainment juggernaut of California; there was and still is nothing like it. Opening in 1955, the theme park is located in Anaheim about 40 miles south of Los Angeles and the middle of a mega-population center of 20 million residents. About 16 million people stream into the park each year, a number equal to about 40 percent of California's entire population.

Of course, as a "destination" location, Disneyland draws visitors not only from California but also from throughout the world. Today the Disneyland Resort (its new name because of recent additions) covers 500 acres, employees 20,000 workers, and brings in more than $1 billion in annual revenues. Near-perfect weather in southern California allows the enterprise to operate 365 days a year. Its components focus on everything from history to fantasy to adventure to the future. The park remains contemporary because fresh attractions correspond with newly released Disney movies; in short, there's always something new to draw visitors, no matter how many times they may have been to the park. Yet, Disneyland is steeped in American tradition, as embodied by Main Street at the entrance and a wholesome environment. Fantasyland reminds people of their dreams, while Frontierland and Adventureland appeal to their sense of adventure—all in a very controlled way, of course. In this sense, Disney authority Neal Gaebler writes, "Disneyland was neither just a park nor even an experience. It was also a repository of values."[54] Disney may not have known it, but his Disneyland offered tranquility to a state on the go and uncertain of its future.

Soon after the park opened in 1955, Disney leveraged his newfound gains into multiple enterprises. His company built similar resorts in Florida, Paris, Tokyo, and Hong Kong. The entertainment empire expanded its capabilities by producing new television shows as well as movies, and eventually merging with the ABC television network. The Disney Corporation even added a cruise line to further market its products. Those developments speak well for the company, but they're not so important in terms of shaping California. Disneyland embodied hope for all who came regardless of economic status, social standing, ethnicity, education level, or any other characteristic, even though the state's reality dictated otherwise. That's the benefit of fantasy.

To be sure, there were other theme parks in California and elsewhere. Knott's Berry Farm and Ghost Town, initially a restaurant featuring Mrs. Knott's fried chicken and berry pies in nearby Buena Park, began adding a "gold mine," Old West theme rides, and other attractions to its dusty streets in 1940.[55] Shortly after Disneyland opened, Pacific Ocean Park (POP) debuted as a water-oriented theme park in Santa Monica. Many others like Legoland, Six Flags, Marineland of the Pacific, and Universal Studios joined them. Some have folded (POP and Marineland), others have found niche audiences (Legoland), and others still have been reconstituted (Knott's Berry Farm), but no theme park has enjoyed the success of Disneyland. The sophisticated interdependent relationship between television shows and movies on the one hand and the theme park experience on the other has assured a continuous flow of visitors generation after generation.

The Lure of Escape

The intrigue of California's residents with entertainment tells us much about the state's complex culture. Without a doubt, the entertainment sector stands out as a valuable staple of the state's economy. On a deeper level, many of the values associated with this sector tell us much about the almost obsessive requirement for Californians to get out from under an unforgiving economy, contentious social system, and collective psychology of disconnectedness. Think about it—at the same time the state's residents run from responsibility to public education and the poor, they embrace the opportunity to pursue sheer fantasy. It's an odd combination, but one that goes a long way toward explaining the uneven culture of the not so golden state.

High Tech

Thus far, we've encountered elements of California that run the gamut between inequality and escape. We now turn to a sector of California riveted on the future: high technology. In this arena, we look to the impact of technological innovation on the state in particular and society in general. In some respects, high tech represents California's potential salvation; in other respects, high-tech visionaries are in a space unto themselves, with neither the desire nor the inclination to relate to the rest of the state, even if their products attract interest from here to the rest of the nation and the world.

Innovation and Entrepreneurship

Silicon Valley is ground zero for innovation in California. The very name speaks of something that is as much a concept as a physical place. There is no zip code for Silicon Valley. Geographically speaking, it covers an area roughly between San Francisco and San Jose, and extends to the east side of San Francisco Bay. Depending upon the product, tentacles of the Valley extend southward to Santa Cruz County and northward to Marin County, along with portions of Alameda County. Some connections go as far east as Boston's Route 128 or North Carolina's Research Triangle. This underscores the fact that in some respects, Silicon Valley is as much a state of mind as a physical entity. Intellectual wafts notwithstanding, the heartbeat of the territory pulsates loudest between Palo Alto and San Jose. Over that 25-mile stretch lies the perfect combination of brain power and venture capital.

True to the very concept of an innovation mindset, Silicon Valley has transcended the name given to it only half a century ago. Then, the region gained its title because of the invention of silicon chips, sand-based wafers capable of powering all kinds of products faster, in less space, and at a much lower cost than anyone could imagine. Originally, silicon chips were manufactured in Silicon Valley, where research and development seemed to reduce cost and size almost on a daily basis. That's changed. First Fairchild, then Intel, along with several smaller operations, perfected these incredibly complex memory-storing jewels.[56] For a few years, massive fab (short for fabrication) plants dotted the area, but that was relatively short-lived. Intel, the largest manufacturer of silicon chips, closed its last fab plant in Silicon Valley in 2010. Most of its production as well as the production of competitors now occurs in Asia and other cost-efficient countries throughout the world. Still, even today, research and development continues in the Valley for a variety of high-tech products and services. But we're getting ahead of ourselves.

Long before Fairchild and Intel, and prior to the region's name, Silicon Valley was the home to personal computation devices. In the late 1930s, David Packard and William Hewlett formed a company with $538 to design and produce electronic instruments—first oscillators and then ultimately personal computers and a host of other devices. Other companies emerged, some dealing with medical instruments, others with biological research, some with complex robotics, others still with a defense and aerospace industry bent. A wave of electronic games and applications followed. More recently, nanotechnology and green technology firms have become part of the ever-growing mix of cutting-edge industries. Other than building "things," the thousands of electronics-related companies have little in common with the corporate mindsets of a generation ago except a cultural thread that supported experimentation and suffered little from failure.[57]

"Experimentation" and "risks" are twin cornerstones of the Valley's ethos, both historically and even in the present day, with the latest wave of social media companies like Facebook and Twitter. These values did not appear by accident. Rather, they are characteristics cultivated by an influential faculty of computer scientists and engineers at Stanford University. Dozens of start-ups owe their beginnings to relationships between Stanford University faculty and graduate students that spawned commercial success stories. No other university provided such intellectual nourishment.[58] The University of California at Berkeley across the bay couldn't come close to matching Stanford's start-up magic. Of course, Silicon Valley didn't invent high tech single-handedly; Bell Labs, MIT, and other places made noteworthy contributions, but more of the collective high-tech energy flowed in Silicon Valley than anywhere else. Anyone who had a worthy idea knew the best place to cultivate it was Silicon Valley.

The results have been impressive. According to *Fortune* magazine, in 2010 four of the top ten revenue-producing companies in the state were housed in Silicon Valley—Hewlett-Packard (2), Apple (6), Cisco Systems (8), and Intel (10). Still, the surge in some ways may be illusory. While *The Wall Street Journal* headline screamed "Tech Revival Lifts Silicon Valley" in late 2010, the results of a comprehensive study only weeks later found that the number of jobs in the Valley remained the same in 2010 at 850,000, despite a population increase of 20 percent. That's because a sizable part of the corporate growth came from jobs sent offshore.[59] Clearly, not all have benefitted from the Valley's resurgence.

Capital Ideas

Ideas come and go, especially in Silicon Valley where creative juices flow on a 24/7 basis. To enable a new concept to blossom, you need to have some kind of outside support, which commonly has been delivered in the form of venture capital. The companies that provide this seed money usually take great risks with their capital. In return for their investment, venture capitalists are given sizable stock positions in the companies that they underwrite. In Silicon Valley, some of the best known of the 500 or so venture capital firms are sequestered along Sand Hill Road, an unassuming street with low-rise buildings, in Palo Alto.

Venture capital firms have little expertise in the companies they fund; their analysts' backgrounds tend to be in finance rather than technology. Because of their training, venture capitalists know a lot about what looks like a winner and what doesn't—at least enough of the time. Few investments provide returns equal to or in excess of the dollars committed by the venture capitalists, but when an outlay pays off, the profits for the investor can be mind-boggling. Most Silicon Valley high-tech companies that have been formed in the past 50 years have relied upon venture capital for early support, and those that have succeeded have earned small (and large) fortunes for their backers.[60] Still, being a venture capitalist is a tricky vocation not for the faint of heart.

Given that backdrop, the presence of venture capital in Silicon Valley is nothing short of astounding. As one account notes, "Capital and attention are lavished on Silicon Valley as in no other place."[61] Nationwide in 2010, venture capitalists poured $21.8 billion into 3,277 investments. About 40 percent of those funds were committed to Silicon Valley companies, with software, "cleantech" energy solutions, and biotech companies scoring most of the support. The size of the investments ranged from several thousand dollars to hundreds of millions, depending upon the stage of the new company's development, its profitability, and its potential for growth, among other factors.

An Uncertain Future

Genius, imagination, and venture capital have made Silicon Valley a one-of-a-kind place. But while the imagination may still be there, the jobs may not. Off-shoring, the concept of U.S. companies structuring manufacturing, production, and even services abroad, has become a mainstay of many large Valley companies. Hewlett Packard, Cisco, Oracle, Google, and countless others have built huge campuses in India, China, Vietnam, the Philippines, Ireland, and dozens of other countries where production and manufacturing costs are a fraction of the costs at home thanks to an abundance of cheap labor.

Off-shoring is not restricted to Silicon Valley high-tech companies, but it's much more common here than elsewhere.[62] According to the U.S. Bureau of Labor Statistics, in 2008 there were 86,000 fewer high-tech jobs in the Valley than in 2001, a reduction in the workforce of 16 percent.[63] Most of those jobs went overseas. These moves have made Valley technological companies among the most profitable in the nation, but their increased profits have come on the backs of tens of thousands lost jobs. Sentimentality doesn't play well here.

DREAMS, DELIVERABLES, AND DISAPPOINTMENTS

Ask ten Californians to define the state's essence or the core values of its residents, and you'll probably get ten different answers. That's both the state's charm and conundrum: in fact, there is very little consensus. No wonder it's so difficult to agree on major policy themes. The social demography of California is anything but flat. Like a never-ending earthquake, the state's residents and their values gyrate in all kinds of directions, at differing rates of speed, and with little continuity.

To the casual observer, California is the trendsetter, the state where things happen, a state that's always turning a page on the future. It seems to be a place where many groups and interests co-exist harmoniously on common ground. But it's not and they don't.

California is a state where too many people struggle over too few resources, and the distribution of those resources is anything but even. It's a state whose residents are so consumed with their financial present that they are willing to sacrifice the next generation. It's a state where people look for simple solutions to complex situations. It's also a state where Hollywood-orchestrated magic masks profound social and economic inequities and a good deal of despair. Yet, in a very uneven and dysfunctional social setting, incredible innovations and breakthroughs unmatched anywhere in the nation or world are born. Struggling for balance between dreams and disappointment, the state churns, with its residents and leaders alike struggling to find some kind of equilibrium.

Just because California never stops moving doesn't mean it's necessarily heading in a healthy direction, or in any one direction, for that matter. Endless cross-currents of activity suck up vast amounts of personal energy. Social trends come and go, some staying around longer than others. Among those who have and those who don't, the chasm seems to grow by the day, leaving few in the middle and most with dark futures. What's a dream for the few is a nightmare for the many. Still, the visionaries come, and some of them make significant contributions to society; others simply struggle to find themselves.

At the end of the day, none of these factors makes California a better place. It's more interesting, perhaps, and certainly more fractured. This is the state's cultural framework—frenzied, fractured, and on the verge of falling apart.

Yes, the canary is in the mine, and its tweet is one of despair, not of delight. And it's in that context that California manages to plod.

ENDNOTES

1. Donald L. Barlett and James B. Steele, *Howard Hughes: His Life and Madness* (New York: W.W. Norton, 1979), p. 176.
2. See Virginia Nicholson, *Among the Bohemians: Experiments in Living, 1900-1939* (New York: HarperCollins, 2004), p. 24.

3. See Daniel Hurewitz, *Bohemian Los Angeles and the Making of Modern Politics* (Berkeley, CA: University of California Press, 1985), pp. 21–39.
4. Ibid., p. 123.
5. Nicholas von Hoffman, *We Are the People Our Parents Warned Us Against* (Chicago, IL: Ivan R. Dee, Publisher, 1968), p. 144.
6. Mark Cramer, *Culture Shock!* (Portland, OR: Graphic Arts Center Publishing Company, 1997), pp. 30–31.
7. Walton Bean and Andrew Rawls, *California: An Interpretive History*, 4th ed. (New York: 1983), p. 441.
8. Richard B. Rice, William A. Bullough, and Rchard J. Orsi, *The Elusive Eden: A New History of California*, 3rd ed. (New York: McGraw Hill), p. 388.
9. Ibid., pp. 381–395.
10. For an in-depth discussion of McPherson and her life, see Matthew Avery Sutton, *Aimee Semple McPherson and the Resurrection of Christian America* (Cambridge, MA: Harvard University Press, 2007).
11. Stephen Winzenburg, "TV Ministries Use of Air Time, 2004," unpublished paper, Grand View College, Des Moines, IA, 2005, pp. 38–39.
12. "Religion: Enterprising Evangelism," *Time Magazine*, August 3, 1987, http://www.time.com/time/magazine/article/0,9171,965155-7,00.html.
13. "Crystal Cathedral's Tale of Two Ministries," *Los Angeles Times*, June 19, 2011, pp. A1, 14.
14. Cathy Lynn Grossman, "Biggest U.S. Churches 'Contemporary, Evangelical,'" *USA Today*, September 17, 2009, http://www.usatoday.com/news/religion/2009-09-16-church-growth_N.htm.
15. http://www.saddleback.com/blogs/newsandviews/index.html?contentID=1502
16. Kenneth C. Burt discusses this support in his *The Search for a Civic Voice: California Latino Politics* (Claremont, CA: Regina Books, 2007), pp. 334–335.
17. Andrew Sullivan, "The Mormon Money behind Proposition 8," *The Atlantic*, October 23, 3008, http://andrewsullivan.theatlantic.com/the_daily_dish/2008/10/the-mormon-fact.html.
18. Duke Helfand, "Pastors Risk their Careers over Gay Marriage," *Los Angeles Times*, July 17, 2008, http://articles.latimes.com/2008/jul/17/local/me-methodist17/3
19. Alejandra Lopez, "Race and Income in California: Census 2000 Profiles," No. 13, June 2003, prepared for the Center for Comparative Studies in Race and Ethnicity, Stanford University, pp. 12, 14.
20. California Current Population Survey Report, 2007, published by the Department of Finance, State of California, Sacramento, CA, 2009, p. 26.
21. "More Californians Living in Poverty, Losing Job-Based Health Coverage," California Budget Project, Sacramento, CA, September 10, 2009, p. 1.
22. "Policy Points," California Budget Project, Sacramento, CA, June 2009, p. 2.
23. Mary C. Daly and Heather N. Royer, "Cyclical and Demographic Influences on the Distribution of Income in California," Federal Reserve Bank of San Francisco Economic Review, 2000, p. 4.
24. "California: State and Local Taxes in 2007," Institute on Taxation & Economic Policy, Washington, D.C., November 2009, p. 1.
25. "California's Tax System," The California Budget Project, February 2009.
26. "California's Fiscal Deficit: The 2011-2012 Budget," Legislative Analyst Office, Sacramento, CA, November 10, 2010.

27. Charles M. Blow, "Empire at the End of Decadence," op-ed in *The New York Times*, February 11, 2011.

28. "State Shares Last Place in U.S. Reading Test," *San Francisco Chronicle*, February 25, 2010.

29. Peter Schrag provides the data and observations in his *Paradise Lost: California's Experience, America's Future* (Berkeley, CA: University of California Press, 1998), p. 41.

30. "A Master Plan for Higher Education in California, 1960–1975," California State Department of Education, Sacramento, CA, 1960.

31. "24% Likely to Drop Out at State's High Schools," *San Francisco Chronicle*, July 17, 2008. For a discussion on funding woes, see EdSource, "School Finance 2009–2010: Budget Cataclysm and Its Aftermath," January 2010.

32. Jim Cummins, "Literacy and English-Language Learners: A Shifting Landscape for Students, Teachers, Researchers, and Policymakers," *Educational Researcher*, 38(5), 382–384, 2009.

33. Belinda I. Reyes, "Demographic Change and the Politics of Education," in Sandra Bass and Bruce E. Cain, Editors, *Racial and Ethnic Politics in California*, Volume 3 (Berkeley, CA: Berkeley Public Policy Press, 2008), p. 225.

34. "No Quick, Cheap Fix for State's Schools," *Los Angeles Times*, March 15, 2007.

35. "UC Tuition Could Rise by Up to 16% a Year," *San Francisco Chronicle*, September 13, 2011, pp. A1, A9.

36. See "CSU Prepares 20% Fee Hike," *San Jose Mercury News*, July 17, 2009, and "Broken Promise," *San Jose Mercury News*, April 18, 2010.

37. "UC: More Freshmen, But Fewer from State," *San Jose Mercury News*, April 19, 2011, pp. B1, B4.

38. "Californians and Higher Education," Public Policy Institute of California, San Francisco, CA, October 2007.

39. See "California's Future Workforce," Public Policy Institute of California, San Francisco, CA, December 2008, and "Degrees Hold Keys to State's Success," *San Francisco Chronicle*, April 27, 2006.

40. Sarah McCally Morehouse and Malcolm E. Jewell, *State Politics, Parties, and Policy*, 2nd ed. (Lanham, MD: Rowman & Littlefield, 2003), p. 325.

41. "California Voters' Reaction to Proposed Cuts in the State's Medi-Cal Budget," prepared by the Field Institute for the California Healthcare Foundation, July 9, 2002.

42. See the Field Poll, "While California Voters Prefer Spending Cuts to Tax Increases to Resolve the State Budget Deficit, Majorities Oppose Cutbacks in Ten of Twelve Spending Categories," Release #2306, April 30, 2009.

43. "California Does Poor Job with Children," *San Francisco Chronicle*, February 2, 2011, p. C1.

44. "U.S. Supreme Court to Decide if California Can Cut Payments to Medi-Cal Providers," *Los Angeles Times*, January 11, 2011.

45. See The California Endowment, "Stability and Churning in Medi-Cal and Healthy Families, Los Angeles, CA, March 2008, and The California Endowment, "4.7 Million Californians to Gain Coverage under Health Care Reform—New CHIS 2009 Estimate," Los Angeles, CA, February 15, 2011.

46. Gretchen Rowe and Mary Murphy, *Welfare Rules Databook: State TANF Policies as of July 2006* (Washington, D.C.: The Urban Institute, 2008), pp. 72–73.

47. "The Foreseeable Harm from Governor Brown's Proposal to Reduce CalWORKS Grants for Children," Western Center of Law and Poverty, March 1, 2011.

48. Schrag, *California,* op. cit., p. 90.

49. Carey McWilliams, *Southern California: An Island on the Land* (Salt Lake City, UT: Peregrine Smith Books, 1946), p. 331.

50. See Paul Monaco, *A History of Modern Movies* (Lanham, MD: Scarecrow Press, 2010), p. 3.

51. "State-By-State Statistics," 2011, http//www.mpaa.org.

52. Martha Jones, "Motion Picture Production in California," prepared for the Select Committee on the Future of California's Film Industry, California State Assembly, March 2002, p. 83.

53. For an excellent overview of Disney's life and career, see Neal Gabler, *Walt Disney, The Triumph of the American Imagination* (New York: Alfred A. Knopf, 2006).

54. Ibid., p. 500.

55. Richard Harris, *Early Amusement Parks of Orange County* (Charleston, SC: Arcadia Publishing Company, 2008), p. 17.

56. For the history of the wafer chip in Silicon Valley, see Tim Jackson, *Inside Intel* (New York: Penguin Putnam Publishers, 1997), pp. 29–30.

57. John Kao, *Innovation Nation* (New York: Free Press, 2007), p. 264.

58. David A. Kaplan cites numerous examples of this special relationship in his *The Silicon Valley Boys and the Valley of Their Dreams* (New York: William Morrow and Company, 1999), pp. 32–33.

59. "Valley's Evolution Leaves Jobs in Lurch," *San Jose Mercury News*, January 2, 2011.

60. Kaplan, op. cit., chronicles the history of venture capital in Silicon Valley in his *The Silicon Valley Boys*.

61. Randall Stross, "It's Not the People You Know, It's Where You Are," *The New York Times*, October 22, 2006.

62. *InformationWeek*, March 3, 2008, http//www.informationweek.com/story/show/Article.jhtml?articleID=206901364.

63. Patrick Thibodeau, "Salaries Up, Jobs Down in Silicon Valley," *ComputerWorld*, September 14, 2009, http://www.computerworld.com/s/article/343078/Salaries_Up_Jobs_Down_in_Silicon_Valley.

Section II

The Demography

3

Immigrants: Cultures and Controversies

All the problems we face in the United States today can be traced to an unenlightened immigration policy on the part of the American Indian.

—Comedian Pat Paulsen

With his dry sense of humor, the late comedian Pat Paulsen reminds us of a simple, yet often overlooked fact: We all are immigrants in one way or another, maybe not directly but certainly indirectly. Some of us are descendants of ancestors who arrived three or four generations ago or more; others of us may be first-generation American citizens; others still may be here temporarily legally or otherwise in hopes of gaining permanent status or citizenship. Plainly stated, no Californian can claim original homestead rights save, perhaps, the Native American Indian.

That seems simple enough. Still, this point is sometimes overlooked by those whose family roots here are deeper than those of others are. Some of these residents view their length of presence somehow as a position of seniority that confers more rights and more legitimacy for them than those who have come here recently or may be new to California altogether. Roy Beck makes this claim in *The Case against Immigration* when he writes, "among the losers from immigration are all Americans who prefer to live in a more middle class and less economically polarized society."[1] Translation: Immigrants are a threat to the rest of us already here, even though "the rest of us" come from descendants who were immigrants themselves.

If Beck is right, there are an awful lot of threatened Californians, much more here than almost anywhere else in the United States. That's because in California, immigrants account for about 27 percent of the population, more than twice the national portion of 12 percent. In addition, whereas immigration has slowed considerably in the rest of the nation, it remains far more significant here. Of the 11 million illegal or undocumented immigrants throughout the United States, 2.7 million live in California alone—far more than any other state. Either way, immigrants are a powerful force in California, not only in numbers but also in the passions that arise with their presence regardless of their accuracy or justification.

But California's population is more than a collection of immigrants. In fact, people from the rest of the United States began coming here long before streams of foreigners. Like the other new Californians, they have added to the state's overall demographic texture through their attempts to live more fulfilling lives by virtue of their acquired educations, vocations, or other opportunities, as well as by contributing new and different layers to the state's social composition.

Two facts are abundantly clear, however, when viewing California's demography. First, the make-up of the people who reside here today is more complex and diverse than the arrangement of the past. They are less white, poorer, and speak numerous languages. Second, the state has ceased being a magnet for population growth. Yes, the number of Californians increased by about 10 percent between 2000 and 2010 to 37,250,000, but the pace was no greater than what transpired in the rest of the nation. Because of "flat" growth, the state's congressional delegation remains at 53 members. The last time California failed to gain at least one new seat in Congress was after the 1920 census. Every other southwest state grew more than California during the first decade of the 21st century. This is another sign that California's golden magnetism has diminished.

The remaining portions of this chapter focus on the make-up of California's population particularly in terms of its changing diversity. We'll look at domestic migration as well as immigration from abroad, tracing where today's Californians originated and why they have come. We'll also explore cultural clashes, and try to determine whether the differences between groups are too great to overcome. And if the answer is "yes," we'll need to consider a more foreboding second question, namely what to do about a state whose population may be too diverse to get along.

DOMESTIC MIGRATION

There's nothing new about people coming to California from other parts of the nation; that pattern has persisted for nearly 300 years. What is new, however, is that recently there's been an exodus of sorts from California by some citizens to other states. A stubbornly weak economy and high cost of living have proven a potent combination for chasing some people out of California to places where they believe there is a better opportunity to succeed. A mild climate may be good for the soul, but it doesn't pay bills.

Before we focus on any new migration tendencies, we need to spend a little time on the past. Most California transplants journeyed to their adopted home in response to a major event either in this state or in their state of origin. By tracing westward movements from other parts of the United States, as well as when and why, we'll add to our understanding of the complex California collage.

The Call of Gold

Few Americans traveled to California until the Gold Rush of 1848. Why bother? It was a pretty hard place to reach, given thousands of miles of inhospitable land between the populated east coast and here. The land mass known as Alta California was part of a large swath of the western part of North America under the auspices of Mexican rule, or ownership claim, anyway. Mexican governance wasn't prominent in the entire west coast but in the case of California, Mexican presence was clearly established, thanks to a string of 21 multi-purpose missions.

Originally constructed by the Spanish, the previous rulers of Mexico, the missions served as sources of religious outreach, land management, and education centers; in some cases, nearby were military presidios, or barracks.[2] In those days, Mexican officials on site had their hands full with generally passive tribes of Native Americans, who after a while, began to resent the ways that Mexicans intruded on their territory, values, and lives.

White Americans were few in number, perhaps 10,000 or less, until the unearthing of gold at Sutter's Mill along the American River, about 50 miles east of Sacramento. The discovery occurred on January 24, 1848, days before the signing of the Treaty of Guadalupe Hildalgo on February 2, 1848, which ended a three-year war between the United States and Mexico over Mexican-controlled land. Under terms of the treaty, Mexico ceded California and much of its southwest claims to the United States. Of course, communication was slow in those days, and word of the great gold find never reached the closing moments of the treaty negotiations and signatures. Otherwise, who knows how matters might have turned out, with the knowledge that potential great fortunes resided in a pastoral location known for farming and little else. In fact, the news did not reach the east coast until August 1848.

Suddenly, California became a valuable destination, with the promise of gold proving to be a magnet for those in search of instant wealth. Over the coming months, about 90,000 people made their way to California; two-thirds were Americans who arrived from all parts of the United States. By 1855, the number of new Californians swelled to a half million; again, they were mostly white Americans, although a few hundred free African Americans also managed to migrate to California in search of gold.

There wasn't much government organization in those days. During the first couple of years particularly, the Gold Rush took place in a "no man's land" legal environment. California was neither part of Mexico nor a state until September 9, 1850. The new arrivals pretty much expropriated what they wanted, when they wanted, and where they wanted with force serving as their "rule" of law. As one historical account of the time notes, "California society in 1848 was at once decentralized, independent, and deferential."[3] Might was right, especially since most of the gold was found in sparsely populated public lands in the hills. With California now separated from Mexico, the miners ignored Mexican rules of ownership and operation.[4]

Much of the Gold Rush vigilantism had a strong racist tinge. Anger was directed with regularity toward Mexicans, Native Americans, and the few Asians, and further codified in the Constitution of 1849 and subsequent state legislation. In Article II of the state Constitution, voting power was given explicitly to white males over the age of 21, leaving out Native Americans, Mexicans, and other nonwhites. Then in 1850, the state legislature passed "The Act for the Government and Protection of Indians," an ironic name because it facilitated removal of Native American Indians from lands contested by whites and placed resolution of any differences between a white and an Indian in the hands of the local white Justice of the Peace.[5] Minorities didn't have a chance, which, some critics would say, was a harbinger of things to come for centuries.

More discrimination was legitimized at the second state constitutional convention of 1879. There a splinter group known as the Workingmen's Party, a discouraged group largely comprised of Irish ex-railroad laborers, advocated for Chinese exclusion from California.[6] Their voices were heard and additional anti-Chinese measures were added to the revised state constitution. Clearly, a pattern was set.

The Railroad

The difficulties associated with Americans traveling to California were eased immensely with the completion of the transcontinental railroad in 1869. At last, people could move from one end of the country to another in a matter of weeks, not months. But transport ease wasn't enough to induce the relocation of Middle America; the attraction of plentiful land was, however. Congressional passage of the Timber and Stone Act in 1878 allowed settlers to purchase up to 160 acres of vacant federal land for $2.50 per acre—an incredible buy in those days. From that point on, the flow of American immigrants was steady, if not overwhelming. Most came from the east coast, specifically New York, Pennsylvania, Massachusetts, and Maine; a few others came from interior states such as Ohio, Indiana, Illinois, and Missouri.[7] Thanks to the railroad, the population of Los Angeles County doubled between 1890 and 1900 to 170,000.

That was just the beginning. During the early years of the 20th century, California became the home to large-scale farmland irrigation, the movie studios, and even a nascent petroleum industry. Many people initially came as tourists, with large numbers deciding to relocate permanently upon arrival. The railroad brought out people to work these new sources of employment as well as other jobs. By 1910, more than half of California's population had transplanted themselves from the Midwest. White, Protestant, and middle class, they identified disproportionately with the Progressive philosophy. Briefly organized as a political party, Progressives espoused "direct democracy," or political participation in the political system by the white middle class to offset corporate domination of the state legislature, while eschewing political involvement of racial minorities, particularly Japanese Americans.[8] As with other eras, the new white Californians pushed others of different races aside, even those who had preceded them.

There were others, although not nearly in the same numbers as middle class whites. Between the last decade of the 19th century and first three decades of the 20th century, a cadre of African Americans also came out to California, although in smaller numbers than did their white counterparts. Many of the men worked for the railroad as waiters and porters, taking up residence in major railroad-served cities such as San Francisco, Oakland, and Los Angeles. In Los Angeles, particularly, the African American population grew from 2000 in 1900 to nearly 40,000 by 1930.[9]

Still, the numbers of African Americans there amounted to less than 4 percent of the city's population of 1.2 million at the time.

The Great Depression

It was bad enough that the Great Depression ravaged the U.S. economy. Worse yet, many farmers in the "Dust Bowl" states of the southwest suffered an agricultural drought without end or parallel. Combined, these two incidents were enough to send hundreds of thousands of poor, disproportionately evangelical white Protestants packing in Oklahoma, Texas, Arkansas, Missouri, and the surrounding areas. Between 1935 and 1940 alone, more than 250,000 "Dust Bowl" victims moved to California, a sizable portion of whom settled in the San Joaquin Valley to grow cotton they had failed to produce in their home states.[10] By 1940, the number of migrants largely from the southwest reached more than 700,000, nearly half of whom settled in rural areas of California.[11] A decade later, their numbers doubled again.[12] Of course, migrants came from the rest of the nation as well, but the people from the southwestern part of the country were by far the largest portion of new Californians. We also know that foreign arrivals were extremely few during this period because of strictly enforced immigration laws and reduced mobility because of the global depression.[13]

Given that 6,950,000 people lived in California at the time of the 1940 census, an infusion of 700,000 people from one part of the country represented a substantial change in the state's demography. The new composition altered the tenor and proportions of the state's racial, ethnic, and religious values. As historian James Gregory explains, "If the arrival of blacks from the South helped turn the northern Democratic Party into the voice of Democratic liberalism, the influx of white heartlanders [into California] has spread lower-middle-class conservatism."[14] Once again, California was changing.

Post-World War II

After World War II, California went through yet another growth spurt. As with previous population metamorphoses, the composition of the state evolved yet again in both quantity and origins. Remarkable changes occurred between 1950 and 1985. Researchers Hans Johnson and Richard Lovelady divide this fertile period into three distinct parts, each with its own combination of demographic characteristics.[15] Between 1950 and 1965, the state grew like crazy. An average of 272,000 people moved in each year, with more than 90 percent from other states. Few Californians left.

Between the late 1960s and early 1970s, the migration pattern changed somewhat. With a sputtering aerospace industry, the state's economy failed to keep up with other parts of the nation. California drew an average of about 40,000 domestic migrants during this period, with international migration averaging 100,000 each year, a staggering 2.5 times the domestic amount. Something else happened during this period: between 1970 and 1972, the state actually experienced its first domestic loss—that is, more people left than came, but the change was temporary.

During the third part of this 35-year period, 1975–1985, the state experienced another surge in population growth. Domestic net migration picked up to an average of 60,000 annually. However, the greatest growth occurred among foreign immigrants, who came to California in numbers averaging 200,000 plus during the period.

The flow of domestic migration to California seesawed during the next decade. Between 1985 and 1990, Johnson and Lovelady note, migration from other states averaged a net gain of 100,000 annually. Then the domestic migration bottom fell out. Between 1990 and 1995, people left California in droves, averaging a net annual population loss of 125,000 during the span.

Beginning in 1995, the battle between net gain and net loss of domestic Americans was over. The redirection happened over a short span of time. Between 1995 and 2000, more than 1.4 million people living in the United States moved to California, while 2.2 million Californians went elsewhere. The lack of well-paying jobs, accented by the dot com bust in 2000 sent people running to what they saw as greener pastures accented by lower cost of living and better quality of life. Other western and southern states gained people from the rest of the nation, and California became one of their donors.[16] The reversal continues to this day.

Losing Curb Appeal

When people shop for new homes, they search for "curb appeal"; they need to feel good about the look of the house, including the lawn, the paint, the roof, the plants—everything—before they walk in. If the house has curb appeal, there is a much greater likelihood that it will entice the interest of the prospective buyer. Otherwise, it's on to the next house on the list. For Americans living elsewhere as well as many of those who reside here, California has lost its "curb appeal." The high cost of living, sketchy job opportunities, a slowly deteriorating infrastructure, scarce resources, and a host of intangibles have led many prospective Californians to look elsewhere, with many here ready to join them.

The exodus is underway with demographics just as interesting as are those of the domestic migrants who arrived here in the first place. Recent data show that more than 70 percent of those leaving California are white, well above the white percentage of the state's population. They have lower incomes than those remaining, less education, and higher unemployment rates.[17] Moreover, the whites who remain in California are older than nonwhites are. The median age for whites is 44, compared with 28 for Latinos. As demographer Hans Johnson explains, whites simply are not replacing themselves; meanwhile, other groups have increased their proportions of the population mix.[18] All this points to a changing California.

IMMIGRANT PATTERNS

Depending upon a range of climatological factors, ocean waves pound the surf with varying degrees of intensity, strength, and volume. That has been no less the case with the flow of newcomers into California. The immigration pattern has been uneven over the past three centuries, but there is a pattern nonetheless. They have landed here again and again, although in varying numbers, for widely divergent reasons, and with widely different outcomes. Some immigrants have come in search of land and fortune; a few have journeyed here because of political regime changes in their former homeland; others have simply wanted a fresh start in a new environment; still others have been lured to California under false pretenses. About the only consistency with the irregular streams of immigrants has been the general lack of acceptance of the newcomers by those already in place—even if the "natives" have been here for a short time.

Immigration brings change to the *status quo*. The presence of newcomers can alter social, economic, and political conditions already in place. Immigrants bring their own experiences to a new environment. There is a kind of awkward social overlay of the old with the new—trying simultaneously to fit in the present while not abandoning the past entirely. The concept is hardly new to the United States, which has received immigrants since its very beginning and has more immigrants than any other nation. But there is a difference between immigration patterns to California and the rest of the United States. Historically, the preponderance of immigration arrivals for most of the United State has originated in various parts of Europe. Not so here, where most of the state's newcomers have come from Mexico and points south, with a few additional arrivals from Asia.

This distinction comes with its own set of challenges. With each new wave of immigration, another level of social complexity and diversity is added to those already rooted in the state. The temporary disequilibrium plays out with different patterns, sometimes with ugly outcomes. What offers hope for the newest arrivals occasionally strikes fear for those with established routines and relationships. Maybe it shouldn't be that way, but it often is. Xenophobia—the fear of strangers—can be a powerful offset to the inclusive outreach of the traditional community "welcome wagon," and nowhere has this emotion been expressed with greater intensity and frequency than in California. It's a collective ugly side of the state that outsiders rarely sense unless they're the new immigrants looking in. The result is a state with sociological fissures as problematic for California's multi-ethnic society as earthquakes are to the land.

Like layers of sandstone that compress over time, each group of immigrants adds something to the make-up of the state in the form of new cultural traditions. Still, the pulsations of new arrivals have impacted California, and continue to do so to this very day. The list is long and shows no sign of ending. It helps to explain how the "new" California is increasingly different from the "old" California.

Native Americans[19]

Native Americans have the oldest ties and have suffered some of the greatest costs. Experts differ on their first entry dates probably from what it is now Siberia—some say 15,000 years ago, others suggest much earlier. Whatever the time of origin, this group clearly reached and established a foothold in California well before anyone else. Historians estimate that between 100,000 and 1 million Native Americans lived here when European settlers first arrived in the mid-1700s.[20] They formed their own tribal governments and welcomed occasional visits from white traders and explorers. Once the Spanish began what appeared to be permanent occupation of Native American land, the welcoming spirit quickly disappeared.

Over time, hundreds of thousands of Native Americans died from exposure to European diseases to which they had no natural immunity. Successive occupiers including Spanish, Mexican, and later California state and U.S. governments expropriated almost all American Indian lands and most of their constitutional rights.[21] Between 1848 and 1865, the U.S. Calvary killed more than 15,000 Native Americans, all in the name of bringing peace to the new state.[22] In the years shortly after California joined the union, tens of thousands of other Native Americans were deported to reservations in other territories. By 1910, the population had dropped to 16,000. During the 20th century, the federal government stepped in with various forms of assistance, often laced with sizable amounts of paternalism.[23] Belatedly, the relationship between Native Americans and the rest of the state underwent reassessment. Approximately 400,000 Native Americans live in California today, although now they represent but a tiny fraction of the state's 38 million residents. Under various treaties, a fraction of their 100 million acres of land has been returned. Native Americans have paid a steep price for their claim to California.

Spanish

In the mid-1700s, both Spanish and Russian explorers cast their eyes on California. Approaching the land from the south and the north, the two groups and their governments ultimately reached dramatically different conclusions. After a brief flirtation with areas near what is now San Francisco from the early 1800s through 1841, Russian traders and merchants retreated to places closer to home; perhaps the supply lines were too thin to justify continued presence.

It was much easier for the Spanish who, because of the proximity to their home base in Mexico, experienced little difficulty in charting a presence in what is now California. Beginning in 1769, seven years before American colonists declared independence from England, Spanish missionaries set up the first of 21 missions in San Diego. Soldiers quickly claimed ownership of the land for the Church, moving further north with each new venue. The final mission completed in 1823 near what is now Sonoma, more than 1500 miles north of San Diego.

As they solidified their positions, missionaries went about their business of "pacifying" the state's Native American population. The new occupiers were relentless in their efforts to convert the native population while subjecting them to near-slavery status.[24] It was a terribly uneven exchange: Spanish colonists seized land while Native Americans died from European diseases to which they had no immunities. Ultimately, the land under control of the missionaries represented about one-sixth of what is now California.

Mexicans

After the Mexicans revolted successfully against their Spanish occupiers in 1821, the new order strengthened its presence in California. The Mexicans ruled the territory differently than the Spanish did. In an attempt to mollify the hostile Native American population, Mexican rulers organized a more secular government system and ceased most of the proselytizing, but they continued the near-slavery status of Native Americans.[25] Equally important, Mexicans controlled large swaths of valuable land.

But their reign over the territory was brief. An end to the Mexican-American War and the discovery of gold brought thousands of Americans to California within months. Mexican rule terminated in 1849, when the relatively few whites already here declared independence as the first step to seeking American statehood the following year.

Mexican influence has been a constant in California. Millions have come often to work in the most menial positions, especially backbreaking farm labor jobs with low pay, abysmal housing, and no benefits. During World War II, the Emergency Farm Labor Supply Program, an agreement between U.S. and Mexican authorities, encouraged Mexicans to work on farms in California and other states to make up for men at war. The farm labor program continued in one form or another through the 1980s, providing a clear path for Mexicans to work not only on California farms but also in factories. Since then, millions of other Mexicans have made California their permanent home, some legally and others not. Today, residents of Mexican descent are by far the largest minority group in California, comprising more than one third of the state's residents.

Irish and Chinese

The California immigration turnstile continued to operate. The unskilled Irish and Chinese were enticed to the state in its infancy with the promise of immediate work. They were brought in during the 1860s as laborers to complete railroads dedicated to connecting the nation—the Irish building tracks for the railroad company moving west, the Chinese building tracks for the railroad company moving east. Dismissed when the transpacific railroad was connected at Promontory, Utah in 1869, neither group had the wherewithal or desire to return to their native lands.

Now out of work and unprepared for anything other than manual labor, most of the Irish and Chinese laborers ended up in San Francisco, where they competed for employment on the bottom rung of the economic ladder. Cities seemed to offer more services and opportunities than rural areas did as well as the potential for employment, which helped to explain why these immigrants sought comfort in the City by the Bay. Today, San Francisco's Chinatown is the largest Chinatown in the United States and the largest Chinatown outside of China.

Japanese

By the turn of the 20th century, Japanese immigrants began arriving to fulfill their dreams of economic prosperity. A few hundred had trickled in as laborers during the last two decades of the 19th century, but the numbers of arrivals did not increase dramatically until the first decade of the 20th century. By 1910, more than 40,000 Japanese lived in California; the population nearly doubled to 71,000 by 1920. Their numbers and their financial successes grew. By 1940, just before the start of World War II, the Japanese American population in California hovered near 100,000.

Japanese immigrants and their families worked hard, especially in agriculture-related enterprises, where they grew produce and flowers. They were hard working and incredibly innovative. Japanese farmers developed the state's first hothouses, which allowed them to grow products with year-round availability. Excluded from labor unions and trade associations because of discrimination, Japanese Americans often lived near each other. Anti-Asian sentiment notwithstanding, many family-run Japanese American enterprises became successful within a generation. Their contributions were stalled in 1942, when in response to the attack on Pearl Harbor by the Japanese military, the U.S. attorney general ordered Japanese Americans to divest themselves of their land and report to "internment centers." After the war and upon release from confinement, many Japanese Americans were able to assume their place in California society, their humiliation notwithstanding.

Vietnamese

After the Vietnam War ended in 1975, the United States admitted more than 1 million South Vietnamese who had been forced to flee their country in the wake of North Vietnam's communist victory over the South Vietnamese-American alliance. Some were associated with the political or military elite, but most were members of the army or peasants who had been loyal to or identified with the South Vietnamese government. Hundreds of thousands fled in small boats, taking little more than the items they could carry on their backs.

The overwhelming percentage settled in California, with 41 percent of the entire Vietnamese Diaspora in the United States and the largest Vietnamese population outside their native country. Even more telling, today 20 percent of all Vietnamese immigrants to the United States live in the Los Angeles metropolitan area. The San Jose metropolitan area is home to another 8 percent. These are the two largest Vietnamese communities in the United States.[26]

Contrary to many immigrant groups, Vietnamese Americans enjoy a higher rate of home ownership in California. Fewer live in poverty, compared to other immigrant groups. Knowledge of the English language remains a nemesis, however; as of 2008, two-thirds of all Vietnamese immigrants had limited proficiency in English.[27] Still, overall, California's newest immigrant group appears to be making an easier adjustment than its predecessors did.

Others

In addition to the groups discussed previously, others from faraway lands have come to California in less dramatic fashion, albeit in fewer numbers and perhaps less dramatic fashion. Indians, Filipinos, and Koreans have been among many from the Pacific Rim who have crossed the ocean to study in American universities or with skill sets in search of new lives.

Eastern Europeans have arrived since the end of the Cold War. In lesser numbers, people from South America, Central America, Central Asia, and Africa also have come to the Golden State.

Illegal Immigrants

Some people call them "aliens," others use the less offensive term "undocumented residents," but whatever the description, illegal immigrants are part of California's population—and not just a small part. No state has as many illegal immigrants as California has, where 2.7 million of the 11 million in the entire nation reside. Here's another way of understanding the numbers: California has about as many illegal immigrants as the total populations of Maine, New Hampshire, and Vermont, *combined.*

Illegal immigrants are hardly new to the United States or to California, for that matter. They have been entering the United States from just about everywhere around the globe almost since this country's founding. Unlike today's commotion-filled setting, illegal immigrants were pretty much ignored altogether until the Chinese Exclusion Act of 1882 because until that time, almost all immigrants were from Europe, a continent with a collective culture similar to ours. But the Chinese were another story; they were different, as were the Japanese who followed, which ultimately led to the Immigration Act of 1924. Both of these pieces of legislation were vital to the interests of white majorities in California.

Skip ahead to the 1920s when, for the next half century, a group of 300,000 or so Mexicans emerged as a sizable part-time agricultural labor force. We say "part time" because they would come in January or February, work their way up the state to harvest various crops, and then leave in September. A small percentage headed further north to assist with harvests in Oregon and Washington, but most returned to Mexico until the next winter, when they would begin the cycle again.

Then conditions changed. Many farm laborers moved to cities, usually taking better and less strenuous jobs in construction, housekeeping, gardening, or in some cases workers on assembly lines in manufacturing plants. With their relative affluence, many decided to plant permanent roots in California. Others from Mexico took their places in the fields before some of those moved away to cities. After all, it was easier to stay rather than go through the hassle of illegal border crossings every year.

The results were stunning in terms of a population shift. Before 1986, nearly half of all Mexican migrants travelled back to Mexico at the end of the harvest season. By 2002, only a quarter of them returned to their homes and families.[28] Nationally, the explosion was palpable. Of the 12 million illegal immigrants in the country at the time, one study estimated that half came to the United States between 2000 and 2008 alone.[29] Beyond farm labor, illegal immigrants now account for sizable percentages of the workforce as roofers, insulation workers, drywall installers, food processers, janitors, restaurant workers, and textile workers.[30]

It would be silly to deny that illegal immigrants have emerged as a sizable constituency among California's population. They have and they are. The question is, does their presence bring harm or benefit to the state? That's where the discussion becomes interesting. Given the huge presence of illegal immigrants here, it's worthwhile to look into the question.

The Case for Illegal Immigrants Remaining in California

Upwards of 60 percent of all illegal immigrants in California are Mexican, with most of the rest coming from Central America and Asia. Commonly with little education and an inability to speak English, illegal immigrants take jobs on the bottom rung of the economic ladder, particularly those associated with farm labor. California growers believe that this group accounts for 90 percent of their labor pool; as such, crops would go unpicked without this labor pool.[31] According to a study by the Pew Hispanic Center released in 2011, illegal immigrants comprise nearly one-tenth of California's entire workforce, and they are anything but a drag on the economy. In fact, the study found that illegal immigrants had an unemployment rate of 9.7 percent in California, considerably below the overall state rate of 12.5 percent.[32] Overall, when considering compensation for services, illegal immigrants actually earn 31 percent less than their legal counterparts earn doing similar work.[33] This inexpensive labor is actually a boon to employers both in terms of worker availability and company profits.

Some observers see benefits beyond filling corporate coffers with cheap labor. In fact, immigrants are consumers, too, whether legal or illegal. In his research on Mexican immigration, Tomas Jimenez observed businesses that discriminate against immigrants hurt themselves because of lost revenues.[34] A recent *BusinessWeek* article described the benefits of illegal immigrants as follows: "The problem for critics of illegal immigration is that corporate efforts to sell to the undocumented weaves them ever more tightly into the fabric of American life."[35] What's so bad about that?

The Case against Illegal Immigrants Remaining in California

Opponents of illegal immigration argue that the state must send them away because of their overwhelming numbers and consumption of costly state services. There is no question that illegal immigrants account for a sizable portion of the state's population. In California's public schools, one out of every ten students is the child of an illegal immigrant, adding to the cost of education.[36] That alone amounted to about $2.3 billion, according to a 2009 state report. In addition, prison expenses for illegal immigrants totaled $834 million and healthcare costs added another $703 million.[37] Together these three categories approach $4 billion. Critics say that money contributes to the state's annual budget deficit problems.

Others view illegal immigration as a threat to American culture. The more immigrants come here, the more they water down traditional norms and values. Writing about this concern, eminent political scientist Samuel Huntington states that for the United States, Mexico is ground zero for the immigration problem: "While Europeans see the immigration threat as Muslim or Arab, Americans see it as both Latin American and Asian, but primarily as Mexican."[38] Clearly, this school of thought fears "strangers," those with values other than the values associated with the European roots of white Americans.

An Issue, Yes; a Problem, No

What do we make of this debate? There's no question that immigrants, legal or illegal, change the social dimensions of California more so than elsewhere in the United States due to the extent of their numbers. The government statistics for various forms of aid are large, to be sure. On the other hand, shouldn't we also consider contributions in terms of revenues?

Because of their status, many illegal immigrants are paid cash "under the table." Still, they use that money to purchase consumer goods and services, like anyone else. Many have bought cars, furniture, and other sizable staples. Those acquisitions usually include sales taxes for state and local governments. Also, by virtue of their purchasing power, illegal immigrants add to consumer demand, which requires companies to employ more people to make those products.

Much of this discussion is logical, but without "hard" numbers. After all, no one asks a customer his or her legal status at the time of purchase. However, there is at least one reasonably concrete number: the Social Security Administration estimated that in 2007, illegal immigrants contributed $12 billion to the system with intentionally invalid Social Security numbers. Given that California has about one fourth of the illegal immigrant population, that number alone comes to about $3 billion that illegal immigrants will never see.

No doubt, the biggest challenge with immigrants—legal or illegal—is in the public schools, as discussed in Chapter 2. Without professional assistance in acquiring English, immigrants are set up for failure, period. To the extent that we provide assistance in learning English, immigrant children will do better in school, acquire skills, and become better equipped to get good jobs that generate more taxes for governments. Sadly, public policymakers and the public alike have not seen the benefits of this investment.

Still, there's a larger question, even more fundamental than economics or education: It's the question of who belongs here and who doesn't, and under what circumstances? What gives some of us the sense that we have more of a right than others do? For whatever reasons—economic, social, or psychological—some people feel threatened by illegal and legal immigrants alike. Such an attitude is unfortunate and an anathema to what our society claims to be, a democracy. In his celebrated work, *The Book of Democracy*, James David Barber ends with assessing the best ways to create and maintain a democracy. One way, Barber notes, is through immigration. Democracies, Barber writes, should permit immigration from other democracies, and not dictatorships. "This would probably motivate the people living in nondemocracies—and perhaps even their leaders—to convert to democracies."[39] So much for the philosophical viewpoint at 35,000 feet.

But let's take a closer look on the ground. Are immigrants the source of our problems, economic or otherwise? No, according to recent survey data. A statewide Field Poll released in 2011 asked respondents about the impact of immigration on their quality of life. While 39 percent said immigrants made their quality of life "worse," 47 percent replied that there was "no change" in their lives and 10 percent actually answered that their lives were improved. When asked about the impact of immigrants in their communities, the results were even more one-sided. About one quarter (26 percent) answered that their lives were "worse," while 62 percent replied "no change" and another 9 percent cited improvement in their lives.[40] Clearly, California's problems do not stem from immigration.

This is not to suggest that the federal government shouldn't act on the immigration issue—it should do so by discouraging border crossings by those without employment and providing an orderly means to citizenship opportunities for those who have otherwise obeyed the laws. The state of California can help, too, by enacting legislation that permits illegal immigrants to acquire driver licenses. By doing so, the state would be better able to monitor the driver behavior of a huge percentage of California.

PERSISTENT DISCRIMINATION

The equality issue extends back to the days before California attained statehood and when the Spanish, and then Mexicans, mistreated the Native Americans simply because of their race and unwillingness to accept western European traditions.[41] Discrimination of Native Americans, a given when Westerners landed in California, continued after the Gold Rush and statehood in 1850. Now whites replaced Mexicans as oppressors.

New victims of discrimination were added over time. Even though California was admitted to the Union as a free, or non-slave state, the few African Americans here were treated as second-class citizens; they weren't allowed to vote until passage of the 15th Amendment, ratified in 1870, and the experience was not always pleasant. Well into the 20th century, they were denied access to housing and schools in white neighborhoods. Some of the discrimination was blatant; most was through intimidation and neglect.[42] Many of these injustices were corrected when the state legislature passed the Rumford Fair Employment Practices Act in 1959 and the Rumford Fair Housing Act in 1963, both authored by the African American assembly member of the same name. But the voters said otherwise in 1964 when they passed a California Association of Realtors–sponsored ballot proposition that specifically allowed renters and sellers to avail their property only to those they deemed suitable.[43] Three years later, the U.S. Supreme Court overturned the California law as a violation of the 14th Amendment of the United States Constitution.

More groups fell to the wickedness of discrimination. After Chinese and Irish foreign laborers completed construction of the transcontinental railroad, they were dismissed without repatriation to their native lands. That led to disproportionate numbers of each landing in San Francisco, where they struggled on the bottom rungs of the economic ladder under the most trying of circumstances. Both groups suffered discrimination, although the nonwhite Chinese endured more grief, no doubt because of their difficulties with English and non-Western appearances.

The Chinese were barred from state citizenship, land ownership, and employment, according to the terms of the revised California Constitution of 1879. Mobs of whites in San Francisco and Los Angeles occasionally tortured the newest immigrants, and received little punishment from government authorities.[44] Some Chinese had set up small farms outside the cities, but their land ownership opportunities were denied, particularly after Congress passed the Chinese Exclusion Act in 1882. Whatever the benefits of wide open California, equality was not one of them.

Discrimination was a mainstay for Japanese immigrants, who arrived in California around the turn of the 20th century as well. Many went into farming and soon were not only producing the best crops, but were envied by white farmers who were unable to produce at the same levels or sell at the same prices.[45] In 1913 and again in 1920, the state legislature passed restrictive laws prohibiting Japanese immigrants from owning land. Congress also passed the Immigration Act of 1924, although those Japanese Americans born here, "Nisei" they were called, continued as successful farmers. A simmering animus of whites toward Japanese Americans boiled over with the start of World War II. Then-California Attorney General (and later U.S. Supreme Court Chief Justice) Earl Warren asked President Franklin Roosevelt to relocate Japanese Americans to places far from California and the Pacific shores. Never mind that most were U.S. citizens—many of them were actually born here. Roosevelt complied with an Executive Order and the whole mess was upheld by the United States Supreme Court.[46] Still, in spite of their persecution by the U.S. government, many young Japanese Americans volunteered to serve their country in the U.S. military. They were packaged into the 442nd infantry regiment, shipped off to the European front regiment and, in a moment of irony, became the most decorated American military unit of the war. After Japan surrendered, the internees were released from their confinement, mostly penniless. Not until 1988 did Congress admit mistake, when each surviving internee was given an official apology and a government check for $20,000. Still, this rectification hardly offset years of involuntary servitude and humiliation.

As for Latinos, their treatment was mixed and has remained so to this day. During the 1930s, Mexicans who dwelled in the cities were routinely segregated and limited largely to manual labor and housecleaning jobs. With labor shortages during World War II, hundreds of thousands came across the California border to become the backbone of the agriculture workforce. For a moment in time, they were welcomed almost as saviors because the state had no one else to pick crops and support the agricultural community.[47] This was no small acknowledgment, given that until that moment, Mexicans had been belittled and segregated just like African Americans. Whites had kept them in their place. But the nation now was at war, and California's fertile land had become its breadbasket. So, large numbers of Latinos were given temporary opportunities to work the fields and carry out other mundane agricultural jobs, not, however, without local authorities reminding them that these new Californians benefitted courtesy of the white establishment.[48] Like other minorities, Latinos remained second-class citizens.

One other point before we leave the topic of discrimination—prejudice has not always been a matter of whites denying opportunities to nonwhites. In some instances, whites have been intolerant of other whites, such as when "Okies" (a disparaging name for Oklahomans) and other mostly poor farmers from the southwest United States moved to California during the 1930s.[49] California also has witnessed discrimination of one minority against another, the results equally harmful to the aggrieved party. One recent study of Los Angeles found situations where African Americans were victimized by Latinos; in another part of the city, profound tension existed between Koreans and African Americans.[50] Similarly, a San Francisco weekly that today describes itself as "The Voice of Asian America," has published a column entitled "Why I Hate Blacks."[51] In California, no one group has a monopoly when it comes to bigotry.

Racism, California Style

The pattern here has been clear: Whatever the state's reputation as a laid-back, "kumbaya" kind of setting, race has been a dominant theme in California throughout its history, and an ugly one at that. Although many of the constitutional issues have been clarified repeatedly in the courts and through legislation, minorities disproportionately find themselves in the worst schools, in the most depressed residential areas, and with the fewest vocational opportunities. None of this is coincidental. Demographic studies show that even today, half of all neighborhoods in California remain segregated.[52] More on these themes later.

STRIKING BACK

When we think of some of the great civil rights battles in recent years, people often point to confrontations like the public school showdown in Little Rock, Arkansas or the lunch counter sit-ins in Birmingham, Alabama during the early 1950s. These are seminal moments in the efforts to overcome racism and move toward equality, where people put their lives on the line, where the state and national governments clashed, and where the nation watched with concern. The issue of racial strife in California often is far from the top of most people's minds, at least in terms of public discussions. Yet, because of the abuses cited previously, California has been the center of its own brutal battles relating to racism.

Zoot Suit Riots

By the 1930s, a sizable Mexican population had developed in Los Angeles. Many Mexicans from poor neighborhoods during that period began wearing "zoot suits," distinctive, baggy garments that identified their heritage. Other minorities, particularly African Americans, wore zoot suits as well, but these clothing sets were most closely associated with Mexicans.[53] Police, elected officials, and a very bigoted print media at the time harassed the Mexican population incessantly, in part because of their attachments to these garments.

Matters were exacerbated during World War II when hundreds of servicemen, sensing protection from the Establishment, began attacking Mexicans in zoot suits on a regular basis. They patrolled Mexican neighborhoods, going after any Mexicans they saw along the way. In a show of racial solidarity, the organized African American community in Los

Angeles joined with Mexican organizers to condemn the vigilantism. The effort, while courageous, further fueled white anger.

Outright rioting ensued in 1943, after nine Mexicans were falsely convicted of a murder. For several weeks, Mexicans fought with whites mostly in an effort to keep whites from harming them. Nevertheless, the exchange led to the trials and convictions of hundreds of Mexicans on a variety of charges, most of which were unfounded. When all was said and done, few servicemen suffered any indignities from the courts.[54]

The zoot suit riots received a good deal of notoriety for a short time; after all, the United States had a war to fight. For the better part of two decades after the war, Los Angeles authorities treated Mexicans as troublemakers. But from that point on, racial lines were drawn and opposed by Mexicans.[55]

Watts and Other Cities

Of course, Latinos have not been the only group to strike back at their condition. Though relatively small in numbers, African Americans have also been victims of persistent discrimination. Like Latinos, historically, most African Americans in California had little education, worked in menial jobs, and lived in racially segregated neighborhoods. The police and other authorities kept them in their place, often through brutal treatment, encouraged by the press, realtors, and banks.[56]

African American groups protested mistreatment for years, largely through nonviolent means, and generally receiving lip service from local leaders in return. One day in August 1965, Los Angeles finally exploded when crowds in Watts, a black portion of the city, erupted against police making a traffic stop. The police chief fueled the flames by referring to the rioters as "monkeys in the zoo."[57] Racial tension remained overt in Los Angeles from that point on, fueled by authorities operating more or less with a policy of racial containment. Describing social conditions during the 1980s and 1990s, Min Hyoung Song notes that local government became "less a tool for properly managing the city, providing necessary social services, and planning for an equitable future, and more a regime of incarceration, retributive justice, and increased surveillance."[58] It was only a matter of time before another explosion would occur.

In April 1992, another riot occurred a year after police pulled over Rodney King, an African American driver who had been speeding. A video showed that almost immediately after King stepped out of his car, four police began pummeling him. But it wasn't just another police beating, which would have been bad enough; it was a spectacle. In addition to the four officers taking shots at defenseless Rodney King, 25 others watched in approval as a police helicopter hovered overhead. Local television news programs carried the event and the African American community simmered. On April 29, 1992, a largely white jury acquitted the four officers. That night, thousands of African Americans took to the street in rage. When the violence subsided, 53 people were killed and property damage exceeded $1 billion.

But brutality against African Americans has neither been restricted to Los Angeles nor diluted over time. A 2005 report by the California NAACP identified a series of unprovoked attacks by police officers throughout the state against African Americans between 1996 and 2005.[59] Referring to housing discrimination against African Americans, Peter Schrag noted "These things were not supposed to happen in California, where blacks lived not in crowded tenements as they did in Newark or Detroit, but in detached little houses."[60] Yet, the pattern has witnessed a long history and little has changed in either perception or practical terms. A full decade after the 1992 riots, half of the respondents in a survey of Los Angeles residents believed that a similar event would occur within the next five years.[61] Expectations are low.

The Fields

The cities have not been the only centers of discrimination and brutality. Farm workers have long suffered from oppressive working conditions, decrepit housing, and minimal compensation. Comprised predominantly of Mexicans, these migrant laborers carry out their backbreaking work for a little more than half the year. They begin south in the Imperial Valley with cantaloupes in March and end in the wine country and orchards to the north part of the state with grapes in October and apples in November. These farm workers became a meaningful part of California agriculture during World War II, when most American men went into the service. Periodically, U.S. immigration authorities have launched sweeps against these workers, commonly referred to as "braceros," only to look the other way when conditions dictated otherwise.[62]

Today, about 500,000 farm workers harvest fruits and vegetables in the state's 90,000 farms. About 70 percent are noncitizens and most earn annual incomes of less than $10,000 per year. From those funds, workers must pay for lodging, food, and other necessities as they travel up and down the state. According to the Bureau of Labor Statistics, as of 2007, the average farm worker earned $8.64 per hour. Try living off that with a spouse and a couple of kids. Moreover, three-fourths of all migrant workers are illegal and, as such, ineligible for government healthcare and unemployment insurance.[63]

For years, groups of farm workers attempted to secure agreements with farmers for better wages and working conditions; their efforts were futile. In 1965, Cesar Chavez and others demanded that farm workers be paid the federal minimum wage; again they were spurned. They went on strike, but strikes in the past had been short-lived before they were broken either by stonewalling growers or the courts. This time, Chavez and his team organized a boycott of California grapes. The agricultural labor group, now named the United Farm Workers, sent members to delivery docks at grocery stores, where they asked fellow union members to leave the grapes in the trucks. The Union also asked consumers to refrain from purchasing table grapes. The strike lasted for two years before a leading agricultural corporation signed a collective bargaining agreement, and another three years before all of the grape growers fell into line and the boycott officially ended. Since then, the union has entered into agreements with growers of other crops. Today, the UFW has 30,000 members. There is even a state holiday commemorating Cesar Chavez and his work. Still, organizing efforts leave much to be accomplished. The battle goes on.

RACE AND ETHNICITY IN CALIFORNIA'S SHRINKING WHITE WORLD

Every day the demography of California becomes less white. That's because for several decades most of the population growth has occurred among racial and ethnic minorities, particularly Latinos but also Asians. Census bureau data show that between 2000 and 2010, California's population expanded by 10 percent, matching the rate of the nation. But that's not the most important part of the story.

Over the 10-year period, the Latino population increased by 28 percent, and the Asian population increased by 32 percent. As for African Americans in California, their numbers increased by only 2 percent. Meanwhile, the non-Hispanic white population actually decreased by 5 percent. Combined, the non-Hispanic white population actually decreased from 46.7 percent to 40.1 percent. Today, Latinos are a close second at 37.6 percent. Combined, racial and ethnic minorities now account for about three-fifths of California's population.

The ever-changing composition of the state impacts both those who are chosen to lead and those who are the recipients of their policies. For example, in the November 2010 elections, whites comprised 65 percent of the voters, far beyond their 46.7 percent of the population. Whites also were 67 percent of the state legislature, whereas the 24 Latinos comprised 20 percent of the two-house body. (More on this in Chapter 8.)

This disconnect won't last forever. As larger percentages of minorities gain election to various offices, past discriminatory policies enacted by elected officials and the voters alike are sure to be revisited. Those changes will be as interesting as the changing demographics of the state. The new representation lines for the state legislature and Congress augur an upswing for the most representation of minorities in state history.

Meanwhile, we can't leave this chapter without stating the obvious: When we ask why the state is "not so golden after all," part of the answer lies in the inability of its diverse society to live with each other harmoniously and thrive. It is a state of profound animus.

ENDNOTES

1. Roy Beck, *The Case Against Immigration* (New York: W.W. Norton, 1996), p. 21.
2. W.W. Robinson, *Land in California* (Berkeley, CA: University of California Press, 1948), pp. 24–25.
3. Malcolm J. Rohrbough, *Days of Gold: The California Gold Rush and the American Nation* (Berkeley, CA: University of California Press, 1997), p. 7.
4. Robinson, op. cit., p. 36.
5. Several anti-Indian, anti-Mexican, and anti-Asian laws were written by the California legislature during the 1850s. See R. Kimberly Johnston-Dodds, "Early Policies and Laws Related to California Indians," CRB-02-014, published by the California Research Bureau, Sacramento, CA, 2002.
6. Charles Postel, *The Populist Vision* (New York: Oxford University Press, 2007), p. 265.
7. Robert M. Fogelson, *The Fragmented Metropolis* (Berkeley, CA: University of California Press, 1993), p. 64.

8. George E. Mowry, *The California Progressives* (Berkeley, CA: University of California Press, 1951), p. 154.

9. Fogelson, op. cit., p. 76.

10. William H. Mullins, Oklahoma Historical Society's *Encyclopedia of Oklahoma History & Culture*, "Okie Migrations," http://digital.library.okstate.edu/encyclopedia/entries/O/OK008.html.

11. Allison Verzally, *Making a Non-White America* (Berkeley, CA: University of California Press, 2008), p. 23.

12. James N. Gregory, *American Exodus* (New York: Oxford University Press, 1989), p. 7.

13. Leah Platt Boustan, Price V. Fishback, and Shawn Kantor, "The Effect of Internal Migration on Local Labor Markets: American Cities during the Great Depression," *Journal of Labor Economics*, 28(4), 723, 2010.

14. Gregory, op. cit., p. 246.

15. The data and analysis over the next few paragraphs lean heavily on their report. See Hans P. Johnson and Richard Lovelady, "Migration between California and Other States, 1985–1994," joint project of the California Research Bureau and the California Department of Finance, Sacramento, CA, November 1995, pp. 7–8.

16. "California Is Seen in Rearview Mirror," *Los Angeles Times*, August 6, 2003.

17. Hans P. Johnson, "Movin' Out: Domestic Migration to and from California in the 1990s," *California Counts*, Public Policy Institute of California, San Francisco, CA, 2(1), August 2000.

18. "Whites in State 'Below the Replacement' Level, *San Francisco Chronicle*, June 5, 2010.

19. A word about terminology. "Native Americans" is the term most commonly used to describe California's indigenous population today. Previous authors have used the words "Indians" or "California Indians." For purposes of consistency, the term "Native Americans" is used in all discussions that focus on this demographic group.

20. Andrew F. Rolle pegs the figure at between 100,000 and 150,000 in his *California: A History* (New York: Thomas A. Crowell Publishers, 1963), p. 28. However, Richard B. Rice, William A Bullough, and Richard J. Orshi estimate the number at between 300,000 and 1,000,000 in their *The Elusive Eden: A New History of California* (New York: Alfred A. Knopf, 1988), p. 25. Either way, the number was substantial for its day.

21. Robinson, op. cit., p. 16

22. Stephanie S. Pincetl, *Transforming California: A Political History of Land Use and Development* (Baltimore, MD: The Johns Hopkins Press, 1999), p. 2.

23. Rolle, op. cit., p. 398.

24. David Wyatt, *Five Fires: Race, Catastrophe, and the Shaping of California* (New York: Oxford University Press, 1997), p. 11.

25. Robinson, op cit., p. 29.

26. Aaron Terrazas and Cristina Batog, "Vietnamese Immigrants in the United States," published by Migration Policy Institute, Washington, D.C., September 23, 2010.

27. Terraza and Batog, Ibid.

28. Edward Alden, *The Closing of the American Border: Terrorism, Immigration, and Security Since 9/11* (New York: HarperCollins, 2008), p. 74.

29. Steven A. Camarota, "Immigrants in the U.S., 2007," Center for Immigration Studies, Washington, D.C., November 2007, p. 1.

30. "Many Employers See Flaws as Immigration Bill Evolves," *The New York Times*, May 27, 2007.

31. "Slim Pickings in Farm Labor Pool," *Los Angeles Times*, August 14, 2005.

32. Jeffrey S. Passel and D'Vera Cohn, "Unauthorized Immigrant Population: National and State Trends, 2010," Washington, D.C.: Pew Hispanic Center, February 1, 2011, p. 17.
33. Laura E. Hill, Magnus Lofstrom, and Joseph M. Hayes, "Immigrant Legalization: Assessing the Labor Market Effects," Public Institute of California, San Francisco, CA, April 2010, p. 7.
34. Tomas R. Jimenez, *Replenished Ethnicity: Mexican Americans, Immigration, and Identity* (Berkeley: University of California Press, 2009), p. 205.
35. "Embracing Illegals," *BusinessWeek*, July 19, 2005.
36. Jeffrey S. Passel and D'Vera Cohn, "A Portrait of Unauthorized Immigrants in the United States," Washington, D.C.: Pew Hispanic Center, April 14, 2009, p. 9.
37. "Deficit May Trigger Anti-Illegal Immigration Ballot Measure," *Los Angeles Times*, July 10, 2009.
38. Samuel P. Huntington, *The Clash of Civilizations and the Remaking of World Order* (New York: Simon and Schuster, 1996), p. 203.
39. James David Barber, *The Book of Democracy* (Englewood Cliffs, NJ: Prentice-Hall, 1995), p. 412.
40. The Field Poll, Release #2370, March 18, 2011.
41. Rolle, op. cit., pp. 135–36.
42. Fogelson, op. cit., pp. 200–201.
43. Proposition 14 amended the California Constitution to state: *"Neither the State nor any subdivision or agency thereof shall deny, limit or abridge, directly or indirectly, the right of any person, who is willing or desires to sell, lease or rent any part or all of his real property, to decline to sell, lease or rent such property to such person or persons as he, in his absolute discretion, chooses."*
44. Kevin Starr makes this point in his *Inventing the Dream: California through the Progressive Era* (New York: Oxford University Press, 1985), pp. 42–43.
45. Pincetl, op. cit., p. 85.
46. Executive Order 9066, issued on February 19, 1942, required 120,000 ethnic Japanese to relocate to residences in guarded camps, officially called "internment centers." The order was upheld by the U.S. Supreme Court by a 6-3 vote in *Korematsu v. United States* 323 U.S. 214 (1944).
47. Peter Schrag, *California: America's High-Stakes Experiment* (Berkeley, CA: University of California Press, 2006), p. 90.
48. Kevin Starr drives home this point in his *Embattled Dreams: California in War and Peace, 1940–1950* (New York: Oxford University Press, 2002), pp. 97–115.
49. Allison Varzally, *Making a Non-White America* (Berkeley, CA: University of California Press, 2008), p. 27.
50. Karen Umemoto and C. Kimi Mikami, "A Profile of Race-Bias Hate Crime in Los Angeles County," *Western Criminology Review*, 2(2), 2000.
51. "Asian Paper's 'I Hate Blacks' Column Assailed," *San Francisco Chronicle*, February 27, 2007.
52. Ali Modarres, "California in Flux: Demographic Trends in the State," in Sandra Bass and Bruce Cain, Eds., *Racial and Ethnic Politics in California: Continuity and Change*, Volume 3 (Berkeley, CA: Berkeley Public Policy Press, 2008), p. 31.
53. Varzally, op. cit., pp. 74–76.
54. For a complete account of the events surrounding the zoot suit riots, see Kevin Starr, *Embattled Dreams*, op. cit., pp. 105–111.

55. For a thoughtful account of this period, see Stuart Cosgrove, "The Zoot-Suit and Style Warfare, *History Workshop Journal,* 18, 77–91, Autumn 1984.

56. Fogelson, op. cit., p. 200.

57. Anthony Obershall, "The Los Angeles Riot of 1965," *Social Problems,* 15(3), 312–324, 1969.

58. Min Hyoung Song, *Strange Future: Pessimism and the 1992 Los Angeles Riots* (Durham, NC: Duke University Press, 2005), p. 58.

59. "Focus on Solutions to Stop Police Brutality in California against African Americans," published by the California NAACP, 2005.

60. Peter Schrag, *California,* op. cit., p. 97.

61. Mara A. Marks, Matt A. Barreto, and Nathan D. Woods, "Race and Racial Attitudes a Decade after the 1992 Los Angeles Riots," *Urban Affairs Review,* 40(1), 4, September 2004.

62. "Faces of Our Fathers," *San Jose Mercury News,* November 30, 2008.

63. Sarah Watson, "California's Agricultural Workers," Insure the Uninsured Project, funded by The California Wellness Foundation, The California Endowment, Blue Shield of California, and L.A. Care Health Plan, July 2010.

4

From Farmers to Assemblers to Engineers

There is science, logic, reason; there is thought verified by experience. And then there is California.

—Edward Abbey, author and environmentalist

Big. That simple three-letter word speaks volumes about California's economy. That's because if separated from the rest of the United States, the totality of the state's economy would be equal in size to the eighth-largest nation in the world. According to the U.S. Department of Commerce, the gross domestic product (GDP) of California in 2009 was $1.74 trillion, an amount equal to the GDP of the entire country of Italy. Given its massive dimensions, any issues relating to California's economy automatically become everyone's issues, wherever they live.

California's prowess as an economic juggernaut transcends to virtually every major source of production and services. Some states have economies that are deeply dependent on a single sector such as farming, mining, automobile manufacturing, or even tourism. Not so here, where many sectors generate goods and products in volumes unimaginable anywhere else. The $40 billion agriculture sector yields more than half of the nation's fruits, nuts, and vegetables.[1] In manufacturing, California has three of the nation's ten largest employment centers: Los Angeles (1st), San Jose (8th), and Orange County (10th).[2] In biotechnology, California commands one sixth of all the industry jobs in the United States and, perhaps more tellingly, 42 percent of the venture capital dedicated to the development of new businesses in this research and manufacturing sector.[3] The significance of these numbers goes well beyond the state's borders. When California's economy hums, most of the rest of the nation zooms.

When the state's economy stalls, the rest of the nation holds its breath in fear of potentially punishing ripple effects. Thus, while the Great Recession of 2008–2010 stunned the nation, the economic downturn brought California to its financial knees. Of the 7.9 million jobs lost throughout the nation during the two-year period, California alone accounted for 1.3 million.[4] In other words, the state with 12.5 percent of the nation's population lost 16.5 percent of the jobs. And when the Great Recession left 23 percent of the nation's properties "under water" with negative equity, California was well above that proportion at 35 percent, leaving the state's homeowners in a world of hurt.[5] We all know that one of the basic laws of gravity is that what goes up must come down. But with California's economy, what goes up can soar almost out of sight and what comes down can land with a punishing thud.

There's another aspect of California's blockbuster economy: The existence of so many huge industries leads to political confrontations over scarce resources such as land, water, and government support through subsidies or tax breaks. Much of this is played out in Sacramento where powerful interest groups use their influence to steer state policies in ways that confer upon them the greatest benefits and fewest obligations. Agricultural organizations, business associations, and technology alliances are among the thousands of interest groups that maintain a strong presence in Sacramento to protect their turfs. Elected officials think twice before taking on many of these sectors, as they do with organized labor and other major interests. We'll cover this issue in depth in Chapter 9. But for now, it's important to know that California's economy is not to be trivialized. This is a powerful commercial machine, albeit one that is fragile and vulnerable to misfire.

Not all sectors thrive today as they have in the past, a reminder that few enterprises are safe in an era dominated by technological innovation and globalization, regardless of where they originated or their previous clout. Competition within many sectors also can be fierce, which has resulted in the victories of agribusiness over small farms and the gobbling up of small companies by large corporations several times their size. Then, there are always examples of companies that begin with a novel idea and soon dominate their competition. SpaceX (a private space shuttle company), Apple Computer, Google, Netflix, and Facebook are just a few examples that readily come to mind among thousands of others.

The remaining sections of this chapter focus on the building blocks of California's economy both in terms of their present operations and in terms of historical development. Some sectors function with generations of tradition, while others are the results of the state's endless innovation mentality. Some corporations have workforces the size of small cities, while others generate billions of dollars of income with relatively few personnel. Regardless, California's businesses are not afraid to throw their weight around in the name of survival. Some bang on government's door for help through tax breaks or subsidies, others bar the door from government intrusion. All told, this is a compelling story worth knowing because of the enormity and types of industries, products, labor pools, and endless innovations that contribute to California's economic might.

THE AGRICULTURAL SOCIETY

With bustling cities like Los Angeles, San Diego, San Jose, and San Francisco, you might not think of California as a major center for American agriculture, but it is. California produces nearly twice as much volume of farm products as its closest competitor, Texas. Today, 25.6 million acres, or about one fourth of the state's 100 million acres, are dedicated to agriculture. Here's another way to understand the immense magnitude of agriculture in California: the amount of California land committed to agriculture is larger in size than the entire state of Kentucky.

The land quality is incredibly generous. The nation's five most financially productive counties all are found in California—Fresno, Tulare, Kern, Merced, and Monterey. Fresno and Kern counties alone account for more than 20 percent of the value of the state's agriculture products.[6] But nowhere is the land more prolific than in the Great Central Valley, that long swath of land 450 miles long that is bounded by the Cascade mountains in the north and the Tehachapi mountains in the south. In their narrative about J.G. Boswell, the once-powerful overseer of a California cotton empire with 200,000 acres in total, Mark Arax and Rick Wartzman recount the land's extraordinary capabilities: "The Valley grew everything...in such staggering amounts that there was no such thing as a single harvest season but rather a constant pick and pack and shipment of fruits, vegetables and grains."[7] The Great Central Valley is the heart of California's farm pulse, but there are other farm centers in the state as well. In fact, more than 350 different crops are grown in California on 81,000 farms, just about everything from avocado to zucchini, yet another indication of the state's agricultural diversity.

In an era that marches to the beat of high technology and innovation, agriculture remains a valuable staple of California's economy. Today, one out of every ten jobs relates directly or indirectly to farming activity, and sales from livestock and agriculture foods and other products yield about 8 percent of the entire gross domestic product of California.[8] In an era when the United States routinely imports more goods than it sells abroad, California agricultural exports account for more than $10 billion annually.

From Small Farms to Agribusiness

Farming has a long history of being big business in California. True, in California's earliest days, some people farmed for self-sufficiency and little more. That's because for a brief period the Gold Rush of 1849 dominated much of the state's economy and command of human resources. While the more ambitious new arrivals mined gold, most of California's economy focused on provisions for miners in the forms of supplies, equipment, food, and lodging.[9] But the Gold Rush was relatively short-lived and by the 1870s, it was a past adventure. People turned to farming in earnest as the state's major industry.

Diversification of the Land

The earliest uses of farmland were devoted to livestock, mostly cattle, long before the days of the Gold Rush. The Spanish, and later Mexican settlers brought cattle to California, where they grazed over vast ranchos in large herds. By 1834, more than 400,000 cattle foraged on endless acres of tall grasses. But water has always been a wild card in California, especially since most precipitation falls in the far north, while most of the state's farmland (and, these days, most of its people) lies to the south. A series of droughts plagued California cattle during the 1860s, 1870s, and 1880s, punctured by rampant disease on several occasions.[10] Together, these tragedies of nature drove away some ranchers altogether and led others to consider more reliable uses of the land. Within a few decades, the cattle ranching industry was supplanted by farming, which seemed to be more resilient and predicable.

Over time, various crops were planted on fertile land that seemingly could grow anything and everything. The earliest farming businesses centered on wheat, but by the end of the 19th century, farmers had taken to growing various varieties of fruit and sugar beets. Extension of the railroad through the length of the Central Valley during the 1880s helped to open new markets for these crops; unfortunately, the terms of transportation were dictated by the railroad often at the peril of the grower.[11] By 1910, 62 percent of all sales were from crops, compared with 38 percent from ranching.[12]

Land use patterns changed, too. In the beginning, most farming was undertaken in the Central Valley. Shortly after the turn of the 20th century, farmers began planting cotton in the Coachella Valley, located in the arid southeast corner of the state near Palm Springs and other future desert communities. The flower and hothouse industries also blossomed during the second and third decades of the 20th century, this time in areas of the state closer to the coast and more temperate climatological conditions. By the early 1940s, various melon crops were cultivated in the Coachella and Imperial Valleys.[13] The state's agriculture industry was diversifying quickly. These days, California produces nearly 100 percent of a dozen crops and between 70 and 99 percent of another dozen crops, including grapes, consumed by Americans.[14]

Sizing Up

Whether large or small, most California farmers historically have viewed themselves as businesspeople hoping to bring their products to market.[15] The sizes of the enterprises run the gamut as well. Cotton and wheat farms tend to be large; orchards, berry, and vegetable plots tend to be small. While sizes and uses of the land continue to vary to this day, there have been some important changes in the industry overall. During the past quarter century, large corporate farms have grown in numbers, and surged even more so in their market share. In 1978, corporate farms comprised 5.3 percent of all California farms; by 2007, corporate farms amounted to 7.1 percent of California's 81,000 farms. But that's not the real story. By the end of the 20th century, slightly more than 1,000 landowners controlled nearly half of the state's agricultural acreage.[16] Combined, these business farms employed 39 percent of all farm workers. Meanwhile, family farms have found it harder to compete because of rising feed prices, expensive equipment, and pesticide and fuel costs, as well as difficulty in matching the prices of large agribusinesses. Moreover, increasingly they are being bought out by the largest farms which have the resources because they are the beneficiaries of a convoluted farm subsidy program that rewards large farms while giving virtually nothing to small farms.[17]

The most significant changes have come in production volume. For example, according to U.S. Department of Agriculture data, corporate farms in 2007 registered 73 percent of the nation's greenhouse nursery sales, 70 percent of all poultry and egg sales, and 50 percent of all vegetable sales. Overall, this relatively small number of farms account for about 40 percent of all farm sales in California. Some farms are beyond belief in size. The first and largest California agribusiness, J.G. Boswell and Company, owns 150,000 acres alone in the San Joaquin Valley dedicated almost exclusively to cotton. This single farm represents about twotenths of 1 percent of the state's entire land mass. Closely behind is Paramount Farms with 120,000 acres. E & J Gallo, a family-owned enterprise, cultivates 15,000 acres of grapes and exports more than half of all California wine. Others operate as both owners and lessees of land; Dole Corporation is a prime example of a company that owns 7,000 acres and leases another 12,000. As a point of comparison, the "average" farm size in California is slightly more than 300 acres.

Farm Power

Their numbers may be small, but clearly, members of the agribusiness community are deeply involved in policy areas that impact their issues. In many cases, they haven't been shy about throwing around their weight, sometimes as individual companies and in other instances through interest group representation. Three areas particularly worth noting are water, labor, and environmental regulations.

Water

Nothing is more important to the survival of a farmer, large or small, than the availability of water. In California, this issue is particularly delicate because many crops such as tomatoes, cotton, and corn are water-intensive, requiring farmers to use large amounts. The problem is that enough water is not always available for these crops.

Most of the state's water originates in the Sierra Nevada snowpack; the second-largest source is the Colorado Aquifer, a massive underground lake that extends under seven western states and provides about 20 percent of California's water.[18] During a year with average rainfall, farmers will receive about 75 percent of all the water available to the state, either through rainfall or delivery. On years with less than average rainfall, the state and federal government agencies allocate less water to farmers so that adequate supplies flow through environmentally sensitive areas and urban populations. When that happens, hundreds of thousands of acres may go without planting, costing farmers in the short run and consumers in the long run.[19] The fact that California has gained millions of people without any changes in precipitation averages has exacerbated the farmer's vulnerability.

Farmers have not taken their plight lightly. They had an easier time of things when California was less populated and the environmental movement was nowhere to be found. But as the state grew, the opportunities for water-starved farmers dimmed. For the past quarter century, farmers have found themselves in a fight with environmentalists over the water that flows through the Sacramento–San Joaquin River Delta. Farmers have argued for a water conduit (commonly called the "peripheral canal") to divert the water for agricultural use; environmentalists have countered that a canal would ruin the state's ecology, specifically endangered fish species.

The California Farm Bureau, an agricultural interest group with 76,000 members in 56 of the state's 58 counties, has taken the lead on pushing for more water, including the peripheral canal. Farm trade organizations such as the California Cattlemen's Association (cattle), Sunkist (citrus), and Nursery Growers Association of California (flowers) also have pressured state policymakers for generous water policies. On other occasions, the state's biggest farmers have successfully argued for federal subsidies to reduce their costs of water. One study by the Environmental Working Group found that in a recent year, the largest 10 percent of California farms received 67 percent of all water subsidies. The result: wealthy farms paid 2 percent of the price that Los Angeles residents paid.[20] Ouch.

Sometimes, powerful individuals have attempted to use their influence to move public policies on water. In 2009, for example, Richard Resnick, owner of Paramount Farms and a major campaign contributor to political campaigns, requested U.S. Senator Dianne Feinstein to promote federal government support for the peripheral canal. Feinstein asked for a federal review of California water practices, although Resnick denied it was because of campaign contributions.[21] Should a renewed effort come forward to build the canal, environmentalists will not let that happen without a fight.

Labor

As noted previously, agribusiness is a complicated enterprise for the family farm, and even more so for the corporate giants that operate vertically (crop management, canning, and distribution) as well as horizontally. Major agricultural companies have sophisticated operations that utilize the latest scientific equipment and weather forecasts. But they also are dependent upon basic elements such as readily available labor at key points during the season.

Relying upon migrant farmworkers as the heart of their labor pool, farm owners have found themselves mired in two perennial problems: assurance of an adequate supply and union organization. Concern over the labor supply backs into the thorny issue of illegal immigration. Inasmuch as many temporary farmworkers come to California each year from Mexico, the idea of closing down the border or restricting illegal immigration is an anathema to farmers, especially the largest companies. Here's how the California Farm Bureau tiptoes on the issue: "Enforcement at the border is important….But the jobs offered on this side of the border are a powerful magnet. Some of those jobs are on farms…."[22] Why is the Farm Bureau so concerned with the plight of immigration? As many as one-fourth of all farm workers are illegal immigrants, according to a recent study.[23] The more border enforcement impedes their entry, the tougher it is for California farmers to harvest their crops.[24]

The second labor issue for California farmers centers on union activism. As discussed in the previous chapter, farm workers historically have worked under onerous conditions for low pay. In 1966, after a long strike against grape growers, the United Farm Workers (UFW) gained a contract with Scherdey Industries, followed by contracts with 32 other growers. Over time, the UFW had some successes, along with several other unions, including the Teamsters. But union gains have been more symbolic than substantive. As of 2010, up to as many as 450,000 people worked on California farms, but only 16,000 full-time workers were union members. Why? The best answer lies in the make-up of the workforce, which has a sizable contingent of illegal immigrants who are likely to maintain low profiles while working in the United States. That contrasts with unionism activism, which is anything but low profile.

For California farmers, the best of both worlds would be a workforce of temporary workers with no standing other than their physical presence. Whether they come illegally or with temporary government permission is of little concern to growers because they come without rights or demands.

Environmental Regulations

What do environmental regulations have to do with farming? A lot more than you might think. In addition to rich soil, fertilizers and pesticides enhance the quantity and quality of the farm products while saving them from insect infestation. That sounds reasonable enough, except farmers and environmentalists are traditionally at odds over the definition of safety, with state and federal government agencies often determining the proper balance through various regulatory policies.

The land mass of California farms equals 3 percent of the nation's farm acreage, yet state farmers use one fourth of the nation's pesticides. For California farmers, pesticides for the land are equivalent to a mother's milk for her infant. The question is, are these deterrents harming more than insects? Farmers and pesticide manufacturers say "No," even though the use of pesticides has increased dramatically in recent years.[25]

Environmental regulations exist to protect farm workers and consumers from contracting pesticide-caused, life-threatening diseases. Is there reason to be concerned? Perhaps so. Studies on the impact of fertilizers and pesticides use different methodologies, which can impede the determination of conclusive results. Nevertheless, there are data worth mentioning, especially since lives are at stake. One of the most comprehensive assessments to date was a comparison between UFW Latino farmworkers and Latinos who did not work on farms. The independent study occurred over a 10-year period. In analyzing the data, the principals found that leukemia and several forms of cancer occurred with much greater frequency among UFW Latinos and California Latinos than in the general population.[26]

Environmentalists not only condemn excessive pesticide use but also blame the state and federal governments for being careless, if not outright derelict, in pesticide oversight. Californians for Pesticide Reform, a coalition of 185 organizations, has accused farmers of using soil fumigants and pesticides not only harmful to crops but also the air, essentially putting everyone in contact at risk.[27] In 2011, the Center for Biological Diversity filed suit against the Environmental Protection Agency for permitting pesticides that threatened more than 200 endangered species of animal and insect life. If history is any guide, they have a good case. Numerous cases of farmworker poisonings and tainted water supplies seem to occur on a regular basis.[28]

Some of the discussion is little more than finger pointing about data, but in a clearly hypocritical instance of regulation, two environmental groups sued the United States Environmental Protection Agency in 2010 for allowing farmers to use chlorpyrifos, a chemical sprayed on grapes, nuts, and other crops, while banning the chemical for household use in 2001.[29] How can such applications be safe in one place and not another? You don't have to be a chemist to see that they can't. No wonder environmentalists are concerned—lives are at stake.

Do Animals Have Rights?

Big farming doesn't always win. For years, animal rights activists and human rights groups have criticized the confined conditions under which farm animals are kept. They have focused on egg-laying chickens and penned calves, among others. State legislators have submitted proposed laws for these groups stipulating criteria for the treatment of farm animals and other livestock, but the powerful farm lobby always has defeated them on the grounds that the animals don't suffer and that such rules would jeopardize productivity and profits—code words for higher costs to the consumer.

In 2008, animal rights groups gathered enough signatures to place a farm animal rights ballot proposition before the voters. Proposition 2, officially known as the Standards for Confining Farm Animals Act, established minimum size living areas for chickens and other penned animals that would allow them to turn around without constraints, lie down, stand up, and fully extend their limbs. Activists in both camps spent more than $15 million on the campaign, with the "yes" side outdistancing the "no" side by a 3-to-2 margin, despite virulent opposition by major farm groups. Proposition 2 carried by a margin of 65 percent to 35 percent. The new law takes effect in 2015. People's lives may be in jeopardy from debilitating pesticides, but when it comes to creature comforts, California's chickens have come to roost! Oddly enough, that incredulous paradox screams volumes about the state's priorities. Only in California.

California Farming: A Lot More than Putting Food on the Table

Clearly, farming has emerged as a major component of California business, and the state's economy has benefitted wildly from its sales. In countless respects, growers' successes here are the envy of the rest of the nation and of the world. But at what cost? And to whom? Farmers must find a way to reconcile their practices with limitations, be they in resources such as water or production enhancements such as pesticides. Farmers must also deal with the immigration issue in a way that goes beyond their own narrow labor needs; otherwise, the complex issue will lack for meaningful resolution. Equally so, state and national governments need to take a closer look at land management practices, given the types of products grown in a challenging water environment. All this underscores the point that farming, while very important, does not operate in a vacuum. Many farmers, like other Californians, have yet to realize this point.

MANUFACTURING—METAMORPHOSES AND MISMATCHES

The role of manufacturing in California today is considerably different from that in the past. For the state's first 50 years, California leaned on agriculture and ranching, and to a lesser extent mineral extraction, as the basis for its economy. Then the framework of the state's economic foundation began to change. By the turn of the 20th century, California was 13th of the then 47 states in the value of manufacturing, and 14th with respect to the size of the factory workforce. The trend toward industrialization continued through the end of World War II, with manufacturing in the state growing at a pace faster than the rest of the nation.[30]

During the post-war years, the nation's economy continued to hum, even more so in California thanks to a series of government initiatives. First, the G.I. Bill of Rights put through college many of the 800,000 veterans who either returned or relocated here; then the Veterans Administration helped them buy homes, which they purchased through their well-paying jobs in defense plants, and later aerospace industries.[31] For the burgeoning middle class, California *was* the Golden State with seemingly endless potential.

By the beginning of the 21st century, California had become the nation's leading manufacturing state with 12 percent of all production and 12 percent of the nation's population. Manufacturing has slowed since then, however. In 2010, California still led the nation with 12 percent of all manufacturing, but now with 12.5 percent of the nation's population. These differences may seem small, but they scream volumes about the state's economic direction.

The industries we see here today are much different from the industries of 50 years ago, much less the state's earliest days. Through the 1960s, Los Angeles County aerospace companies alone employed more than 40 percent of the county's workforce. Today, aerospace and defense are much smaller portions of the manufacturing sector. Boeing's commercial aviation production, long a staple in Long Beach, was phased out in 2006 along with 6,000 jobs; military aviation production has slimmed down considerably as well. Other changes have occurred, too. During most of the 20th century, four automobile manufacturing plants produced between 100,000 and 200,000 cars annually. Several plants in Los Angeles alone built more than 6.5 million vehicles between the end of World War II and the early 1990s.[32] Now automobile manufacturing has disappeared altogether, except for a fledging Tesla Motors plant in Fremont. California shipbuilding, which had employed as many as 200,000 workers during World War II, now has less than 10,000 workers on various payrolls scattered throughout the state.

Then there are those industries that have prospered irrespective of the state's economic ups and downs. California's ocean ports come to mind as such an example. With tremendous increases in the volume of goods between the United States and Asia, the state's port facilities have thrived. As of 2010, Los Angeles ranked first in volume with 7.9 million cargo containers, followed by Long Beach with 6.3 million containers.[33] More than 40 percent of the nation's imports come through these two facilities alone, which account for more than 100,000 port-related jobs. Oakland ranks fifth with the movement of 2.3 million containers. Although not manufacturing per se, these facilities play vital roles in moving shipments in and out of the United States.

Ports move goods, but they are not necessarily transported in and out of the state in the same proportions. These days, much more comes in than goes out. For 2009, California ports welcomed 73 million tons of goods, while shipping out 51 million tons—a proportion similar to the nationwide average.[34]

To a great extent, increased global trade is a by-product of increased global competition. Many industries that were spawned and nurtured in California have lost a good deal of their ability to compete as other nations with similar capabilities have offered the same products for less—ship-building, automobile production, and airplane manufacturing are three such examples among many. Historically, these industries have provided well-paying jobs with health care and retirement benefits. Combined, these changes have redesigned much of California's economy. In the next few paragraphs, we'll focus on the transformed industrial base, skill-set issues, and global challenges.

The Waning Industrial Base

Over the past decade or so, the industrial base has shifted once again. Less certain is the extent to which the problem is nationwide or more dramatic in California than the rest of the country. Data compiled by the Milken Institute found that between 2000 and 2007, U.S. manufacturing employment declined by 21 percent to 13.9 million workers from 17.6 million workers. Yet, according to the Milken findings, manufacturing employment in California declined by 26 percent from 1.9 million workers to 1.5 million workers.[35]

Some industries were hit particularly hard. The three areas that lost the most jobs were apparel manufacturing, until recently the fourth-largest manufacturing segment in the state, which shrunk by 67 percent; the printing industry, which dropped by 29 percent; and computer and peripheral equipment manufacturing, which fell by 23 percent.[36] Combined, these three sectors alone lost 140,000 jobs over a seven-year period. They have not returned.

Some industries gained jobs during the period, although not nearly enough to offset the losses. The three industry sectors that gained the most jobs between 2000 and 2007 were the beverage manufacturing sector, which grew by 30 percent; other food manufacturing, which gained 24 percent more employees; and the pharmaceutical and medicine manufacturing sector, which expanded by 17 percent. Together these industries added 22,500 positions.

Two points emerge from these comparisons: first, the number of manufacturing jobs lost in California far outpaced the number of jobs gained; that is accounted for in the state's overall unemployment data, which remained about three points beyond the national period during the entire decade. Second, the only sector offering quality compensation was in pharmaceutical and medicine manufacturing. The other categories were unskilled blue-collar jobs that form the economic foundation of the middle class; in these subsets, there were more losses than gains. But there is a third point that bears discussion, namely, that the best and most financially rewarding jobs have been lost to other *nations*, not to other states, contrary to the claims of other governors. More about this concern shortly. Simply put, the movement of jobs, particularly those in the manufacturing sector, is much more complicated than adding and subtracting numbers.

Other evidence supports the loss of manufacturing jobs in California as part of a national collapse rather than a California-centric disaster. According to the U.S. Bureau of Labor Statistics, between 2006 and 2009, manufacturing in California declined by 14.7 percent, which is below the national decline of 16.3 percent. In fact, manufacturing declined in all of the top ten manufacturing states, including Texas, although the Lone Star state had the lowest dip at 9.7 percent.[37]

Behind Job Losses

How do we reconcile these data? Moreover, to the extent that California has experienced a reduction in manufacturing jobs, how can a state rich in so many ways lose quality jobs and quality people with them?

One school of thought contends that companies and their jobs have moved out of California because of an unwieldy and costly regulatory environment. That's what the Milken Institute study concluded when the researchers wrote that manufacturers in California suffered from "the high cost of doing business due to an onerous regulatory climate and some of the highest taxes in the nation."[38] In support of this claim, an *Orange County Register* article in 2010 listed 100 companies that left California for other states during the decade because of "high taxes, undue regulation, workers' comp costs, a legal environment stacked against businesses and lengthy and costly construction permitting requirements."[39] If true, one wonders why any business would be caught anywhere near the state.

Many accept this analysis as gospel. But is there merit to the claim? True to the call, in 2011 a delegation of Californians including Lieutenant Governor Gavin Newsom and several members of the state legislature went to Texas to study why the state had drawn 165,000 new jobs between 2008 and 2010 as California was losing 1.2 million jobs, according to one

Republican state assemblyman.[40] If we consider the kinds of jobs "lost," as reported in the Milken study, the data take on a much different meaning than one might otherwise expect.

The lost jobs claim may have some merit but the missing workforce hasn't necessarily relocated in Texas or other states, for that matter. In fact, upon close examination we learn that California has lost manufacturing jobs, but to other nations. We know this because of data far more comprehensive than the Milken study. In 2007, the nonpartisan Public Policy Institute of California (PPIC) conducted an exhaustive study of workforce movement in and out of California between 1992 and 2004. Comparatively, the data set was much larger and conducted over a longer period than the Orange County information. The PPIC study found that of the 18 million jobs in play over the 12-year period, 11,000 jobs, or 0.06 percent, were lost because of businesses relocating to other states.[41] As for high taxes, the Tax Foundation data in 2011 found California ranked 10th in corporate tax rates, with four other states at just about the same level. For the most part, companies aren't fleeing California for other states; rather, they're adding jobs outside the country altogether.

So, then, why have the jobs gone away, even if to other countries? The job drain exists for two different reasons. Part of the answer lies with a lack of qualified people for available jobs regardless of whether they are housed in California or anywhere else. In other words, there's a mismatch between the skill sets of the unemployed workforce and the skill sets that companies need. In 2011, the *Wall Street Journal* found that although there were four people looking for every job vacancy, tens of thousands of openings in software engineering, computer science, accounting, and finance were without applicants.[42] In other areas, a survey by the National Association of Manufacturers found that 90 percent of manufacturing respondents had difficulty finding people to fill positions such as machinists and technicians. All of this fits in with our earlier discussion of the lack of commitment to education and training in California. These days, schools are not offering classes in support of these jobs and students think they are inferior in wages, even though this is not the case.[43]

In other cases, companies are relying on workers elsewhere because the cost of labor is substantially less than they would pay in the United States. The vocations at issue run the gamut from typing services to accountants to medical technicians to legal services.[44] These jobs will stay away as long as there are substantial differences in labor costs. Chalk that up to globalization. As Thomas Friedman observes, "Companies have never had more freedom, and less friction, in the way of assigning research, low-end manufacturing, and high-end manufacturing anywhere in the world."[45] Further, Friedman notes, "The cold hard truth is that management, shareholders and investors are largely indifferent to where their profits come from or even where the employment is created."[46] To this point, leading business organizations advocate moving manufacturing jobs abroad as "good business."[47] With that kind of leadership, manufacturing states like California are bound to suffer.

Globalization will not go away, that's for sure. Truth be told, it's hard to fight an international economic environment that has lower costs of production in some places than others. Still, it's clear that we are not preparing people for the jobs that exist, jobs that need qualified workers. That dilemma exists everywhere in the United States, but it's exacerbated in California by the state's pitiful commitment to public education and the predictable poor preparation of today's students for the jobs that are available in the working world. Even if our public policies on regulation, taxing, and spending have contributed to companies looking elsewhere to have their manufacturing needs met, we can help people develop other skill sets if we're committed to investing in the state's educational infrastructure.

NAFTA and California Manufacturing

Although we sometimes believe almost narcissistically otherwise, California is not an island unto itself. The state is tied to the rest of the nation politically, economically, and, most of all, constitutionally. Many Californians have a hard time with this concept for a variety of reasons usually relating to value differences between mainstream California and Main Street U.S.A.

But the union is just that—a compact of the 50 states to share many goals as articulated in the U.S. Constitution, with the ultimate responsibility for many policies in the hands of the federal government. Regulation of foreign trade, for example, is a policy area that the Constitution clearly places at the national level. To the extent that Congress signs on to trade agreements with other nations, California must comply along with the other 49 states. One arrangement with great impact on California is the North American Free Trade Agreement (NAFTA).

Launched in 1992, NAFTA was designed to facilitate increased trade between Canada, Mexico, and the United States by eliminating nearly

20,000 different tariffs. Some of the tariffs had reduced the flow of commerce to a trickle. For example, Mexican tariffs on U.S. trade items ranged as high as 250 percent of value, making U.S. products prohibitively expensive. Meanwhile, the United States had few tariffs with Mexican products. From the standpoint of moving goods, NAFTA has been a smashing success. Agricultural trade between the United States and Mexico nearly tripled from $7.3 billion in 1994 to $20.1 billion in 2006.[48] The San Diego area particularly has flourished as an entry point for Mexican products entering California and continuing to the rest of the nation.[49]

But there is another side to the NAFTA story. Although American companies have benefitted by virtue of eased entry to new markets, American labor has suffered. An examination of the impact of NAFTA by the Economic Policy Institute 10 years after the treaty took effect found a net loss of 879,280 American jobs, 78 percent of which were in manufacturing. California had the largest losses of the 50 states, with 115,723 jobs eliminated as an outcome of the trade pact.[50]

The root of the problem stems from the emergence of the *maquiladora* industry in Mexico. Operating in Mexico along the U.S. border, *maquiladora* factories accept raw American goods such as cloth, wood, steel, or other materials, process or assemble finished products, and then export them back to the United States. Under the terms of NAFTA, Mexican-run companies—often subsidiaries of American companies—pay no tariffs; nor do the American companies that receive the finished goods. Between 1980 and 2006, the number of people working in *maquiladora* facilities soared from 120,000 to 1.2 million.[51] As of 2010, there were 1.6 million *maquiladora* employees; 182,000 were in Baja California immediately south of the California border.[52] Clearly, the industry is thriving. While there are no official statistics on compensation, informal estimates suggest that *maquiladora* workers earn between 15 and 25 percent of what comparatively trained employees earn in the United States. With dramatically reduced labor costs, this exchange mechanism allows Mexican labor to replace American labor.

California Manufacturing in Perspective

It is fair to acknowledge deterioration of the manufacturing sector in California, but it must be done in concert with the loss of manufacturing throughout the entire nation. And it must be noted that other states have not gained at California's expense. In fact, according to a study conducted by the Congressional Budget Office between 2000 and 2008, job losses in California and throughout the nation were attributed to two factors: improved productivity and increased foreign competition through arrangements such as NAFTA.[53] In other words, California was no more or no less competitive than any other state, irrespective of what some in the business community might claim. Still, could the state have done a better job in correcting the imbalance between available jobs and the workforce through better education and training? Absolutely, and unfortunately California now ranks near the bottom of the 50 states in making such an effort.

But there's another point to remember. Just because jobs are lost—in California or elsewhere—does not mean that American companies are necessarily suffering. That's because they have moved jobs elsewhere. Just compare the huge positive corporate balance sheets in 2011 with American unemployment that averaged above 9 percent and it's difficult to conclude anything else.

TECHNOLOGY AND DOT COMS

If there's a bright spot in California's economy, it's in technology. From invention of the silicon wafer to the disk drive to solar batteries, technology has become the shining province of California. There are other places where technology has played a vital role, to be sure. Washington state has Microsoft, Idaho has Micron, and Texas has Texas Instruments, and in all these and other cases, the collection of industries that complement the key players. But California has more types of technology building blocks than anywhere else, period.

Ground zero for technology is Silicon Valley, where entrepreneurialism, capital, and university-supplied brainpower create endless high tech success stories in ways duplicated nowhere else. Of course, California has other centers of technology—Orange County and San Diego come to mind—but no region carries the clout of Silicon Valley. You've heard of many of the big ones—Hewlett-Packard, Cisco, Apple, Intel, Applied Materials, Adobe, Oracle, Ebay, and more recently Google and Facebook, but these are just the tip of the technology iceberg. It's hard to know an exact number because companies form, merge, and disband on a daily basis. But the Silicon Valley Web Directory, a noncommercial website, calculates there are more than 1,000 computer industry companies alone in the Valley.[54] With respect to semi-conductor materials and equipment makers, of the more than 1,200 companies in the United States, 43 percent reside in California. No other state has this kind of critical mass.

All this translates to jobs—lots of jobs. As of 2008, the 11 leading high sectors in Silicon Valley employed 435,000 people, about one sixth of the region's private employment, with an overall payroll of $58 billion. And that doesn't include support firms such as attorneys, accountants, and clerical workers. While New York and the Washington, D.C. area actually employ more high-tech workers, Silicon Valley easily outdistances the two locations in terms of per capita employment.[55] Simply put, high tech is the cornerstone of the Valley's economy, and many would say, in turn, the driver of the state's economy.[56]

Corporate Presence in Name Only?

Despite the large presence of high-tech employees in Silicon Valley, their numbers have taken a beating in the past decade. Between 2001 and 2010, high-tech employment in Silicon Valley fell by 73,000 jobs, or 14 percent.[57] During this period, a small portion of the work has been shifted to other states, but the largest exodus by far has been carried out through offshoring to other nations. This process, now in its third decade, has cost the state in a variety of ways from devastating job losses to depleted state revenues. And with a shrunken tax base, the state has had little choice but to cut back support for public education, transportation, land preservation, and basic but critical social services. The linkage between offshored jobs and a decaying state infrastructure is a story that no one—particularly corporate California—wants to talk about, but it's vital to understanding at least a contributing factor to the decline of California.

Whether computers, software, cell phones, or other high-tech products, these 21st century implements tend to be popular because of their reduced costs courtesy of cheap foreign labor. And with huge profit margins from low costs, the concept of offshoring is wildly popular with corporations. But the loss of jobs at home is a highly sensitive political and economic issue, although "official" offshore employment data are hard to find. Add the fact that companies often hire out rather than establish a formal presence elsewhere and the ability to collect hard data becomes even more difficult. Still, there are some numbers, and the likelihood is that they represent the tip of the offshore iceberg.

Take the case of Apple, a California-based company that had more than $32 billion in revenues in 2009. Recent estimates put the number of Apple employees at between 36,000 and 40,000. Yet, according to one study, only 12,000 to 14,000 of those jobs are in the United States. That means that between 26,000 and 28,000 are outside the country.[58] Then there is California-based Intel, the largest semi-conductor chip company in the world with revenues of more than $37 billion. Yet, half of its 45,000-member workforce is located outside the United States.[59] Those are only two examples of California companies who look overseas for their workforce. Together, they alone account for job losses of more than 50,000 employees. Add Oracle, Cisco Systems, Hewlett-Packard, Applied Materials, Adobe Systems, Intuit, Yahoo, and dozens of others and you're talking big numbers well into the hundreds of thousands of well-paying jobs that started here but were moved offshore for the sake of greater profit margins.

Defenders of these reassigned employee assets explain the development as a result of benign relationships between the California companies that design the high-tech devices and those that produce them downstream.[60] That's great for the companies, but it's crippling for former employees and their families.

To be fair, not all of the state's job losses have been in the high tech sector of the economy. California-based pharmaceutical company Amgen, with more than $15 billion in revenues in 2009, has shifted all its clinical trials offshore to India and Hong Kong as a means of reducing costs. Even entertainment, long a cornerstone of California's economy, has seen the offshore light, with Walt Disney looking abroad for skilled animation jobs. With respect to the entire movie industry, between 1996 and 2010, film production days dropped by 62 percent,[61] leading to the departure of nearly 40,000 jobs. Add to the lost employment all of the support services—restaurants, catering, set designers and movers, hair salons, dry cleaners, automobile facilities, and the like—and the numbers swell even more.

It's important to acknowledge that offshoring is a national epidemic and other areas such as Detroit (automobiles) and the southeast (textiles) have suffered because of companies unable to contend with foreign competition. But California's case is different. Rather than companies going bankrupt, the high-tech companies here have come from extremely profitable companies taking their high-paying jobs to low-paying environments so that the companies can make even higher profit margins. And while their earnings may have soared in recent years, those gains have been on the backs of unemployed U.S. workers who have the skills but cost too much. There's the disconnect.

Meanwhile, to the extent that they have a continued presence in the state, these same companies expect good roads, a steady energy supply, and excellent public education at their disposal, as well as police and fire services. They also benefit from the research and development carried out at tax payer-supported public universities. That's hard to justify here when so many companies are sending their workforces and potential income tax revenues elsewhere.

H-1B Workforce

Amid the intentional shifting of California jobs abroad has existed a counter movement to bring legal, temporary foreign workers to California. Most of the effort has existed under the auspices of the H-1B visa program, a system that allows companies to import specialized labor not available in the United States for up to six years. Whereas most illegal immigrants enter the United States with relatively few skills to take jobs at the bottom of the economic ladder, H-1B workers tend to be highly educated in specialized disciplines. More than 40 percent of the workers come from Asia, with about a quarter coming from Europe.

About 65,000 H-1B slots are available annually, although the annual number has been as high as 195,000 in recent years. Companies pay the U.S. government about $4,000 per H-1B employee, with the money dedicated to training for domestic workers. High tech and accounting companies have been most aggressive in seeking these slots, with California-based corporations particularly active. Other specialized fields include physicians, nurses, accountants, and attorneys. In fact, the applications have been heavily skewed toward technology. Of the 10 most active companies seeking H1-B permits in 2008 and 2009, 7 were California-based high tech companies that collectively requested 6,971 jobs.[62]

The H-1B program has wallowed in controversy almost since Congress established it in 1990, when Congress made available temporary immigration opportunities for highly skilled workers in specialized professions with shortages.[63] Proponents claim that H-1B workers fill important specialty gaps which, if unfilled, keep companies from conducting research and generating products. They also contend that H-1B employees lead to the hiring of more support personnel at home, thereby increasing overall employment. In addition, companies with H-1B employees say that without the ability to bring them in, the companies would have to outsource elsewhere, thereby draining their American workforce.[64]

Opponents have a different take. Rather than create jobs, those against H-1B visas say that these temporary employees take the jobs of those already here and prepared to work. John Mirano of the Center for Immigration Studies presents information that shows an inverse relationship in California between the foreign temporary labor pool and job growth.[65] A similar assessment comes from a report published by the Economic Institute that points to an increase of H-1B computer programmers precisely at the time when the pool of American computer science graduates swelled enormously. The study cited the 25,000 layoffs by Hewlett-Packard in 2008, half of whom were offshored, while the company brought in another thousand H-1B workers.[66] And they come in at salaries beneath their counterparts in the United States. Can all this be coincidental? Hardly. Such activities suggest a repositioning of labor, something particularly costly in California.

All this has taken a toll on the state's labor force. Even the nonpartisan U.S. Government Accounting Office in an independent review has concluded that at a minimum, "the H-1B program presents a difficult challenge in balancing the need for high-skilled foreign labor with sufficient protections for U.S. workers."[67] The dimensions of that "balance" are not only huge in California but costly to hundreds of thousands of workers who have lost out via offshoring or H-1B imports.

The Power of Green

There has been at least one glimmer of positive workforce news in recent years, and it starts and ends with the color "green," as in green or energy-saving industries. Clean technology, solar power, energy-efficient batteries, and other alternative energy products fall into this category. Between 1998 and 2009, the number of jobs relating to environment-related products and services grew by 18 percent—this, even though the state's unemployment nudged upward.[68]

The ascendance of "green" employment is particularly significant when compared to other portions of the economy. To begin with, green technology has become a magnet for venture capital, with most of it going to California. In 2008, of the $4.1 billion invested by venture capitalists in green technology, 57 percent of the money went to California projects; Massachusetts, a distant second, received 10 percent.[69] Those investments had to provide jobs, lots of them. Between 1995 and 2009, green jobs increased by 56 percent, while employment in general grew by 18 percent.[70]

Solar technology has become a mainstay of the green energy movement in California. As of 2009, California collected 528 megawatts in solar energy, two-thirds of all the solar energy harnessed in the United States. New Jersey was a distant second with 70 megawatts, followed by Colorado with 36 megawatts.[71] Each megawatt generates enough energy for 750 homes. And while the amount collected represents only about one fourth of 1 percent of all the energy used by California, it's the fastest growing of all the energy sectors.

Clean energy can't come too soon in California. In 2011, the state legislature passed a new law requiring that one third of the state's energy come from non-fossil fuel sources by 2020, replacing the 20 percent requirement already in place. Most of the clean energy additions will come from the solar energy sector, including two projects so large that they will add about 500 megawatts, courtesy of two large U.S. Department of Energy grants covering about one third of the costs.

The green technologies industry may help California's economic revival down the road, but the road is likely to be long. These impressive numbers notwithstanding, the jobs in this sector account only for about 1 percent of the state's employment.

Tax Breaks to Keep Businesses Here

While major corporations have been shifting jobs offshore, state officials have been working hard to keep jobs in California. Their carrot has come in the form of massive tax breaks. Corporations have benefitted immeasurably, yet less certain are any benefits that have accrued to the state in the form of jobs remaining here. The breaks have been enormously helpful to business, with taxpayers footing the bills. Consider a few of the more outrageous examples courtesy of the state legislature:

- $100 million annually to the movie industry in tax credits to keep productions in California;

- $120 million annually through waived sales taxes for companies that buy custom computer software programs;
- $125 million annually through sales tax waivers on purchases of agriculture-related equipment;
- $500 million annually in tax breaks to businesses with facilities in special "enterprise zones" in exchange for them hiring unemployed workers;
- $1.5 billion annually to allow California corporations to pay income and sales taxes only on the products sold in California rather than on all their sales.

These tax breaks might be worthwhile if the state benefitted from new tax receipts or jobs. In fact, neither case has occurred. Consider the matter of tax breaks for employment in "enterprise zones." The concept behind the idea is that tax revenues created the jobs created in enterprise zones would more than offset the costs. Yet, according to a comprehensive study by the nonpartisan PPIC, enterprise zones "have no statistically significant effect on either employment levels or employment growth rates."[72] But perhaps the biggest ruse centers on the $1.5 billion tax breaks awarded to corporations in 2009 to keep their employees in California. Reformers attempted to repeal the tax break in 2010 via a ballot proposition on the grounds that the state's huge budget deficit could not permit such a change. Corporate California fought the ballot proposal and the voters defeated it at the polls. Shortly thereafter, tax breaks in hand, several corporations announced that they would be shifting employees out of California. They include Genentech and Comcast, both of which had vigorously opposed the reform measure.[73]

One possible change in the other direction has centered on California's effort to collect sales tax revenues from Internet-based retail companies. This drama has been years in the making and may not be clarified for years to come. At issue is whether the state should be able to force out-of-state-based companies to collect sales taxes upon the sale of merchandise to people in California. Companies such as Amazon have long maintained that they are exempt from such taxes because of a 1992 U.S. Supreme Court decision that states can collect sales taxes only if Internet-based companies have some kind of presence in the state. The question then becomes, what do we mean by "presence"? Several states have passed legislation that calls for the collection of sales taxes, while meeting the criteria handed down by the court. California joined the group in 2011, with tax experts believing that the state could collect more than $1 billion annually for its starved treasury.[74] Amazon strongly argued otherwise. More on this in Chapter 9.

Empty State Coffers

Lost jobs translate into lost government revenues. In addition, the California companies that have sent those jobs abroad have sent their earnings abroad, too. By parking their profits in other countries, these companies are able to dodge paying California corporate taxes, not to mention their federal tax obligations.

The absence of corporate participation in the state budget is staggering. According to a study by the California Franchise Tax Board, of the three major sources of state revenue during the 1987–88 fiscal year, 15.3 percent came from corporate taxes. By the 1993–94 fiscal year, corporate taxes accounted for 12.3 percent of the major revenue sources. And for the 2001–02 fiscal year, corporate taxes slipped to just 8.6 percent of the revenue pie.[75] State corporate taxes have hovered near 9 percent ever since. Further research by the California Budget Project shows that between 1981 and 2006, the share of corporate income taxes fell by nearly half.[76]

Add up these missing dollars for a couple of decades along with the missing taxes from those out of work, and it's easy to see a primary source for California's fiscal crisis. If companies are making less money here because they have shifted jobs overseas, they're going to pay fewer taxes. And they are.

Trying to Stop the Bleeding

Some people have put together the relationship between offshoring exodus and dilapidated state coffers and actually attempted to legislate otherwise. A few years ago, state legislators passed several bills to prevent the state from doing business with any company that used foreign workers to fulfill the responsibilities of a contract, but then-Republican Governor Arnold Schwarzenegger vetoed the proposed legislation on the grounds that it would hurt California's economy.[77] If fact, the bills were written because offshoring had ravaged the state's economy.

In his work, *Global California*, Abraham Lowenthal notes that although foreign policy is typically the responsibility of the federal government, numerous California-based actors conduct themselves in ways that impact international issues. Lowenthal lists corporations, banks, labor unions, the entertainment industry, media, environmental protection groups, and others almost as parts of a pluralistic, free-flowing interaction that form the basis of the state's "foreign policy."[78] Yet, the disproportional clout of California-based corporations indicates that while they are surrounded by other players, collectively they are the key player in California's economy—and their efforts are designed to benefit profits first, with the public good a distant second.

CALIFORNIA'S ECONOMY: GOOD FOR THE GEESE BUT NOT FOR THE GANDER

Just because California's economy is big does not mean it's strong—in fact, it's downright wobbly and fraught with conflicting objectives. Agriculture is booming, one of the few areas of predictable success each year, assuming the rain gods cooperate well enough. Still, there is a price for our bounty in the form of questionable processes used to produce the food we eat. Is the price too high? Perhaps so, if the quality of life is at stake.

Our manufacturing capabilities have soured, with low-end jobs often moving to lower cost states and high-end jobs either dispatched abroad or carried out here by specialists from other countries. In many cases, only corporate headquarters and high-end management personnel remain in the state. NAFTA has sent another 100,000 jobs to Mexico in yet another defeat for California's workforce.

Then there's the question of the great disconnect: our research and development is as strong as ever, as witnessed by the large numbers of patents and endless infusion of venture capital. But the manufacturing and assembly jobs that result from our product development capabilities increasingly are found elsewhere. There's something wrong with a situation that provides government assistance in the form of tax breaks and research and development subsidies, only to see the benefits from the discoveries accrue elsewhere.

Not all is bleak. California continues to be a leader in green technology, an emerging leader with tremendous capabilities to produce hundreds of thousands of jobs. This is a great start. But even green-tech jobs will not be enough to bail out a state that has sent so many well-paying jobs to other countries. To better connect jobs with residents, we must invest in education as we have never done before to prepare future generations and retrain those who have had careers that are no longer viable. But this is a huge challenge in itself, given the stubborn resistance by public policymakers, practitioners, and the voters alike to create sensible education initiatives and fund them through more taxes.

Like so many elements of California, our economy has potential. But potential alone doesn't hire employees whose earnings will provide taxes to pay the state's bills. Until we turn potential into real productivity, California's economy will teeter like the rest of the nation—hardly a desirable circumstance for the world's eighth largest economy.

ENDNOTES

1. "An Overview of California Agricultural Production Statistics," California Department of Food and Agriculture, 2011, p. 1.
2. "2011 Manufacturing: Still a Force in Southern California," Los Angeles County Economic Development Corporation, Los Angeles, CA, 2011, p. 3.
3. These data appear in "California Biomedical Industry: 2010 Report," prepared by PriceWaterhouseCoopers, 2010.
4. Sylvia A. Allegretto, "The Severe Crisis of Jobs in the United States and California," Center on Wage and Employment Dynamics, University of California, Berkeley, August 2010.
5. Frank James, "Nearly One In Four U.S. Homes With Mortgages 'Underwater,'" http://www.npr.org/blogs/thetwo-way/2009/11/one_in_four_us_homes_underwate.html, November 24, 2009.
6. USDA Economic Research Service, State Fact Sheets: United States, December 16, 2010, http://www.ers.usda.gov/StateFacts/US.htm#FC.
7. Mark Arax and Rick Wartzman, *The King of California: J.G. Boswell and the Making of a Secret American Empire* (New York: Public Affairs Press, 2003), p. 92.
8. Warren E. Johnston and Harold O. Carter, "Structural Adjustment, Resources, Global Economy to Challenge California Agriculture," *California Agriculture* 54(4), 16–22, July-August 2000.
9. Malcolm J. Rohrbough, *Days of Gold: The California Gold Rush and the American Nation* (Berkeley, CA: University of California Press, 1997), pp. 130–134.
10. Hazel Adele Pulling, *San Diego Historical Society Quarterly*, 11(1), January 1965.
11. Frank Norris vividly describes the extent to which the Southern Pacific railroad dominated farm life as well as almost every other facet of California in his novel, *The Octopus* (New York: Doubleday and Company, 1901).
12. "The Changing Structure of California Agriculture, Statistics, and Financial Indicators: 1950-1960," Giannini Foundation Special Report 04-1, 2000, giannini.ucop.edu/CalAgbook.htm.

13. George L. Henderson, *California and the Fictions of Capital* (Philadelphia, PA: Temple University Press, 1998), p. 10.

14. "California Agriculture: Feeding the Future," Governor's Office of Planning and Research, Sacramento, CA, 2003, p. 3.

15. Richard A. Walker, *The Conquest of Bread: 150 Years of Agribusiness in California* (New York: The New Press, 2004), p. 79.

16. Kevin Starr, *Coast of Dreams: California on the Edge, 2000-2003* (New York: Vintage Books, 2006), p. 495.

17. See "Stuck in a Growing Rift," *San Francisco Chronicle*, September 23, 2007, pp. A1, A12.

18. The states are Arizona, California, Colorado, Nevada, New Mexico, Utah, and Wyoming. Under the terms of the Colorado River Compact (2003), California is entitled to about one-fourth of the water each year.

19. "Crisis On Tap: California's Water Reckoning," *The Press Enterprise*, March 21, 2009, http://www.pe.com/reports/2009/water/stories/PE_News_Local_S_water22.19771d4.html.

20. Dan Bacher, "Corporate Farms Get Massive Water Subsidies in California," Organic Consumers Association, December 30, 2004, http://www.organicconsumers.org/.

21. Lance Williams, "Corporate Farmer Calls upon Political Allies to Influence Delta Dispute," Center for Investigative Reporting, December 6, 2009, http://center forinvestigativereporting.org/articles/corporatefarmercallsuponpoliticalallies toinfluencedeltadispute.

22. "Family Farmers Press for Meaningful Immigration Reform," California Farm Bureau Federation, http://www.cfbf.com/issues/ImmigrationReform.cfm.

23. Jeffrey S. Passel, "The Size and Characteristics of the Unauthorized Migrant Population in the U.S.," Pew Hispanic Center, Washington, D.C., March 7, 2006.

24. See "Border Policy Is Pinching Farmers," *Los Angeles Times*, September 26, 2005.

25. "Pesticide Use Rises, but Farms Shift to Less Harmful Varieties," *Los Angeles Times*, November 26, 2006.

26. Paul K. Mills and Sandy Kwong, "Cancer Incidence in the United Farm Workers of America (UFW), 1987-1987," conducted for the Cancer Registry of Central California, May 22, 2001, p. 11.

27. "Healthy Children and Green Jobs: A Platform for Pesticide Reform," A Pesticide Brief for the Brown Administration, prepared by Californians for Pesticide Reform, San Francisco, CA, November 2010.

28. Walker, op. cit., pp. 185–187.

29. "Ban Sought for Pesticide Used Widely by California Farms," *Sacramento Bee*, July 24, 2010.

30. Paul W. Rhode, "The Evolution of California Manufacturing," Public Policy Institute of California, San Francisco, CA, 2001, p. 13.

31. Lawrence Culver, The Frontier of Leisure: Southern California and the Shaping of Modern America (New York: Oxford University Press, 2010), p. 201.

32. Patrice Apodaca, "L.A. Makes Its Last Car: End of the Road for GM's Van Nuys Plant," *Los Angeles Times*, August 28, 1992, http://articles.latimes.com/print/1992-08-28/business/fi-6132_1_van-nuys.

33. "Ports Surge Back from Recession," *Los Angeles Times*, December 30, 2010, pp. B1, B4.

34. http://aapa-ports.org/Industry/content.cfm?ItemNumber=900&navItemNumber=551.

35. Ross C. DeVol, Perry Wong, Armen Bedroussian, Candice Flor Hynek, and David Rice, "Manufacturing 2.0: A More Prosperous California," prepared for the Milken Institute, Santa Monica, CA, June 2009, p. 25.

36. Ibid., p. 29.

37. "2011 Manufacturing: Still a Force in Southern California," op. cit., p. 2.

38. Ibid., p. 46

39. "List Names 100 Companies Leaving California," *Orange County Register*, February 24, 2010.

40. "Newsom Joins GOP's Trek to Texas for Lowdown on State's Business Rep," *San Francisco Chronicle*, April 9, 2011, pp. C1, C3.

41. Joel Kolko and David Neumark, "Business Location Decisions and Employment Dynamics in California," prepared for the Public Policy Institute of California, San Francisco, CA, 2007, p. 2.

42. "Labor Shortage Persists in Some Fields," *Wall Street Journal*, February 7, 2011. See also "Where the Jobs Are," *Time*, January 17, 2011.

43. "Factory Shift: Manufacturers Struggle to Fill Highly Paid Jobs," *Los Angeles Times*, August 14, 2006.

44. "Office of Tomorrow Has an Address in India," *Los Angeles Times*, August 29, 2004.

45. Thomas L. Friedman, *The World Is Flat* (New York: Ferrar, Strauss and Giroux, 2005), p. 209.

46. Ibid., p. 211.

47. "Chamber of Commerce Leader Advocates Offshoring Jobs," Associated Press, July 1, 2004.

48. Andrea Ford, "A Brief History of NAFTA," *Time*, December 30, 2008, http://www.time.com/time/nation/article/0,8599,1868997,00.html.

49. Abraham F. Lowenthal, *Global California: Rising to the Cosmopolitan Challenge* (Stanford, CA: Stanford University Press, 2009), pp. 66–67.

50. Robert E. Scott, "The High Price of 'Free Trade,'" Economic Policy Institute, Washington, D.C., November 2003, p. 7.

51. Paul R. Bergin, Robert C. Feenstra, and Gordon H. Hanson, "Outsourcing and Volatility," NBER Working Paper, 13144, prepared for the National Bureau of Economic Research, June 2007, p. 2

52. "Spotlight: Maquiladora Employment," Federal Reserve Bank of Dallas, Second Quarter 2010.

53. "Economic and Budget Issue Brief," Congressional Budget Office, Washington, D.C., December 23, 2008, p. 1.

54. Silicon Valley Web Directory, http://gocee.com/valley/s1_compi.htm.

55. "After the Dot-Com Bubble: Silicon Valley High-Tech Employment and Wages in 2001 and 2008," Regional Report, U.S. Bureau of Labor Statistics, August 2009.

56. Pui-Wing Tam, "Tech Revival Lifts Silicon Valley," WSJ.com, December 20, 2010, http://online.wsj.com/article/SB10001424052748704073804576023630025435842.html.

57. Ibid., and "After the Dot-Com Bubble: Silicon Valley High-Tech Employment and Wages in 2001 and 2008," op. cit.

58. Alan S. Brown, "A Shift in Engineering Offshoring," *Mechanical Engineering*, March 2009, http://memagazine.asme.org/articles/2009/March/Shift_Offshoring.cfm.

59. Sarah Johnson and Tim Reason, "Chipping Away at Intel's Seemingly Good News," *CFO.com*, February 11, 2009, http://www.cfo.com/printable/article.cfm/13095637.

60. David G. McKendrick, Richard E. Doner, and Stephan Haggard, *From Silicon Valley to Singapore* (Stanford, CA: Stanford University Press, 2000), pp. 8–9.

61. "Filing in L.A. up 15% in 2010," *Los Angeles Times*, January 12, 2001, B3.

62. The companies and their rankings were: Qualcomm (1), Oracle (2), Intel (3), Google (4), Yahoo (5), Cisco Systems (6), and Apple (9). http://www.myvisajobs.com/H1B-Visa-CA-2009-ST.htm.

63. For a history of the program, see Margaret L. Usdansky and Thomas J. Espenshade, "The H-1B Visa Debate in Historical Perspective: The Evolution of U.S. Policy Toward Foreign-Born Workers," The Center for Comparative Immigration Studies, University of California, San Diego, Working Paper 11, May 2000.

64. Much of this is summarized in "H-1B Visas and Job Creation," National Foundation for American Policy, Washington, D.C., March 2008.

65. John Mirano, "H-1B Visa Numbers: No Relationship to Economic Need," Backgrounder, Center for Immigration Studies, Washington, D.C., June 2008, p. 6.

66. Ron Hira, "The H-1B and L-1 Visa Programs: Out of Control," Briefing Paper, Economic Policy Institute, Washington, D.C., October 14, 2010.

67. "H-1B Visa Reform," Highlights, General Accounting Office, Report Number GAO-11-26, Washington, D.C., p. 2.

68. "California Leading Growth in Green Jobs, Report Finds," *Los Angeles Times*, June 11, 2009, p. B2, and "Green Jobs up 3% in 2008," *San Francisco Chronicle*, January 19, 2011, pp. D1, D4.

69. The 2009 California Green Energy Index.

70. David Baker, "Green Jobs up 3% in 2008, Next 10 Report Finds," *San Francisco Chronicle*, January 19, 2011, http://articles.sfgate.com/2011-01-19/business/27036351_1_green-jobs-green-economy-collaborative-economics.

71. "With Push toward Renewable Energy, California Sets Pace for Solar Power," *The New York Times*, July 16, 2009, p. A17.

72. Jed Kolko and David Neumark, "Do California's Enterprise Zones Create Jobs?" Public Policy Institute of California, San Francisco, CA, June 2009, p. 14.

73. See Dan Morain, "Reply to Tax Breaks Was Rude," *Sacramento Bee*, November 21, 2010, p. 1E, and Michael Hiltzik, "A State's Lesson on Corporate Breaks," *Los Angeles Times*, December 8, 2010, p. B1.

74. "Amazon Backs End to Online Sales Tax in California," *The New York Times*, July 12, 2001, p. A12.

75. Allen Prohofsky, "Trends in California Tax Revenues," *State Tax Notes*, 30(3), 627–637, November 17, 2003.

76. "California's Tax System," California Budget Project, Sacramento, CA, February 2009, p. 7.

77. "Governor Vetoes Bills on Offshoring Jobs," *San Francisco Chronicle*, September 30, 2004, p. B1.

78. Lowenthal, op. cit., pp. 12–13.

5

Life in the 'Burbs—Where There Is No There There

In Los Angeles, by the time you're thirty-five, you're older than most of the buildings.

—Delia Ephron, screenwriter

Ever since the earliest days of the Republic, Americans have had a special relationship with their local governments. Close to home, presided over by neighbors, and within physical proximity of most citizens, local governments have been viewed as the true laboratories of representative democracy.[1] Seemingly, there are few barriers to citizen participation at the local level. There are decision-making centers where everyday people can congregate to support or oppose public policy proposals that affect our lives directly day in and day out.

In California, city council and county board of supervisors meetings dominate the inventory of local government organizations, although there are a few thousand others less well known to the public. In most settings, governance is simple and direct; there are no sergeants-at-arms or long-winded parliamentary efforts to gain hidden advantages, just the town clerk who has had the part-time job for 40 years and the city council or board of supervisors members who have day jobs as homemakers, salespeople, business owners, lawyers, or other "normal" vocations. Few run for local office intending to make politics a career; rather, they run to serve their neighbors and make their town or county a better place. Granted, this stereotypical description plays out much better in towns like Arbuckle (population 2613, Colusa County) or Lake of the Woods (population 935, Kern County) than in Los Angeles (3.8 million), where largesse has a way of formalizing the otherwise informal, but that's the view most people share about local government.

This almost romantic description of people controlling their destiny in a town hall-like fashion has been nurtured further in recent years with the devolution of power that has taken place between the federal government and the states. These days, many see a shift of responsibilities in major policy areas from the national level to the states, and inasmuch as cities and counties are sub-governments of the states, some of that power, presumably, has transferred to them, too.[2] That's the popular theory, anyway.

Whether local governments are depositories of real citizen control is anything but an open-and-shut question. Sure, with city hall or the county building down the block or just on the other side of town, citizens find it fairly easy to have their say about issues of importance to them; the barriers to political participation are few. But having your say and having your way are two different circumstances altogether. In California, most local governments employ city managers who play substantial roles in crafting major public policies. In addition, major power interests just beyond the meeting halls of local governments often enjoy incredible influence over the policymaking process with few observers the wiser for it, other than the occasional investigative piece, which generally has a very short life. Land developers, realtors, public employee unions, cable companies, and homeowner associations are some of the groups that attempt to assert their influence over taxing, spending, and other local government priorities, often succeeding in ways that few of us know.

Although we feel close to local governments, most of us really don't understand their powers, interaction, and limitations. More often than not, residents are baffled over which local government unit has responsibility for various policy issues; after all, they all sound an awful lot alike. There's a reason for such befuddlement. In actuality, local governments operate with precious little independence or autonomy. They are mentioned nowhere in the United States Constitution, leaving local governments almost as wards of the state. As such, these units often operate with little independent authority on major issues of the day, yet they are responsible for managing a variety of important programs and services vital to the needs of their communities. That description may not be flattering and is certain to draw the ire of hard-working local government officials, but it's accurate nevertheless.

Actually, the state has the right to intercede and even assume control of local governments on a temporary basis, should they be unable to execute their responsibilities. In 2003, the state superintendent of public instruction took over Oakland's bankrupt school system, ousting the local superintendent in the process. In 2007, the state attorney general investigated management of an alleged rape case by the Santa Clara County District Attorney, but found no culpability or negligence. In 2011, the state controller ordered an audit of the financial records of the City of Montebello over questionable accounting methods. In fact, the state intervenes in the affairs of local governments on a routine basis. Only in matters of bankruptcy, such as Vallejo's in 2008, does the state back away from involvement because California law prevents the state from assuming local government debts, lest the public be stuck with the tab. Think about the disconnect in state/local relations: the state can take control of local government affairs but accepts no responsibility for assisting local governments in financial trouble.

All of this suggests a less than idyllic picture of local self-rule, to be sure. "Local control" often exists in name only. Local governments live in perpetual political purgatory along with their constituents, even though neither the managers nor the unsuspecting citizens may realize their fate until disaster overcomes them.

The remaining sections of this chapter attempt to demystify the essence of California's local governments and their relationships to the people. The focus here is not so much on the benefits and drawbacks of such governing parameters as charter cities versus general law cities, city managers versus strong mayors, or district elections versus at-large elections; those assessments are covered elsewhere and are worthwhile investigations for people interested in the nuts and bolts of local government management.[3] Rather, the intent is to take a more global view of local governments in terms of expectations, results, and overall performance. To mine this objective, we'll look at the fractured divisions of authority, uneven sources of power, and behind-the-scenes struggles for influence. We also explore the growing demands of local governments, along with their decreasing abilities to respond to the pressing needs in 21st century California—an irony that becomes more burdensome every day. When all is said and done, we may need to replace any idealistic perceptions of local governments with the realities of how they actually work and how they don't, as well as for whom and why.

A TALE OF FEW REAL CITIES AND MANY PRETENDERS

California is filled with thousands of local governments. As of 2010, the state's 58 counties housed 481 cities ranging in population sizes from the hundreds to the millions. But the numbers don't end there. In addition to cities and counties, there were 1,043 school districts and 4,776 special districts that deal with everything from airports to zoos,[4] bringing the total number of local governments to 6,358. A caveat here: the past tense use of the word "were" is intentional; that's because the numbers of local governments rarely remain the same for very long. Whether it's a rare merger of services or, more likely, a new government that sprouts up, the numbers are anything but stable. But more important than precise numbers is the extent to which so many local governments overlap in responsibilities while falling short in capabilities to provide much needed services for their citizens. Combined, California's local governments resemble the political equivalent of a jigsaw puzzle whose pieces will never quite fit as expected because of extensive overlap.

East Coast Cities Grow Up, California Cities Grow Out

Historically, land has been one of California's greatest assets. That there is so much makes it easy for people to spread out and establish residence in a location where the physical distance from a city's core often translates into affordable housing. Timing enters into the history of the land use picture, too. California's greatest population growth didn't commence in earnest until the dawn of the 20th century when the manufacture of automobiles proliferated on a mass basis. That development enabled larger numbers of middle class Americans to buy the improved means of transportation. As the purchase price for cars went down and the availability of cheap housing increased, California developed its own special formula for suburban living. Another equally impressive population spike occurred after World War II, when hundreds of thousands of military personnel settled down in California's suburbs. Given the state's climate, why would anyone return to Buffalo, New York or Kansas City, Kansas, to name only two of hundreds of locations?

That unique sense of openness is also the state's demographic bane. Whereas the relative unavailability of land in proportion to the number of residents has forced densely populated east coast cities to become vertical, California's cities have always grown out, and thinly so. The differences in density are substantial: according to 2010 census data, New York City packs in 26,303 residents per square mile, Chicago has 12,750 residents per square mile, and Philadelphia has 11,234 per square mile. The existence of so many people in comparatively contained areas has allowed these and other eastern cities to provide high levels of public services because of widespread tax bases.

Compare the density patterns of eastern and mid-western cities with California and the rest of the picture becomes clear. Los Angeles, with nearly 4 million residents, has 7,877 people per square mile, and even that number has emerged only over the past quarter century. San Diego, California's second largest city, encompasses 3,772 residents per square mile; San Jose, California's third largest city, contains 5,118 residents per square mile. And so it goes, with relatively sparse populations stretching through large tracts of urban boundaries. Only San Francisco bucks this trend, with 16,636 residents per square mile. Hence, the term "suburban sprawl" applies to most of the state.

Missing Public Services

The absence of density in California in urban areas other than San Francisco has thwarted efforts to provide adequate levels of services found in more mature cities. Because of high costs relative to small, spread-out population bases, roads, electricity, senior centers, water systems, public schools, parks, public transportation, and other services associated with modern life have been extended to the outlying areas usually at grudgingly slow rates, and even then in a much less comprehensive fashion than those in fully developed, densely populated urban communities.[5] Efforts to control horizontal growth almost always fail because of the value of empty land, the power of builders and realtors to promote development, and the inability (or lack of interest) on the part of most local governments to stop it.[6] The sprawling result costs dearly in the form of commute times, a polluted environment, expensive road programs, costly water delivery programs, and other sketchy public services.

Nothing is more demonstrative of this point than the painfully anemic development of mass transit in California, other than a handful of light rail networks. Consider Los Angeles. With a land mass covering 469 square miles, the second most populated city in the country has been ever so slow to build a much needed subway system—79 miles as of 2011 for a system that didn't even begin to operate until 1990. New York, with twice the population at 8.2 million living within a land mass of 305 square miles, has 648 miles of subway track. San Francisco stands out as the California exception to providing modern public transportation. With a population of 800,000 and a land mass footprint of only 49 square miles, the city has 72 miles of subway in a system that began operation on a much smaller basis in 1917. On a much less significant level, the 104-mile Bay Area Rapid Transit system serpentines through four northern California counties, with 37 miles operating underground. Except for these examples, no other California city has a semblance of a subway system.

Moving Out and Staying Behind

The automobile provided transportation independence, but not for all. It was, perhaps, one of earliest agents of separation between the haves and have-nots in California. Beginning in the earliest years of the 20th century, whites moved to the expanding suburbs to escape Latinos and other minorities who took up residence in the city cores with the largest array of social services. This pattern was particularly clear in Los Angeles, where "the Anglo population left downtown and East Los Angeles to the foreign-born, Mexicans and blacks,"[7] relying upon artificial housing patterns to perpetuate *de facto* segregation.

Racially divided communities remained so throughout the 20th century. In southern California, for example, Latinos and African Americans continued to live in largely segregated areas, according to 1990 and 2000 census data. Asians also lived in segregated areas, although not as stark as those of Latinos and African Americans.[8] Another examination finds that residential segregation of Latinos, African Americans, and Asians was particularly strong in Los Angeles, San Diego, and San Francisco throughout the 20th century.[9] Such creative configurations continue to this very day. In Orange County between 1990 and 2010, more than 226,000 whites moved out, while 450,000 Latinos and 290,000 Asians moved in.[10] According to economist Leah Boustan's work, the pattern extended to African Americans: In every decade, cities that received a larger flow of black migrants also lost a larger number of white residents.[11]

"White flight" has not been the only basis of separation between races and ethnic groups. In San Francisco, African Americans have altered the city's racial composition by moving out to the suburbs in large numbers. Between 1970 and 2005, the African American proportion of the city's otherwise stable population shrunk from 13.5 percent to 6.5 percent.[12] In southern California, Chinese Americans have moved from L.A.'s core to suburban communities such as Monterey Park and Alhambra, leaving the city's center to Latinos and newly arrived Asians.[13] It seems commonplace that some group is always moving away from others who are left behind in undesirable neighborhoods.

It's Still Segregation, No Matter How You Frame It

Those observers who are dismayed or offended by the claim of segregation will respond that such housing and education patterns stem from economics and "market forces." In other words, they claim that people move where they can afford to move; as their incomes go up, they find better housing. But what they omit in their analysis is the powerful connection between race, education, and economics. Studies show that, generally, whites are more educated and, hence, wealthier than nonwhites. With such attributes, whites have more mobility than nonwhites do, which allows them to move to enclaves where their incomes support good schools.[14] Therein lies the dividing line between groups—a line that is just as defined today as it was prior to the *Brown v. Board of Education* desegregation verdict unanimously handed down by the U.S. Supreme Court in 1954, despite the mandate of that decision.

But the differences are about more than housing patterns. Segregated public schools have accompanied the population movements, as attested in Chapter 2. In addition, recently white students have been moving to private schools in disproportionate numbers, leaving Latinos and other minorities behind as large majorities in public schools.[15] This shift is important because schools and their student compositions set the tone for future individual behavior, social relationships, and economic patterns. Education is a powerful tool, but one that benefits some groups much more than others in California. Moreover, this pattern plays out repeatedly from one end of the state to the other.

In effect, suburbanization of California has exacerbated the differences between people of various races and ethnicities. Thus, in his description of the "cocoon process" in Los Angeles, urban planner William Fulton notes that suburbanites come together "not so much by what they are heading toward as by what they are running from, and what they are running from is their perception of the ugly realities of urban life."[16] Still, there's a subtlety here that few actually see but many experience. Increasingly, cities show the presence of different ethnic groups to the extent that a superficial examination would suggest mixes and a potpourri of cultures, so to speak. Instead, segregated neighborhood enclaves of one group or another develop, with few real signs of assimilation.[17]

Herein lays one of California's many contradictions. Technically, the state may be more diverse today in overall numbers, but there are few signs that different racial and ethnic groups live comfortably in the same communities. Again, just look at the population make-ups of the public schools if you actually believe otherwise. So much for any notion that California is the "great melting pot" of American society.

FRACTURED LOCAL GOVERNMENTS: UNNECESSARY COSTS AND DUPLICATIVE RESPONSIBILITIES

When people decry the high cost of government, some point fingers at the huge federal bureaucracy; others wring their hands over wasteful management practices in Sacramento.[18] In fact, these critics are looking in the wrong places. By far, the most pervasive waste is found in the stewardship of local governments, not because of graft or corruption but because of unnecessary and costly duplication of services in countless areas of service.

Sometimes we forget the extent to which modernity has changed the way we manage our everyday lives from our work place environment to modes of travel. The same thing goes for local government services. Today, communication is effortless and immediate, whether through the telephone or instant messaging, rather than through the Pony Express or a telegram. Distances between cities are journeyed in minutes, not days. Similarly, citizens can keep track of city council meetings or other government online or via a television cable community access channel, rather than by showing up at city hall. Yet, while technology has changed society immeasurably, cities, counties, and special districts operate as individual islands with virtually no connection to any other nearby entities. That stubborn independence comes at great cost, both in terms of dollars and political accountability.

Artificial Barriers

With each city or county its own political island, a community organizes and maintains its own police force, fire department, school system, parks and recreation programs, recycling facility, and so on. In this matter, the gates of collaboration remain shut, and for good reason. Massive local bureaucracies exist to manage the unique needs of their communities, which is soothing to residents. After all, if Montebello merges its functions and services with next-door Monterey Park, Latinos would have to co-exist with Koreans, and vice versa. The residents of each former locality might complain about different levels of service. Likewise, if Oakland shares programs with Berkeley, increasing numbers of Latino and African American children could be in the same after school or summer programs. What might happen then? And how would Berkeley residents feel about a merged police force that might be less effective because of a higher crime rate in Oakland?

It's not only about race. Divisions between communities occur in terms of income patterns, public education communities, zoning characteristics, and numerous other factors. But at the end of the day, different groups are wont to accept conditions bordering on true neighborhood assimilation, lest they lose their distinctive characteristics or sense of advantage over the others.

The Costs in Dollars

All this parochial autonomy comes at a financial cost to local communities, and a very steep one at that. Duplicated bureaucracies mean unnecessary costly managers, excessive pension commitments, and underutilized expensive equipment ranging from school buses and adjacent community playgrounds to fire trucks and police communication systems. The scenario is played out in one form or another throughout the state, hundreds if not thousands of times over.

Consider Orange County, a 789-square-mile rectangular patch of land that contains slightly more than 3 million people who live in 34 cities. In an area about 40 miles long and 20 miles wide, 15 cities contract with the Orange County Sheriff's Department for law enforcement, but 19 others have their own police departments. For fire protection, 22 cities use the services of the Orange County Fire Authority, but 12 have their own fire departments. The worst overlap is in public education, however, where 28 school districts provide education—some unified (kindergarten through 12th grade), some elementary, as well as a few high school districts. Further, this single county has four community college districts. Imagine the cost savings with one school superintendent, one police chief (or perhaps the county sheriff), and so on. Okay, even if one bureaucracy seems too consolidated, what if the county was divided into two or three jurisdictions for the same services? The savings would be huge.

Is it possible that Orange County is an aberration? Hardly. Let's look at Alameda County to the north, on the east side of San Francisco Bay. With a land mass of 738 square miles and a population of 1,510,000 residents, the county consists of 14 cities and another half dozen unincorporated communities. Here, each city operates its own police department, while the unincorporated areas are protected by the county sheriff's office. Eleven different fire departments operate throughout the county, along with 18 independent school districts. Imagine the savings that would accrue with the consolidation of services.

But these examples pale when compared with the duplication found within the borders of Los Angeles County. With 9.8 million residents, it is the most populated county in the nation and teeming with bureaucratic overlap. Forty-five police departments operate in 88 cities, with almost all of the rest opting for protection from the Los Angeles County Sheriff's Department.[19] Perhaps the most bizarre case is found in the "city" of Vernon, which has 53 officers for 112 residents and is completely surrounded by the city of Los Angeles. To be fair, Vernon is almost exclusively an industrial area, but why should it be separate from Los Angeles? What unique services might Vernonites receive that they couldn't get from the city that completely surrounds them? It makes no sense.

With respect to fire protection, 26 cities in Los Angeles County have their own fire departments; most of the rest rely on the county for protection, although at least one city, Sierra Madre, houses a volunteer fire department.

But the most egregious duplication is found within public education: no fewer than 79 school districts provide education in this single county. Some overlapping jurisdictions truly defy any semblance of logic. For example, Whittier is a city of 85,000 residents, located about 10 miles east of Los Angeles. Within the boundaries of that single city lie Whittier School District, Whittier Union High School District, East Whittier School District, and South Whittier School District! Think of all the unnecessary expenses at a time when schools are overcrowded because of massive teacher layoffs and other cutbacks due to revenue shortfalls. Taxpayers, parents, and children are paying a huge price for their "local" school districts.

While most counties have overlapping and duplicative jurisdictions, San Francisco stands out as an exception. At 49 square miles, the City by the Bay is the state's only city and county housed within the same geographical boundary. As such, the territory has one school district, one fire district, and one police department. Even San Francisco has its quirks, however, because along with a police department, the city also has a separate sheriff's department. Still, compared to the operations within the state's remaining 57 counties, San Francisco seems well organized.

There is a remedy for these costly and unnecessary bureaucracies: consolidation of governments and mergers of key programs and services. This proposal isn't just an untested, abstract theory; it has worked in locations throughout the nation. In some cases, cities and counties have consolidated into one governmental unit; such successes have occurred in Nashville/Davidson County (Tennessee), Jacksonville/Duvall County (Florida), Indianapolis/Marion County (Indiana), and Louisville/Jefferson County (Kentucky).[20] In other cases, smaller city-sized units have merged. The savings can be substantial while improving the level of services at the same time. An assessment of the Nashville/Davidson County consolidation found increased revenues and reduced operating costs.[21] Specialized governments such as school districts have merged with similar successes. In 2009, two districts with 2,500 students in suburban Pittsburgh, Pennsylvania merged and saved $1 million in the first year, more than 3 percent of the previously combined budgets.[22] In tough economic times, these kinds of savings can go a long way in making up for inadequate tax revenues.

In fact, we're beginning to see the first signs of merged services in California, although what's happened to date barely scratches the surface of what can be accomplished. Even though citizens, local elected officials, and bureaucrats don't like giving up proprietary turf, they are even less enamored with paying more taxes to keep their independence. In 2011, four small cities in San Mateo County moved to create a single county fire department, with total annual cost savings approaching $4 million.[23] In the same year, Half Moon Bay, a city also in San Mateo County, disbanded its police department and turned over law enforcement responsibilities to the San Mateo Sheriff's office. Result: an annual savings of $500,000.[24]

Granted, San Mateo County is reasonably compact at 449 square miles and 720,000 residents, but the efforts of its local governments demonstrate that savings can accrue. Perhaps a better example on a larger scale would be in Los Angeles County, where the city of Lakewood, population 90,000, has contracted out police, fire, and garbage services with the county at costs considerably lower than if the city provided its own services.[25] The point is that these arrangements can be done if people are willing to trade autonomy for reduced costs.

Mergers and consolidation aren't meant for everyone. Sometimes geographical distances between communities are too great or community services in adjacent cities are provided under radically different circumstances. There are also very real political threats. Reorganized efforts can threaten protectors of the status quo, ranging from assistant city police and fire chiefs to organized labor. But clearly, great opportunities for savings exist at the local government level and plenty of real life examples bear out the point. Beyond cities and counties, the greatest potential for major savings resides with the more than 1,000 school districts in the state, where redundancies abound. Of course, high-level managers and teacher unions alike are likely to resist anything that might alter the status quo. Just as important, with so many districts segregated in one form or another and widely differing levels of local property tax commitments, mergers will be difficult without the state playing a heavy role through truly equalized funding. More on that in Chapter 11.

Weak Ability to Perform

A second problem with fractured local governments exists in their weak ability to carry out their public responsibilities. That's because although these units are tasked by the legislature with providing badly needed social services, they lack the financial means to raise the necessary revenues to provide those services. It's a catch-22 if there ever was one. Oddly enough, the public has had a substantial role in creating this impossible set of circumstances.

Proposition 13

Much, although not all, of local government impotence stems from the passage of Proposition 13 by the voters in 1978. Officially described on the ballot as "The People's Initiative to Limit Property Taxation," Proposition 13 established that counties could not collect property taxes of more than 1 percent of the value of the parcel as of 1975 or any time afterward when the property changed hands. In addition, any future considerations of special tax increases at the local level would require a two-thirds vote of the people to pass. This last point is particularly ironic. Think about it: Statewide ballot propositions in California pass if they obtain a simple majority, and Proposition 13 easily eclipsed that requirement by garnering 65 percent of the vote. But the proposition required future tax increases at the local level to be decided by a two-thirds vote—a higher threshold than the vote required for the proposition's passage! Something is terribly wrong here. Using a simple majority process to require a two-thirds vote in future elections seems inherently unfair, although the California State Supreme Court upheld the measure as constitutional.[26]

Upon passage, Proposition 13 reduced local government taxes by 57 percent because of drastically reduced property assessment values. Leaders of the Howard Jarvis Taxpayers Association, the group that initially spearheaded the campaign (under a different name at the time) and has remained its political guardian ever since, proudly point out that property owners have saved more than $500 billion since the law's enactment.[27] That may be well and good for the taxpayer who has few expectations from government. But we should remember that these local taxes were used to pay for police, fire protection, K–12 public education, libraries, parks, street maintenance, and a plethora of services traditionally provided by local governments—services they could no longer deliver, at least at the levels prior to passage of the ballot proposition. Of the $7 billion in property tax savings the first year after Proposition 13, schools lost $3.5 billion; other county and city services lost the bulk of the rest. Those losses have continued to build ever since, year after year. As a result, the state has had to step in to make up at least some of the missing revenues, although recent annual state budget shortfalls have decreased that ability considerably.

The Consequences

Two interesting outcomes emerged from Proposition 13. First, the powers relative to local financing decisions migrated to the state.[28] Oddly enough, most Proposition 13 architects were decidedly anti-government at any level of authority, so the transfer "up" was somewhat disheartening particularly because state authority is a big step away from local control. Second, local governments and the state, combined, have never been able to replace all of the taxes lost through Proposition 13. The deterioration of social services, including public education, can be traced to this critical juncture in state history.[29]

Since Proposition 13, the public has tied the hands of local public policymakers repeatedly by passing new programs and services and restricting the ability of local governments to collect revenues. That's an impossible combination when you think about it, but the problem is that few people do. For example, on the programmatic side, in 1986, the electorate approved Proposition 65, which required state and local government to enforce safe drinking water standards, among other obligations. In 1992, passage of Proposition 163 expanded the nontaxable foods list to include candy, snack foods, and bottled water, costing counties a cool $120 million annually. In 2000, the voters passed Proposition 21, which expanded categories of juvenile crime at a cost to local governments of $100 million annually. All these programs cost money, which has to be found somewhere.

At the same time that voters have enacted new programs, they have increased the difficulty of funding them. In 1986, the voters passed Proposition 62, which required city councils and county boards of supervisors to obtain a two-thirds vote before placing local measures on the ballot. In 1996, the voters passed Proposition 218, which prevented local governments from creating any new taxes without approval of the voters. And in 2010, the voters passed Proposition 26, the Supermajority Vote to Pass New Taxes and Fees Act, which denies local governments the ability to impose fees and levies without a vote of the people.

Too Much Democracy?

Simply put, these days local governments are prevented from adding new revenue sources without public approval. That may sound democratic, but it may be *too* democratic, given that the voters don't hesitate to pile on unrealistic services without the ability to pay for them. It leads one to wonder why we have elected local officials at all if virtually every fiscal decision is subject to the whims of public sentiment on narrow issues about which the public may know little or nothing in the first place!

Misplaced Blame

All this has taken its toll as local governments try to pay for services with dwindling resources. In recent times, some have turned to government employees as the source of local government difficulties. The thinking is that there are too many at too great a cost for what the public can afford. Yet a recent study shows that bureaucracy in California ranks 48th of the 50 states, not exactly an indictment of waste or excess.[30]

Still, problems have been particularly onerous with public employee salaries, healthcare, and pensions—many of which have increased faster than the abilities of local governments to generate revenues and adequate retirement funds. In some cities, elected officials and public employee unions have renegotiated contracts, with the results being higher employee contributions to healthcare and retirement, reduced pay, and higher retirement ages for new employees. In other cases, unions have been unwilling to negotiate, especially if they have already negotiated contract reductions. When the two groups haven't been able to find agreement, local government leaders have chastised unions for being selfish; union officials have criticized local government managers for not putting in their share of retirement funds all along and for overpaid higher management.[31] The stalemate has been exacerbated by a large plurality of Californians believing that public employee benefits are too generous.[32] Yet, data show that public employees' salaries and pensions combined earn about the same amounts as private sector employees when controlled for education, according to a massive study by economists at U.C. Berkeley and Rutgers University.[33] Clearly, there's a massive disparity between perception and reality, perpetuated in part, no doubt, by a general public that has suffered from the state's sour economy.

Despite continued expectations for robust public school programs and community services, voter endorsement for limited taxes at the local government level has remained strong. In 2008, 30 years after the passage of Proposition 13, a Field public opinion poll found that voters still favored the measure by a margin of 57 percent to 23 percent.[34] Yet, the voters continue to lament the poor quality of public services provided by state and local governments, and they blame public officials for this outcome even though much of it has occurred because of voter-approved limitations on revenue collection.

PRIVATE INTERESTS TAKE CHARGE

Thus far, most of our attention has focused on the activities of local governments and their leaders, whether elected or appointed. But just past the apparent openness of public deliberations, citizen input, and periodic elections are the thousands of individuals and interest groups that utilize their vast resources to bend the benefits of public policies in their directions. Private interests tend to present themselves as guardians of the public good, although the policies that follow in the wake of their pressures seem to accrue disproportionately to their advantage. These interests vary in both power and success, but their efforts often alter the policies of local governments in ways unequalled by individual petitioners. Most of the time, they are connected with the use of land, whether in the form of transportation, construction, zoning, or development. Private interests don't always get what they want from local governments, but the relatively little public notice of their activities coupled with immense financial clout certainly stacks the deck in their favor. A few examples may help to make the point.

Ripping Up Trolley Tracks in Los Angeles

Traffic congestion is a mainstay of California history, but the means of transportation have changed over time. Before the automobile assumed its place as king of transportation in California, urban areas struggled to find the most efficient ways of moving their people and goods. A major breakthrough came with the availability of electricity as a power source. Clearly, San Francisco was the role model for this effort, but Los Angeles developed a mass transit system, too.

Beginning in the late 1880s, two streetcar companies emerged as replacements for horse-drawn wagons in the "City of the Angels." Powered by electricity via overhead wires, these companies ultimately operated on more than 1,100 miles of track—the largest interurban rail system in the nation at the time. The immense transportation network extended from the Pacific Ocean west of Los Angeles to the San Bernardino Mountains to the east, and from the San Gabriel Mountains in the north to Newport Beach in Orange County. In all, the trolley network covered several hundred square miles.

The streetcar system worked like a charm. As historian Kevin Starr notes, "turn-of-the-century Southern California grew because it had a remarkable rapid transit system."[35] By the 1920s, the public transportation arrangement carried a million passengers per day annually. (By way of contrast, Los Angeles County's rail system carries about 300,000 daily passengers today.[36]) With most trains moving through the city's downtown area in grid-like fashion, Los Angeles had the basis of a true urban core and the means of moving people to and from it.

Then things changed. Increased reliance upon gasoline-powered motor vehicles altered the transportation tradition in Los Angeles, but not without help. As the growing number of automobiles approached the "critical mass" stage, the newly formed Automobile Club of Southern California spearheaded a campaign for the city to build massive roadways, soon dubbed "freeways," as fluid arteries for quickly moving large numbers of motor vehicles without stopping at intersections.[37] The desire to move out was aided by the arrival of increasing numbers of African Americans and immigrants to the city's core—groups considered undesirable by the middle class whites already there.[38] The development of a freeway system allowed them to drive to and from work from their distant enclaves much more efficiently than if they used streetcars.[39]

In a way, the horizontal architecture left the city little choice, with the automobile becoming the transportation means to bridging long distances between places of employment and places of residence. Los Angeles, it seemed, practically invented urban sprawl.[40] Decades later, the city began to reconstruct a combined light rail and subway system, which today is a fraction of the size of its predecessor and hundreds of times the cost. Still, one wonders what might have happened in the 1940s and beyond, had the city committed to expanding mass transit with the same vigor as building freeways.

San Francisco Tweets

Although Silicon Valley is ground zero for high tech, San Francisco has a small, but prestigious share of cutting-edge companies, particularly in the "social media" space. Among these enterprises is Twitter, a mass media company with an application that allows users to type messages of 140 characters (usually letters) or less on their phones or computers. Twitter has become immensely popular in its short life. As of 2010, the company had 350 employees, 175 million users, and a valuation of $3.7 billion.[41]

With expectations that its workforce would double within a couple of years, Twitter was hot—very hot. By early 2011, venture capitalists revised Twitter's value sharply upward to $10 billion,[42] although as a private company the profits were not made public. Profitable or not, the company has been able to generate oodles of capital. And with such cachet, the social media company did not hesitate to use its clout to gain special favors from the city in the form of tax breaks.

In 2011, an expanding Twitter needed more office space to accommodate its growing workforce, but the company considered San Francisco rents excessive. Twitter executives threatened to leave San Francisco for another less expensive location unless the city provided special tax breaks to curb its costs—costs for a company now valued at $10 billion! The claim of excessive taxes seemed a bit odd, inasmuch as studies show that taxes generally account for only about 4 percent of business relocation decisions, compared to 75 percent for labor and transportation.[43]

Meanwhile, San Francisco had its own problems. Looking ahead to the 2011–2012 fiscal year, San Francisco faced a projected deficit of $380 million out of a $4.1 billion budget. The city needed every dime it could generate to balance its books. Anything less would mean cutbacks in public health clinics, police and fire personnel, public education commitments, and basic infrastructure maintenance.

The city's problems notwithstanding, Twitter was not about to be denied. After lengthy debate, the San Francisco Board of Supervisors voted to freeze the city's 1.5 percent payroll tax at the current employee level for six years to any company operating in the part of the city that Twitter wished to locate[44]—hardly a coincidence. For Twitter, assuming the projected rate of workforce expansion, the savings will amount to $16 million over 6 years, or about $2.7 million per year. Critics excoriated the decision for opening a "Pandora's box" for any other local tech company seeking the same benefits.[45] Yelp and Zynga, two other companies occupying similar social media space with the same start-up issues, could be equally justified in making similar claims for a "much-needed" tax break. And what about other companies claiming to be struggling?

San Francisco Mayor Ed Lee defended the tax relief as "a powerful tool that will help us bring in much-needed jobs, services and retail,"[46] yet there was no study to substantiate the claim. Meanwhile, for San Francisco, the tax revenues will shrink, and that outcome is indisputable. One can only imagine what policies (and revenue losses) will result from future corporate threats. In the meantime, while San Francisco struggles, Twitter has been exempt from some of its tax-paying responsibilities.

Development of Newhall Ranch

Even though California has plenty of land, some tracts are more desirable for development than others because of their proximity to urban areas or other destination centers. Newhall Ranch represents such a valuable piece of real estate. Sitting on thousands of acres of land an hour's drive from the heart of Los Angeles, Newhall Ranch remains one of the last undeveloped areas close to a major urban center. For that reason, developers have been hungry to transform the property into a planned community of homes, and manufacturing and office space. Now, after nearly two decades of lobbying local governments and fighting off court suits, developers are about to reap the benefits of their efforts.

Newhall Ranch began as a Mexican land grant prior to California's independence. In the late 1800s, Henry Mayo Newhall purchased the ranch at an auction. The ranch, totaling 38,000 acres, remained in the family until the 1920s, when it was sold to William Randolph Hearst. The ranch changed hands several times thereafter, with most of the land dedicated to cattle grazing and farming. As Los Angeles grew, city leaders cast their eyes on the property for annexation as a means of expanding the tax base, but Los Angeles County officials turned down the proposal. By the 1990s, the land was taken over by the Lennar Development Corporation, the second largest homebuilder in the United States. Lennar proposed turning much of the ranch into a planned community of 12,000 acres that would house more than 20,000 housing units and a population of 60,000 people. Another 6,000 acres would be set aside for public parks.[47]

As an unincorporated area, the Newhall Ranch area remained under the control of Los Angeles County. The company pursued approval of its proposal by county officials, who were lukewarm to such a massive development because of environmental and infrastructure issues. Neighboring Ventura County opposed the project because of increased urbanization in what had been a rural area. Environmentalist organizations also opposed the development because of threats to endangered species, over-reliance on the nearby Santa Clara River and other water sources, and threats to air quality. Added to the controversy were conflicting assessments of the proposal by the U.S. Environmental Protection Agency and the Army Corps of Engineers. Whereas the Corps accepted Lennar's belief that modification of the Santa Clara River would protect the area from flooding, the EPA rejected the claim and called for a smaller project footprint.[48] In 1998, the Los Angeles County Board of Supervisors approved the development request with modifications.

Since then, the Newhall Ranch project has been mired in legal purgatory. In 1999, Kern County filed a lawsuit, claiming that the development would bring environmental harm to the region; the claim was dismissed after a hearing. In 2004, Newland Land Company settled another lawsuit with three environmental groups by agreeing to provide annual reports of projected water use and disposal of its farmland. And in 2011, a coalition of environmental groups sued the state of California for approving development of the planned community on the grounds that the project would harm water resources, historic Native American sites, and rare vegetation, once again putting a stop to any development.

Meanwhile, the Lennar Corporation has continued to promote the development of Newhall Ranch through an aggressive public relations campaign. The company has promoted the planned community as "Awesometown" for its "awesome schools, awesome walking paths, and awesome town center."[49] Awesome or not, the rollout of the full development remains on hold pending resolution of the latest lawsuits.

El Toro Marine Base—When Right Beats Might

Over the past two decades, the United States government has shut down more than 100 military installations, about one-fourth of which have been in California.[50] The closures have impacted California and other states in various ways. Many have suffered economically because of nearby businesses forced to close; others have actually prospered through the availability of significant swaths of land for community development. One such closure was the El Toro Marine Air Station, a base 4,682 acres in size. The base had four long runways, two of which extended 10,000 feet and able to accommodate all commercial aircraft. The military facility was officially decommissioned in 1999, but long before its transition different groups began plotting its future use.

Those favoring development wanted to convert the former base into a new Orange County airport. The current facility in use, John Wayne Airport, covered 500 acres with a runway only 5,700 feet long and unable to handle passenger jets larger than a relatively small Boeing 737. Only eight miles to the north and west of El Toro, John Wayne Airport was hemmed in by development and unable to expand; meanwhile, Los Angeles International Airport was rapidly reaching its saturation point, opening up the opportunity for new a facility between Los Angeles and San Diego.[51]

The loose alliance of airport proponents consisted of traditionally powerful groups in the region, including the Orange County Chamber of Commerce, the Building Industry Association, local realtor groups, construction unions, and land developers. The Southern California Association of Governments (SCAG), a loose regional government of several nearby counties, joined the Orange County Board of Supervisors to pursue conversion of El Toro to a civilian airport. To the north, the city of Los Angeles officially supported a new facility as part of the effort to offload increasing traffic from Los Angeles International airport.

But there was another side to the issue. The local governments of nine cities surrounding the El Toro facility formed the El Toro Reuse Planning Authority (ETRPA), a regional government dedicated to preventing airport development. They called for a huge regional park in place of the airport, one that would be funded from developer fees for about 15 percent of the land that would be set aside for an industrial park or similar purpose. Dozens of neighborhood groups joined in opposition to a new airport. Even the 81-member Clergy for Wholesome Communities protested that building a new airport would be hazardous to the region's spirituality. In the words of the group's leader, "I think it's (the airport proposal) a biblical question. What is the quality of life here?"[52]

While some prayed for divine intervention, others lobbied for constructive change. Backed by a $24 million war chest, ETRPA sued SCAG for setting up the new airport priority without conducting adequate environmental impact reports or holding public hearings. They argued that the proposed airport had dangerous flight path patterns, would be excessively noisy, and posed serious environmental risks to south county communities. Over the course of the struggle, ETRPA filed 15 lawsuits to stop development. On three occasions, anti-development ballot propositions circulated by opponents were voided by the courts, adding to their woes.

Opponents would not be dissuaded. In 2001, allies friendly to ETRPA circulated a fourth ballot petition, which qualified for the March 2002 election; the essence of the petition was that El Toro would be converted into the proposed regional park at an estimated cost of $5 billion, rather than a major international airport. The voters approved Measure W by a margin of 57.8 percent to 42.2 percent. There would be no airport in an area now dubbed the Great Irvine Park, which was annexed by the City of Irvine in 2006.[53]

Postscript: More than a decade after the now-famous 2002 vote, few changes have occurred at the now-abandoned El Toro Marine Base. Developers have not come forward to build. Local authorities have asked for but failed to receive any funds from state and national governments. Other than toxic waste removal, the area remains barren except for 19.5 acres on the northern fringe that have been coifed for hiking and biking trails and a temporary soccer field. In response to critics, one park supporter said, "We've been very clear that this is a long-term project— Central Park (in New York) took 20 years to build, and San Diego's Balboa Park took 75 years to build."[54] Still, whatever the disappointment on park progress, there's not an airplane in sight.

Who's Really in Charge?

Clearly, the playing field often is far from level when considering public policy decisions in local governments. As the previous examples show, more times than not, powerful interests exert enough pressure to have their way on issues important to them. Sometimes there are public benefits in the form of new housing or land set aside for parks or even new tax revenues, but that's not the point. The major concern is that at the local level, news doesn't travel well and strategically connected interests can take advantage of the void, leaving everyone else at a decided disadvantage.

MAKING LOCAL GOVERNMENTS WORK

Years ago, Thomas "Tip" O'Neill, then-Speaker of the U.S. House of Representatives, explained that a member of Congress fares best by understanding that "all politics is local." With that statement, O'Neill was suggesting that people care much more about how their lives are affected at home than by what happens thousands of miles away in Washington, D.C. That same concept applies to the way Californians assess the power and responsiveness of their governments. Sure, they know that the president and Congress contemplate the big issues of the day, often deferring action from one year to another, and so on; it's all so fuzzy. And they appreciate existentially that state legislators make laws relating to myriad topics, while the governor nominates judges and appoints administrators. But all those things are far away from underperforming schools, unsolved local crimes, and cracked pavement on local sidewalks. To which people ask, why isn't the government fixing those things?

City Leaders and Competing Definitions of the Public Good

The irony is that most of the time people don't know who should fix "those things" as much as they're not fixed, period. It's in that no man's land of politics that local elected officials in California operate. On the one hand, their accomplishments—perhaps reduced crime or improved garbage collection—are often buried deep in local newspapers or mentioned almost as afterthoughts on television news, if at all. On the other hand, much of their capabilities are defined, regulated, and monitored by the state. Put those two facts together and you have governments that attempt to function in limited areas with limited authority and lots of accountability.

But whereas local leaders have some say over land use and other community resources, they are largely impotent on the question of taxation and revenue collection. Sure, they can take positions on things like school parcel tax elections and the occasional proposed general sales tax increase, but the outcome of such matters are either defined by the state or determined by the voters.

The political handcuffing of local government officials began with Proposition 13 in 1978 and has continued ever since. Recently, the voters added yet another insult to many injuries with the passage of Proposition 26 in 2010, which now requires approval of the electorate on any kind of local tax or fee increase. Yet, as elected officials try to think of efficiencies in the form of consolidation or merged services, many more times than not, the same people who have restricted their ability to finance government keep them from making better use of fewer dollars.

Unconnected Dots

Given these limitations, local governments increasingly have been unable to provide badly needed local services in policy areas extending from public education to public safety, and just about everything in between. As for the residents, those with the financial means escape to the suburbs, put their kids in private schools, or purchase protection through residences in gated communities. Those without the means are left behind to live in underserved communities with inferior public education and tattered infrastructures. It's not just "a tale of two cities," to borrow from Dickens' fictional account. It's "a tale of two Californias" within the same geographical boundary. In the end, it's a story without a happy ending.

ENDNOTES

1. Terry Christensen, *Local Politics: Governing at the Grassroots* (Belmont, CA: Wadsworth Publishing Company, 1995), pp. 334–335.
2. Kevin B. Smith, Alan Greenblatt, and Michele Mariani, *Governing States and Localities*, 2nd ed. (Washington, D.C.: CQ Press, 2008), p. 21.
3. Terry Christensen and I devote a chapter to such material in *our California Politics and Government: A Practical Approach*, 11th ed. (Boston, MA: Wadsworth Cengage, 2011). See Chapter 9.
4. Because special districts provide targeted services for relatively small populations, they are not the focus of our discussion. For information on these micro-governments, see California Legislature, "What's So Special about Special Districts? A Citizen's Guide to Special Districts in California," 4th ed., October 2010, Sacramento, CA.
5. Robert Gottlieb makes this point concerning the shortage of trees and parks in sprawled areas such as Los Angeles. See Robert Gottlieb, *Reinventing Los Angeles: Nature and Community in the Global City* (Cambridge, MA: MIT Press, 2007), pp. 44–48.
6. William Fulton, *The Reluctant Metropolis: The Politics of Urban Growth in Los Angeles*, 2nd ed. (Baltimore, MD: The Johns Hopkins Press, 2001), pp. 345–346.
7. Stephanie S. Pincetl, *Transforming California: A Political History of Land Use and Development* (Baltimore, MD: The Johns Hopkins Press, 1999), p. 125.
8. John R. Logan, "Hispanic Populations and Their Residential Patterns in the Metropolis," May 8, 2002, http://mumford1.dyndns.org/cen2000/HispanicPop/HspReportNew/MumfordReport.pdf, p. 8.
9. William A.V. Clark, "The Geography of a Mixed-Race Society," Growth and Change, 40(4), 565–593, 2009. http://onlinelibrary.wiley.com/doi/10.1111/j.1468-2257.2009.00501.x/full.
10. Ronald Campbell, Doug Irving, and Peggy Lowe, "O.C. Lost Whites, Gained Hispanics and Asians, Census Shows," *Orange County Register*, March 8, 2011, http://www.ocregister.com/news/county-291335-census-population.html?cb=1299709457.
11. Leah Platt Boustan, "Was Post-War Suburbanization 'White Flight'? Evidence From the Black Migration," *The Quarterly Journal of Economics*, February 2010, p. 417.
12. John Ritter, "San Francisco Hopes to Reverse Black Flight," *USA Today*, August 28, 2007, http://www.usatoday.com/news/nation/2007-08-26-urban-blacks_N.htm.

13. John Holton, *The Politics of Diversity: Immigration, Resistance, and Change in Monterey Park, California* (Philadelphia: Temple University Press, 1995), p. 80.

14. See Gary Orfield, Genevieve Siegel-Hawley, and John Kucsera, "Divided We Fail: Segregated and Unequal Schools in the Southland," The Civil Rights Project, University of California, Los Angeles, March 18, 2011, http://civilrightsproject.ucla.edu/research/metro-and-regional-inequalities/lasanti-project-los-angeles-san-diego-tijuana/divided-we-fail-segregated-and-unequal-schools-in-the-southfield.

15. http://www.nais.org.

16. Fulton, op. cit., p. 338.

17. Gottlieb, op. cit., pp. 294–295.

18. See "Californians and Their Government," Public Policy Institute of California, San Francisco, CA, September 2009, pp. 11, 20.

19. The City of Santa Fe Springs contracts for education services from neighboring Whittier.

20. John J. Harrigan and David C. Nice, *Politics and Policy in States and Communities*, 8th ed. (New York: Pearson Longman, 2004), p. 146.

21. Eric Bradner, "Merger Effort by Nashville & Davidson County, Tenn., in 1962 Bears Economic Fruit," *Evansville Courier and Press*, August 16, 2010, http://www.indianaeconomicdigest.net/main.asp?SectionID=31&SubSectionID=82&ArticleID=55658.

22. Brian David, "Central Valley Celebrates Merger," *post-gazette.com*, July 6, 2009, http://www.post-gazette.com/pg/09187/982079-57.stm.

23. "San Bruno, Millbrae Take Steps to Merge Fire Services," *San Jose Mercury News*, April 4, 2011, p. B6.

24. "In a Beachside Tourist Town, a Wrenching Decision to Outsource," *The New York Times*, April 4, 2011, p. A12.

25. George H. Cox and Raymond A. Rosenfeld, *State and Local Government: Public Life in America* (Belmont, CA: Wadsworth Publishing Company, 2001), p. 16.

26. The case was *Amador Valley Joint Union High School District v. State Board of Equalization* (1978) 22 Cal. 3rd 208.

27. Howard Jarvis Taxpayers Association, 2009, www.hjta.org/index.php.

28. Jean Ross, "Proposition 13 Thirty Years Later: What It Has Meant for Governance and Public Services," in Jack Citrin and Isaac William Martin, Eds., *After the Tax Revolt: Proposition 13 Turns 30* (Berkeley, CA: Berkeley Public Policy Press, 2009), p. 136.

29. Jeffrey I. Chapman, "The Continuing Redistribution of Fiscal Stress: The Long Run Consequences of Proposition 13," working paper, The Lincoln Institute of Land Use Policy, 1998, pp. 44–48.

30. "Looking for Waste," *Economist*, May 1, 2010, p. 33.

31. For some insight into the tension, see "Mayor Sounds Fiscal Alarm," *San Jose Mercury News*, May 14, 2011, pp. 1, 10.

32. "More California Voters Now View Public Pension Benefits as Too Generous. Narrowly Oppose Taking Away Collective Bargaining Rights of Public Sector Employees. Majority Support for a Number of Reform Proposals," The Field Poll, Release #2369, March 17, 2011, p. 3.

33. "Public Workers Highly Paid? Not Exactly," *San Francisco Chronicle*, October 19, 2010, pp. A1, A8.

34. "Thirty Years After Its Passage, Prop. 13 Remains Highly Popular With Voters. Most Proposals To Change Its Provisions Face Stiff Opposition," The Field Poll, Release #2274, June 6, 2008, p. 2.

35. Kevin Starr, *Inventing the Dream: California Through the Progressive Era* (New York: Oxford University Press, 1985), p. 70.

36. http://www.metro.net/news/pages/ridership-statistics.

37. Fulton, op. cit., pp. 132–133.

38. Robert M. Fogelson, *The Fragmented Metropolis: Los Angeles, 1850-1930* (Berkeley, CA: University of California Press, 1967), pp. 178–179.

39. Ibid., pp. 274–275.

40. Carey McWilliams, *Southern California: An Island on the Land* (Salt Lake City, UT: Gibbs-Smith Publisher, 1946), p. 236.

41. Amir Efrati, "Profit Elusive, but Twitter Gets $3.7 Billion Value," *The Wall Street Journal*, December 10, 2010, http://online.wsj.com/article/SB1000142405274870482 8104576021954210929460.html?KEYWORDS=twitter+valuation.

42. Olivia Oran, "Twitter Valued at Up to $10 Billion: Report," *The Street*, February 10, 2011, http://www.thestreet.com/print/story/11004049.html.

43. See "Editorial: No Tax Breaks for Twitter," *San Francisco Bay Guardian Online*, February 1, 2011, http://www.sfbg.com/print/bruce/2011/02/01/editorial-no-tax-breaks-twitter.

44. "Twitter Gets a 6-Year Payroll-Tax Break from San Francisco Board of Supervisors," *Los Angeles Times*, April 6, 2011, http://latimesblogs.latimes.com/technol-ogy/2011/04/twitter-gets-6-year-payroll-tax-break-from-san-francisco-board-of-supervisors.html.

45. "Twitter Deal Sends S.F. Down a Slippery Slope of Tax Breaks," *San Jose Mercury News*, May 10, 2011, pp. A1, A6.

46. Quoted in "Twitter Will Get Payroll Tax Breaks to Stay in S.F.," *San Francisco Chronicle*, April 6, 2011, p. A1.

47. "Newhall Project Advances; Ventura Plans Legal Fight," *Los Angeles Times*, March 24, 1999, http://articles.latimes.com/1999/mar/24/local/me-20651.

48. Louis Sahagun, "EPA, Army Corps of Engineers are at Odds over New Hall Ranch," *Los Angeles Times*, February 3, 2011, http://articles.latimes.com/2011/feb/03/local/la-me-adv-newhall-epa-20110202.

49. Alana Semuels, "'Awesometown' Ad Campaign Spurs Buzz for Valencia," *Los Angeles Times*, September 23, 2010, http://articles.latimes.com/2010/sep/23/business/la-fi-0920-awesometown-20100920.

50. See "California Institute Special Report: California's Past Base Closure Experiences and the 2005 BRAC Round," California Institute for Federal Policy Research, Washington, D.C., 2005 and Appendix Q, Text of the 2005 Defense Base Closure and Realignment Commission and Approved Recommendations, Defense Base Closure and Realignment Commission, Washington, D.C., 2006.

51. M.L. Shettle, Jr., "Historic California Posts: Marine Corps Air Station, El Toro," The California State Military Museum, http://www.militarymuseum.org/MCASElToro.html.

52. Matthew Ebnet, "Battle Over Airport Takes a Religious Turn," *Los Angeles Times*, February 22, 2000, http://articles.latimes.com/print/2000/feb/22/local/me-1343.

53. For a chronology of events, see "Orange County Park: Whose Park Is It?" Orange County Grand Jury, 2005–2006.

54. Sarah Peters, "A Slice of the Great Park," *The Daily Pilot*, October 2, 2010, http://articles.dailypilot.com/2010-10-02/news/tn-dpt-1003-park-20101002_1_great-park-soccer-fields-soccer-practices.

6

Infrastructure on the Brink of Collapse

Physically, the infrastructure is pretty much destroyed, but the battle is now on the ideological front.

—Nawaf Obaid, Saudi Foreign Minister

Foreign Minister Obaid made those comments about post-war Iraq after the U.S. attack to rid the nation of Saddam Hussein and his military forces in 2003. Roads, schools, government buildings, power transmissions lines, and the prized oil refineries and delivery systems—the economic lifeline of the country—were among the infrastructure components that were all but obliterated. At the war's end, Iraq was in pieces.

To compare the condition of California's infrastructure with post-war Iraq would be ludicrous, of course. But curiously enough, there are some common themes. First, California's infrastructure is a far cry today from its condition 50 years ago; some elements have deteriorated, other simply haven't kept up with the explosive needs of a growing population. Second, the battle today is not only over the condition of the state's infrastructure but its value to Californians. In other words, how much do we want to commit scarce resources to roads, the power grid, and the like? How much are we willing to accept mediocrity in lieu of collecting more taxes? These questions often manifest in public opinion polls, legislative activity, and state bond elections. The answers are disturbing to anyone who feels pain from California's fall from grace as a driver in the global economy and provider of quality amenities to its population.

Physically, an infrastructure network provides the necessary assortment of facilities and services necessary for society to function, or at least that's what it's supposed to do. Most of us don't spend much time thinking about these components unless there are power blackouts or tainted water supplies or bridges that succumb to earthquakes. Only when something goes amiss do we demand to know what happened, why, and how soon could it be fixed? In fact, governments invest in infrastructure all the time to guard against anything going wrong. That's the case in California, too.

On the surface, California's infrastructure seems stable. Most of the time everything works as we expect it to. With rare exceptions, everyday 38 million residents expect to wake up to enough electricity, drive to and from work on groomed highways, and have ample amounts of water to shower everything from their bodies to their lawns when they return home. But things are not as they seem. Congested roadways extract a price in the form of lost productivity, illness, and environmental pollution. The water system in the Sacramento Delta that sends much of the state's water south depends on protection from antiquated levies, some of which are 100 years old. The electricity grid is taxed to the point that on hot days, we often suffer rolling brownouts.

These problems are not merely inconveniences; they can play havoc with manufacturing, stop traffic, flood large expanses of valuable agricultural land, and leave us in the dark. They can even cost elected officials their offices. Then-Governor Gray Davis found out as much in 2003 when he was recalled from his post by an angry electorate that blamed him for his mismanagement of an electricity shortage, even though scarcity was caused by greedy power companies.[1] It doesn't matter when you're expected to keep things right.

Infrastructure elements are expensive; rarely can governments pay for these massive undertakings in one fell swoop. Just as a typical homeowner finances (and often refinances) the purchase of a home over several decades, state public policymakers often ask the voters to bankroll projects like dams or prisons through the sale of interest-bearing bonds for as long as 40 years. To pay for these things upon construction would be prohibitively expensive in as much as their costs can be in the billions. The Diamond Valley Dam, California's newest dam, was completed in 2003 at a price tag of $1.9 billion. The state broke ground on its newest prison in 2010 with an expected budget of $906 million. Generally, this elongated bonding process winds up costing twice as much as a one-time purchase, but often it's the only way to finance an infrastructure component. "Often" is not "always," however, and California policymakers have tended to foist too many decisions they should finance on an ongoing basis into a stretched out bond.

These days, California is in a double bind with its infrastructure. On the one hand, over the past decade state voters have approved tens of billions of dollars in infrastructure projects to keep the state safe and up to date. As a result, the annual California state budget has been dedicating an increasing portion of the shrinking state revenues to paying interest on infrastructure projects, leaving less for schools and safety net programs. On the other hand, the state's unmet infrastructure needs have not kept up with a soaring population. It's an unenviable combination of problems.

Still, we rarely connect expectations with costs. In 2011, a Field poll interviewed Californians about what was then a $25 billion state budget deficit, and asked whether we should raise taxes or cut spending. The survey respondents opposed new taxes, but recommended cuts in only 2 of 14 service areas. Don't cut spending, majorities said, on highways, parks, public transportation, and water storage. Fair enough. Then a majority of the respondents added, don't raise our taxes, either![2] That's the conundrum. More to the point, that's the lack of reality suffered by most Californians.

This chapter focuses on California's infrastructure—the physical foundation of the state's organization. The news is not good. Lack of funds, competing objectives, and an absence of honest political leadership have combined to leave California falling further and further behind in providing good roads, reliable electricity, a viable system of public parks, and enough water for the state's residents. The federal government's involvement on the suitability of our state prison system has added to a list of unmet needs. Meanwhile, the public wonders why it is that taxes seem to go for everything except what's important. We'll explain what's happened and what we can do to bring California's infrastructure into the 21st century before the next century comes around.

PARKING LOTS FOR HIGHWAYS

If it seems like you have been taking your car to the repair shop for an alignment with increasing frequency, it doesn't necessarily mean you're a bad driver. Chances are that it's because of California's inadequate and poorly maintained road system. It costs a lot to build and maintain roads, but it costs even more by not keeping them in good condition. That's one of the hidden costs of living in not-so-golden California. While we're keeping our taxes down to minimize expenditures, we're paying more to keep our cars on the roads. And because we have not added very many highway lanes or built new roads in proportion with an increasing population, it takes us longer to travel—a cost that extracts its own special toll in both time and money.

It didn't used to be this way. Fifty years ago, the state viewed its planned freeway system as an infrastructure cornerstone. Kevin Starr, perhaps California's best recorder of state history, has written how in the late 1950s and early 1960s state leaders not only planned out a multi-billion dollar freeway system, but found a way to pay for it on a pay-as-you-go basis through increased gasoline taxes, higher motor vehicle registration fees, and increased weight taxes for trucks.[3] There was no serious thought to borrowing from the future to pay for what the state needed at the time. That's changed, and even though the state has turned to bonds in recent years with greater and greater frequency, it still has not been able to keep up with the transportation demands of a growing population.

Dilapidated Roads

Good roads are important to a state's infrastructure; they facilitate better gas mileage, keep motor vehicles in good condition, and discourage unnecessary accidents. Good roads also are important for moving goods. More than ever, Californians travel on poorly maintained roads. A study by the American Association of State Highways and Transportation Officials finds that California roads rank 49th of the 50 states in operating condition. Only New Jersey has worse roads, and not by much. That's saying a lot, given that California has nearly 50,000 miles of paved thoroughfares and more than 12,000 bridges.

The differences between the quality of roads in California and the rest of the nation are stark, if not downright depressing. According to the report, only 18 percent of California's roads are in good condition; 35 percent are in poor condition, and the rest are somewhere in between. The situation is even worse when considering how California's major cities stack up against their counterparts elsewhere in the country. With 64 percent of its roads rated in poor condition, Los Angeles ranks as the number one large city for bad roads; at 61 percent each, San Jose and San Francisco/Oakland are tied for second. San Diego delivers a slightly better transportation grid with "only" 53 percent of its roads rated poor, enough to place that city seventh among the nation's cities with the worst roads. Here's the kicker: Nationally, 52 percent of all roads are in good condition, while only 13 percent are in poor condition.[4] Clearly, California has not kept up with other states, and we're all paying for it one way or another.

Unwilling to Pay

California's lack of good roads stems from the unwillingness of policy-makers and the public to dedicate enough funds to construction and maintenance. Data published by the CQ State FactBook in 2007 has California state and local highway spending ranked at 47th, approximating the road condition ranking cited previously. Whereas the national per capita average was $536, California spent $308 per capita.[5] Only Tennessee, Hawaii, and Georgia spent less. Translation: We get what we pay for. Moreover, the future looks even bleaker than the present—if that's possible. In 2011, the California Department of Transportation estimated that the state would need $7.4 billion annually over the next 10 years just to *maintain* California's roads in their current sorry condition. Nevertheless, the department projects available funding of $1.8 billion, or 24 percent of the actual need.[6] Translation: We're falling further behind every day.

There's more. Along with spending little for roads, we have incredibly congested transportation networks. In a 2008 study of peak hour volume-to-capacity ratios conducted by the Transportation Research Board, 51 percent of all urban transportation areas throughout the nation were congested during rush hour. In California, the congestion rate was nearly 80 percent, the highest of the 50 states.[7] Congestion means lost time and lost time translates into lost productivity, not to mention unnecessary additional pollution and a terrible mood.

The bulk of California's revenues for roads comes from a gasoline tax paid at the pump. The state collects 18 cents per gallon, which is tied for 30th among the 50 states. That tax has not been raised since 1994, or nearly 20 years because of the state's general anti-tax mood. California also collects sales taxes on gasoline purchases, but those dollars are not earmarked for transportation; rather, they are set aside for general fund expenditures.

Hidden Costs

We pay a steep price for poorly maintained roads in California. The Road Information Program (TRIP), a nonprofit research organization that sponsored groups associated with promoting safe highway travel, estimates that poor roads cost the average California driver an average of $590 annually, nearly twice the national average of $335. And it's worse in the state's major cities, where the average additional cost for motorists exceeds $700 because of their disproportionately poor condition. When added up, the amount of money lost by Californians to poor roads totals $13.5 billion—each year! That's more than twice as much as the funding shortfall cited by the state Department of Transportation. Imagine if the state collected enough taxes to pay for road needs, we all would be paying less in the long run, but not too many Californians think that way.

There are other hidden costs. Nearly one-third of California's 12,000-plus bridges are structurally deficient or obsolete, well above the national average of 26 percent. Only four states have more bridges in disrepair. That means trucks with goods must carry lower weights or take longer routes to reach their destinations. These obstacles cost consumers in the end, one way or another.

Then there's the issue of congestion. According to a recent study by the Texas Transportation Institute, the average American driver loses 34 hours per year—almost a work week—just from traffic tie-ups. But for folks driving in the Los Angeles area, the typical annual delay is 63 hours, the third highest wait in the nation and nearly twice the national average. Drivers in the San Francisco area do slightly better at 49 hours.[8]

Combined, our not-so-hidden costs stem from accelerated vehicle depreciation, otherwise unnecessary repair costs, increased fuel consumption, and faster tire wear.[9] Come to think of it, we pay an awful lot of money for electing not to spend more on California's roads.

Toll Roads—Solution or a Bigger Problem?

As the state's budget woes have mounted, public policymakers have not been able to meet California's many needs because of their unwillingness to raise revenues. This is true with highways as much as any other aspect of state government. Thus, they have looked for creative ways to expand and maintain California's highways. One recent approach has emerged with the construction and management of toll roads through public/private partnerships. Although toll roads have been fixtures in other states for decades, most are operated by state or local governments, rather than the for-profit private sector. The concept has a short history here and has become a bit controversial along the way.

In what was considered something of an experiment at the time, the state legislature authorized privately operated toll roads in 1989. The new law provided for the construction of four roads totaling 81 miles in length, with slightly different models of operation in each case. In most cases, problems have emerged. For example, a special 10-mile stretch of State Route 91 in Orange County was carried out with private funds only. The private toll road opened in 1995 but the Orange County Transportation Authority purchased ownership in 2002.[10] In another instance, State Route 57 in Orange County, a dispute between the private contractor and the state led to a termination of their relationship in 2003, and the state assumed management of the 11-mile toll road. In a third case, the 40-mile Mid-State Tollway in Alameda and Contra Costa Counties, the agreement with the original private contractor was terminated in 2001; once again, the state assumed control of the road prior to its opening in 2007. State Route 125 in San Diego County, a 10-mile thoroughfare, has operated without controversy since its opening in 2007. Clearly, public/private partnerships have not worked with respect to toll roads, with government taking over the operation in three of the four instances.

In addition to construction delays and questions of ownership and management, toll road authorities have come under criticism for unwarranted or mistaken fines of drivers because of transponder issues. In 2009, a group of California drivers won a lawsuit that required the Orange County Transportation Agency to waive $41 million in unpaid fines and set aside another $1.4 million in restitution payments.[11] For the most part, the toll road experience has not worked out as planners have hoped, much to the chagrin of those who have wanted to move highway management to the private sector.

Separating the Haves from the Have-Nots...Again

Aside from ownership and governance, toll roads may not be as successful as their sponsors envisioned. SR 91 in Orange County has attracted less traffic than expected, forcing the management authority to raise toll rates.[12] In addition, at least one credit agency has downgraded the value of the bonds sold to finance construction of toll roads, thereby making investment a risky proposition.[13] Still, they seem to be taking root as a means for attracting funds to build new roads, while discouraging those who can't afford them from traveling on the roads.

In 2010, the Los Angeles County Metropolitan Transportation Authority, the county agency for managing traffic, committed to a program of converting high occupancy vehicle (HOV) lanes to toll lanes during rush hour. The idea was to move more traffic while developing new revenue sources for roads. As one account summarized, such a program is highly regressive in nature: "For the wealthy, an extra couple of bucks will not put a noticeable dent in their budgets. But for the working poor, the cost for the solo HOV lanes may not be affordable."[14] The policy may work as a magnet for new funds, but if it catches on, it may well serve as yet another wall of divide in California.

WATER: TAPPED OUT

Few elements are as important to Californians as water. Beyond the daily consumption by 38 million residents, this special ingredient is used by agriculture and high-tech manufacturing in voluminous amounts. Courtesy of a geographical quirk, California's population and water sources are at odds with one another. About 75 percent of the state's water originates from areas north of Sacramento, while 75 percent of the demand for water occurs south of Sacramento. That incompatibility has created huge logistics issues for the state.[15] One other fact: While California's population has soared to be the largest in the nation, the water supply, of course, has remained the same—that is, within the variations between dry and wet years. Still, the same amount of water for a growing population equals a potentially massive distribution problem, period.

California has several sources of fresh water. To begin with, the snowpack in the Sierra Nevada is the state's largest natural "reservoir." In a typical year, melting snow flows into the state's rivers and becomes about 40 percent of California's overall water supply. Groundwater from winter rain is also collected and in some cases pumped into local storage facilities. In addition, the state receives some water from the Colorado aquifer, a massive underground lake that stretches through seven states, although California's share has been sharply reduced in recent years with the growth of other western states. Ultimately, however, it's the Sierra snowpack that is most critical to the state and moving the water to where it's needed most can be a challenge.

The Geographical Challenge

Years ago, state leaders recognized the potential problems from water shortages. Although the federal government built the north-to-south Central Valley Project in 1937, demands for water were fast outstripping the capacity of that water-moving system. In 1959, then-Governor Pat Brown and the state legislature placed a $1.75 billion bond on the ballot for voters to approve development of a massive statewide water distribution system. That dollar amount may seem relatively inconsequential today, but at the time it was almost equal to the size of the entire state budget (think $90 billion today). Known as the California Water Project, the voters passed the proposal, thanks to the large turnout from arid, yet populated southern California.[16]

But it was agribusiness that thrived most from the new water distribution commitment. Huge swaths of previously vacant tracts in the Central Valley now had access to the one element they had previously lacked, water. The availability of water produced stunning results. Prior to the development of these two systems, the Valley had 4.4 million acres under irrigation. Today, the figure is more than 9 million acres.[17] But, once again, demand has begun to outstrip supply. Add to that dilemma an increasingly fragile water delivery system, which has not been upgraded for decades, and the picture becomes all too clear: California's water infrastructure is in a precarious state.

In a typical year, these two pumping networks transport 10 million acre feet of water, 7 million through the federal government's Central Valley Project and 3 million through the California Water Project. Likewise, in a typical year, 80 percent irrigates agriculture and 20 percent meets the needs of urban populations and industrial users in southern California. It's a substantial undertaking by any standard.

But there are few "typical" years when discussing California water. For example, water runoff from the Sierra snowpack can vary dramatically from year to year. When there is drought, managers of the two water systems allocate less water to farmers so that there will be enough for personal and commercial consumption. Reduced distribution can cause havoc in every respect from employment to crop production, and it ripples all the way to the consumer in the form of higher food prices. Matters became so severe during the three-year drought of 2006–2009 that the managers of the Central Valley Project were able to deliver only 10 percent of the necessary water for farmers in the San Joaquin Valley. In Fresno County, traditionally the most productive agricultural county in the nation, lost farm revenue dropped $900 million and cost the region 30,000 jobs.[18] Conditions improved in 2010 and 2011, but after three years of economic despair, the area had a lot of catching up to do.

Warring Interest Groups

Money is one reason that dam construction has ceased in California, but concerns registered by environmentalists have emerged as well. In recent years, environmentalists have spoken out against new dams as artificial barriers to both the natural flow of water and the preservation of various fish species, some of which are endangered. They claim that if farmers grew less water-dependent crops, the state wouldn't need to pump more water for agriculture or develop costly dams. In fact, there's merit to such an argument. Research by The Pacific Institute finds that field crops like alfalfa, rice, cotton, and sugar beets use 56 percent of all agriculture acreage and guzzle 63 percent of all agriculture water, but account for only 17 percent of California's farm revenues. Meanwhile, vegetables use only 16 percent of all irrigated acreage and consume 10 percent of the state's agricultural water, while providing 39 percent of the state's crop income.[19] The Institute maintains that simply by changing crops, California could save more than 1 million acre feet per year, equivalent to the addition of a large dam.[20] This solution is a unique approach to conservation.

Farmers counter that the problem stems from the overreach of environmental regulations, increased urban population growth, and industrialization. They claim that California suffers from a lack of adequate water storage. This may seem odd, given that the state has 144 dams and reservoirs. But of that amount, 102 are owned either by individual users, local governments, local water districts, or power companies; moreover, they tend to be small and designated for use by specific customers. Of the remaining 42 dams, either the U.S. Bureau of Reclamation or the U.S. Army Corps of

Engineers own 35; the state of California owns 7. These facilities serve the public. More to the point, only one has been constructed since 2000, even though the state's population has grown by more than 10 percent.

Because of the stalemate, farmers and ranchers, the groups that have consistently fought for more water, have been stymied in their bid to increase water production. In the process, they have not only found themselves at odds with environmentalists, but also urban dwellers whose increasing numbers have placed larger claims on ever more scarce and unpredictable water resources. Without serious conservation or modified farming practices, there just isn't enough water to go around.

The most recent confrontation between these warring forces has centered on construction of the proposed Auburn Dam, a massive 700-foot high facility that would store 2.3 million acre feet of water by walling off the north fork of the American River in northern California. If built, the Auburn Dam would become the third largest water storage facility in the state. It was intended to complement Folsom Dam downstream (constructed in 1956) to fully prevent flooding in Sacramento and other areas downstream in the Valley. But discovery of a seismic fault underneath the proposed dam led to reconsideration of the project. In 2008, despite $325 million invested in preliminary work by the federal government over a quarter century, a coalition of environmentalists and geologists persuaded the California State Water Resources Board to stop the project by invoking a state law.[21]

Yet another factor has entered the debate over dams in recent years: climate change. Some scientists have pointed to long-term trends that have the potential to make California's water supply less reliable than ever. They worry that global warming will lead the snow pack to melt sooner in the year than in the past. Without more reservoirs to store the water, it will flow into either San Francisco Bay or other places at too fast a pace, leaving farmers and city dwellers alike clamoring for water later in the year.[22] If true, this problem could split the environmental movement and open reconsideration of a redesigned Auburn Dam site or a site elsewhere in northern California.

Sacramento–San Joaquin Delta: A Pending Disaster

Different groups may debate the wisdom of new water resources in California, but one issue is beyond debate: the condition of California's levees in the Sacramento–San Joaquin Delta. Between the confluence of the Sacramento and San Joaquin Rivers and the upper reaches of San Francisco Bay lay 1,000 miles of navigable tributaries and channels, supported by unreliable earthen berm levees that are designed to keep some of the fresh water they collect from draining into the San Francisco Bay.

Considerable debate has centered on whether more or less of the fresh water should be diverted from the Delta for agriculture use through a "peripheral canal," a 43-mile long ditch that would reroute as much as 70 percent of the water from the Sacramento River. Large growers and southern California developers have heralded the concept, while environmentalists and Delta dwellers have feared ruination of the region because of excessive saltwater intrusion.[23] Some reports suggest that reconfiguration of fresh water movement has already led to the extinction of species that used to populate the area,[24] adding to the debate over how the entire area should be managed.

The berms are intended to prevent flooding and assure an orderly flow of water into the Bay. More than 600,000 acres of rich farmland lay just on the other side of the levees, some of which are more than 100 years old; a few go back as far as the Gold Rush days.[25] Just how important is the levee system? It protects the safety of 500,000 people, 2 million acres of agricultural land, and about 200,000 structures, which have a total value of $47 billion.[26] But it's not only the immediate area that has so much at stake. Fresh water that runs through the Delta wetlands serves 28 million Californians downstream. And its condition is suspect.

Over time, many levees have broken down; others have been disturbed or threatened by earthquakes. Soil engineers have attempted to repair the breaks, but others have occurred elsewhere in the system. All told, there have been approximately 60 breaches since their development, and some have been costly. In 1997, levee breakthroughs forced 120,000 Valley residents in Sacramento to flee their homes.[27] In 2004, a levee broke, causing $100 million in crop losses and water pumping costs.[28] Other breaks causing varying amounts of damage have occurred since. In addition, geoscientists have calculated that there is a 63 percent chance that an earthquake of 6.7 magnitude or greater will occur nearby within the next 20 years.[29] That kind of event could do irreparable harm to California agriculture and the state's water supply.

What should be done? One answer would be to repair the levees to make them safe and earthquake proof; experts believe the price tag would be

$750 million—tough money to find in California's present financial condition. An even more radical suggestion would be to build the "peripheral canal," not very likely, however, given the historical resistance and continued push back.

Finding a "win-win" for all parties concerned about the Delta will be difficult because each has a different need. The problem is compounded because, explains a policy analyst for the Natural Resources Defense Council, "water supply, ecosystem health, flood management—all these issues are connected."[30] Still, if left as it is, the Delta levee system will be a disaster waiting to happen. Somewhere, somehow the state's planners need to think about not only warring interests with different agendas, but also how to manage a scarce resource that is only likely to become more problematic over time. California can't be all things to all people.

THE ENERGY STRUGGLE

Californians have a love/hate relationship with electricity. On the one hand, we crave it for our manufacturing, our homes, and for powering our toys (adult and child alike), whatever they may be. On the other hand, we're oh so finicky about how our electricity is generated. We loathe coal-fired plants because of the negative impact of effluents on the environment, we question hydroelectric power because of the impact on various species, and we oppose offshore drilling because of potential harm to marine life. Concerns are just as large about nuclear power, so much so that California became the only state to shut down a nuclear power plant in 1989 after a local public vote.[31] Considering all of these obstacles and points of resistance, finding enough energy is an immense challenge in this state. Yet, given that energy is the lifeblood of the state's infrastructure, finding enough of it is an imperative.

The California Model for Clean Air

Historically, energy generation in California has come at a great environmental cost, both in terms of individual health and pollution. It's not that Californians are energy guzzlers. In fact, the state has been incredibly responsible in limiting energy use. On a per capita basis, California uses about half the energy consumed nationally;[32] that's an enviable record. Nowhere is this better demonstrated than with our consumption of oil, the largest percentage of which is used by automobiles. Although Californians represent about 13 percent of the U.S. population, we operate 26 percent of all hybrid automobiles.[33] Still, the combination of dependence on gas-guzzling automobiles by 23 million drivers (nearly twice that of #2 Texas) and a topography of populated valleys ringed by mountains has led the state to be an unintentional major polluter.

California has worked hard at curbing its air pollution problem. Since the discovery of smog in the 1940s, the state has made improvements, thanks in large part to a clean electricity commitment and tough rules for automobile exhaust. The changes have been rather dramatic. In 1977, Southern California had 121 Stage 1 smog alerts (there are three stages, from bad to worse); that number dropped to 79 in 1986. By 1997, the area suffered only seven Stage 1 alerts.[34] That progress shows the extent to which California has become a leader in environmental issues.

Generating Clean Electricity

Generating enough electricity for Californians has been a tough task for decades. That's because we depend on sources outside the state for most of our electricity. The primary energy component of our electricity is natural gas, little of which is produced here; in fact, 87 percent comes from outside the state, according to the California Energy Commission.[35]

Meanwhile, California doesn't have the luxury of most other states, which often rely on cheap and abundant coal to produce electricity. Because coal is a major source of pollution, it is an anathema to the environmental conditions of this state. Coal accounts for less than 2 percent of the state's electricity, with the rest coming from natural gas (57 percent), the state's two nuclear power plants (15 percent), hydroelectric facilities (12 percent), and renewable energy sources (14 percent).[36] That 2 percent is on the verge of becoming history.

In 2007, the California Energy Commission ordered all state utilities to cease energy acquisition from coal-fueled plants; only a few long-term contracts prior to the order remain in place.[37] In 2002, the state legislature passed SB 1078, the California Renewables Portfolio Standard Act, which required the state's major utilities to generate at least 20 percent of their electricity from renewable sources by 2010; as discussed previously, the goal has since been increased to 33 percent by 2020. Because of the state's commitment to clean electricity, our per capita greenhouse gas emissions are at about half the national average and heading down thanks to leading edge legislation.[38]

Reliance on outside sources means that electricity costs more here than elsewhere, about 35 percent more,[39] which is an irritant to businesses and other commercial users. That's the bad news. The good news is that natural gas is a very clean energy source, generating little pollution. The latest estimates are that the United States has a 200-year supply of natural gas,[40] although in times of peak, or strongest demand, the state energy producers often turn to harmful emissions-belching, diesel-generated electricity plants to provide short-term needs. Reducing pollution helps everything from people with respiratory diseases to global warming, although "bottom line" bean counters don't necessarily appreciate those benefits.

Still, being dependent on other states or nations to any extent is a cause of concern for two reasons. First, there's a lot of competition throughout the world for the same sources, which can increase cost especially when demand outstrips supply. Second, and more important, there can be disruptions in the supply, which can cause havoc for the state's energy customers whether they are businesses or individual consumers.

The task of keeping sufficient supplies of energy became even more difficult during the 1990s when the state gained an average of 600,000 people per year. During that decade, California's energy generating capability actually decreased by 2 percent, while electricity sales increased by 11 percent.[41] The combination forced the state's three major power companies—Pacific Gas and Electric Company, Southern California Edison Company, and San Diego Gas and Electric Company—and independents to import more electricity from other states.

Electricity Shortages

From 1997 on, electricity production declined in part in California because of a new law that deregulated the industry. Years later, when California's energy prices soared beyond belief, public officials blamed one another, particularly then-Governor Gray Davis, for California's debacle. In fact, the deregulation law, AB 1890, passed *unanimously* in both houses of the state legislature prior to Davis' signature.

With companies outside California offering to sell energy at rates much lower than the prices here, consumers in the state abandoned the three major utilities for better deals. Soon they were purchasing electricity directly from the likes of Enron, Dynegy, Williams, Reliant, and a few other firms located outside the state with the capacity to provide electricity cheaply and at will. Then the roof fell in. In 2000, the state declared 55 energy emergencies because of unavailable electricity, followed by incredibly expensive electricity suddenly made available by the out-of-state companies. Usually, each cry for help was accompanied by rolling blackouts of power, leaving industries and individuals alike in various states of panic and desperation. Another 70 emergencies were declared in 2001, with the same two-part routine ensuing: first shortages, then suddenly found electricity available at sky-high prices.[42]

Governor Davis screamed to the Federal Energy Regulatory Commission that thievish energy companies were plundering California, but the George W. Bush Republican majority pushed back and saw no chicanery. Meanwhile, a study by the Massachusetts Institute of Technology in 2000 found that the outside energy providers made billions of dollars in excess profits by cutting back power generation and creating artificial shortages.[43] It was a dark time for California in more ways than one. There was little consolation years later when the federal government finally agreed and brought major players to trial.

Lingering Challenges

Perhaps the biggest challenge with our electricity is the ability to move it where it's needed when it's needed. Here we focus on the transmission and delivery system, sometimes known as the "grid," the network of towers and wires that carries electricity from the point of generation to its destination. During the energy crisis of 2000 and 2001, part of the state's problem was the lack of infrastructure capacity to move electricity quickly and efficiently. One prominent transmission bottleneck was in central California. Known as path 15, the bottleneck was the result of several transmission lines from the northwest part of the country narrowing down before the energy was distributed further south—think of an hourglass as a visual. That problem was corrected in 2004, thanks to a new $190 million, 83-mile transmission line.

Other problems remain. Most of the transmission equipment in California is well beyond its intended life expectancy and suffers from more than three decades of under-investment;[44] that means major costs ahead, and better sooner than later. Given projections of as many as 50 million California residents within the next 15 years, new capacity must be built. For California alone between 2011 and 2015, one recent private study calculated that the state must invest $12 billion in the transmission to keep up with needs.[45] That's quite a bit of money over a short period of time. Yet, according to a 2009 report issued by the California Energy Commission, California's transmission plans remain disjointed and uncoordinated, and fail to meet future statewide transmission infrastructure needs. Moreover, the report finds, "The lack of a guiding transmission plan will give rise to a suboptimal outcome—from both a cost and an environmental perspective—and it will slow efforts to meet greenhouse gas emissions reduction and renewable energy goals."[46] The state is a long way from resolving long-term infrastructure electricity issues.

On a more optimistic front, California continues to lead the way in securing alternative sources of energy that will be clean and fossil-free. According to the U.S. Department of Energy, the state is first among the 50 states in generating renewable power, energy from biomass, geothermal energy, and solar energy; California ranks second in generating wind energy.[47] These statistics are promising in the long term, but at present they comprise small amounts of the state's energy sources. And finding that energy is taking longer than some had hoped. In 2011, the three major utilities announced that they failed to meet the 20 percent renewable energy quota generated by legislation in 2002, although two came close.[48] Unfazed (and perhaps equally desperate), the state legislature pressed on in 2011 and increased the renewable energy requirement to at least 33 percent by 2020. At least one utility, PG&E, fought the new law as a contributor to high prices, but environmentalists won the day.[49]

Automobile Exhaust

The automobile long has been identified as a major source of air pollution in California. That's because automobile exhaust accounts for about 40 percent of the greenhouse gas emissions in the state. Given this unwelcome addition to the environment, state public policymakers have sought to curtail these emissions for the past half century, often to the chagrin of Detroit automakers. The state first acted on automobile exhaust in 1966 with adoption of a first-in-the-nation law that regulated the content of

tailpipe exhaust. Ever since then, California has led the nation in auto pollution legislation. California's Air Resources Board, the state's principal
emissions control agency originally formed in 1967, upped the ante on
automobile exhaust by requiring catalytic converters in 1975, again to the
objection of American automakers.[50]

Not all of these changes were totally the brainchildren of environmentally minded state policymakers. In fact, passage of the Clean Air Act of
1970 required states to meet new federal anti-pollution standards. For
California, management of automobile emissions became a cornerstone of
that objective because of the prominence of automobile-caused pollution
in the state. Ever since 1970, California and the federal government have
both been active in regulating automobile exhaust, but not always from
the same perspective.

Most of the time, the state has enacted regulations in excess of
national law because of waivers granted from the Environmental
Protection Agency; since 1970, the EPA has granted California 44 such
exceptions in deference to the state's commitment to advanced clean
air standards. But in 2007, the EPA administrator appointed by then-
President George W. Bush balked at California's request to further
reduce greenhouse emissions from automobiles beginning in 2014 on
the grounds that there was no evidence that such gasses were pollutants,[51] much to the delight of the American Petroleum Institute, the
primary lobby group for the oil industry. Stunned, California regulators and their contemporaries in 16 other states sued the George W.
Bush administration for not carrying out the EPA mandate to reduce
pollution in the nation.

After a two-year journey through the federal judiciary, the U.S.
Supreme Court upheld California's claim. By a 5-to-4 vote, the justices
wrote that the EPA needed to fulfill its mandate to help states curb
emissions—that meant clarifying any doubts about the contents of
automobile exhaust. It was an embarrassing moment for both the Bush
administration and the EPA. Immediately, California again applied for
a waiver, which was granted. In 2009, the Barack Obama administration
accepted California's new standards as the model for national standards,
effective in 2016. The new requirements raised fuel economy standards
by 30 percent and reduced tailpipe emissions by 38 percent.[52] It was a
good day for environmentalists.

AB 32—The New Standard for Environmental Protection?

In 2006, state policymakers again grappled with the question of environmental protection. In a rare moment of agreement between the legislature and then-Governor Arnold Schwarzenegger, the parties enacted the Global Warming Solutions Act. The legislation was touted as a breakthrough for those committed to stopping global warming. While extensive lobbying by energy producing companies and energy-using businesses has led to the defeat of this proposal in Congress for several successive years, the new law has remained on the books in California. This legislation was the signature piece of the Schwarzenegger administration, which otherwise had little success in finding common ground with legislative Democrats and Republicans alike.

The basic objective of AB 32 is to reduce greenhouse gas emissions in California to 1990 levels by 2020 under the direction of the California Air Resources Board, perhaps the state's most powerful regulatory body. The law includes a controversial "cap and trade" provision that will allow energy-polluting companies to purchase energy pollution "units" from those that don't use all the energy to which they are entitled. However, the total amount of pollution emissions available will be reduced each year to meet state goals. If successfully implemented, the law will result in a 30 percent decline of emissions by the target date, with an 80 percent reduction by 2050.

AB 32 overcame serious opposition en route to becoming law. A business-friendly group, the Coalition of Energy Users, claimed that the new law would cost California as many as 1.1 million jobs and the average small business an extra $49,691 because of the new energy use rules. But not all experts agreed. An independent energy-auditing firm calculated that inasmuch energy costs amount to 1.5 percent of small business revenues, "any increase in the price of energy (electricity, natural gas, and transportation fuels) will have only a modest financial impact."[53]

In 2010, out of state oil interests, the Howard Jarvis Taxpayers Association and the National Federation of Independent Businesses waged a battle against the law by qualifying an initiative opposing the law. If passed, Proposition 23 would have prevented implementation until the state unemployment figure reached 5.5 percent for a full year—something that has occurred only twice since 1990. The voters rejected the proposal by better than a 3-to-2 margin, even though proponents outspent opponents.

Whether AB 32 becomes a role model for national climate control policy remains to be seen. For now, the legislation represents a bright spot in attending to California's otherwise blighted infrastructure.

PRISON OVERCROWDING

Incarceration has become big business in California. That's because of the phenomenal growth of the state prison population, which has occurred at a rate much faster than the state's overall population increase. In 2009, 1 in 36 California adults were under "correctional control," whether in state prison, county jails, parole, or probation. That's just under 3 percent of the adult population. The proportion has almost doubled since 1982, when 1 out of 69 California adults were in custody under the same circumstances.

Of the four custodial categories, state spending on prisons easily consumes the largest percentage of crime-related outlays. Like a vacuum cleaner, this category has sucked up funds from other areas ranging from public education to public transportation. In 2012, the straitjacketed California state budget dedicated $9.8 billion to state prisons, making it the third highest expenditure area after public education and healthcare. For the 2000–2001 fiscal year, corrections accounted for 6.6 percent of the budget, and 10 years before that spending on corrections totaled about 5 percent of the state budget. No other part of the budget has soared so much over such a short time span.

Why Growth of the Prison Population?

The rate of crime is not much different in California from the other 49 states; the difference, however, lies in the punishments connected to the crimes. The signature piece for prison sentencing in California is a law known as "Three Strikes and You're Out." Passed by the legislature in 1994, this law was a response to a heinous kidnapping and murder of a 12-year old girl by a felon on the loose for parole violation, a crime that might otherwise add a year or two to his sentence. In order to make sure that repeat offenders stay in prison, the "Three Strikes" law provides mandatory 25 years to life imprisonment for a defendant convicted of any felony or misdemeanor reclassified as a felony if the defendant has been convicted of two previous felonies. The voters ratified the "Three Strikes" law by an overwhelming 3-to-1 margin in November 1994.

The theory behind "Three Strikes" is the concept of deterrence. The belief is that if people see the costs they are likely to bear from their crime, surely they will think twice before acting. Maybe so, but more than 40,000 Californians are in prison for "strike" offenses, including nearly 9,000 who are serving sentences of at least 25 years. Many of these sentences relate to drugs. More than 28,000 people in the state are imprisoned for drug-related offenses, and 10,000 of those are for nothing other than simple drug possession.[54]

But does the "Three Strikes" law deter violent crime? Not according to a study by the Center on Juvenile and Criminal Justice, which found that "higher rates of imprisonments for all strikes or third strikes were not associated with any significant reductions" in felonies.[55] In other words, putting people behind bars for longer periods of time does nothing to discourage future criminal activity. Surely, this speaks to an issue bigger than time behind bars—perhaps a different approach to rehabilitation.

The Price of Incarceration

It costs close to $50,000 per prisoner per year for incarceration in California prisons. If you think that's a lot, multiply that number by the 142,000 inmates and pretty soon you're talking serious money. Nearly half of all incarceration costs in California are spent on the prison guards who supervise the inmates and maintain order in the facilities. In addition, more than 20 percent of the cost is for health care. The remainder is for the variety of components concerned with prison life such as prison upkeep, supplies, food, prisoner training programs, and miscellaneous products and services.[56]

But the core of the price tag resides with the "Three Strikes" law discussed previously, especially over time. A recent study by the Legislative Analyst's Office calculated that at $46,700 per inmate, a 25-year "Three Strikes" sentence would cost the state $1.1 million per inmate; a life sentence would cost $1.8 million. When adding together "Three Strikes" and life sentence prisoners, the cost comes to a staggering $10 billion for the next 25 years.[57] That's a lot of dough for something that doesn't work!

Race

Incarceration in California is impacted not only by the types of crimes that put people there, but the make-up of prison society itself. The collective racial composition of the California prison population hardly reflects the composition of the state. In fact, the composition is highly predictive, given the social backgrounds of the state's inmates. Latinos, the largest group, constitute 39 percent of the inmate residents, followed by African Americans at 29 percent and whites at 26 percent; other races make up the remaining 6 percent.

Remarkably, these data correspond with high school dropout rates. Data compiled by the California Dropout Research project show a white dropout rate of 13.7 percent, compared with a 33.3 percent rate for African Americans and a 31.0 percent rate for Latinos. The study shows that California "inmates in prisons and jails are disproportionately comprised of dropouts."[58] All this helps us to understand some of the root causes associated with crime and punishment.

We already know that California schools are segregated and that schools with white kids are better funded than those for nonwhites (see Chapter 2). It doesn't take a rocket scientist to put 2 and 2 together: California prisons are comprised disproportionately of minorities thanks to a public school system that has disproportionately let down minorities. Imagine what might happen if, rather than spend nearly $50,000 per prisoner, policymakers would provide a few more thousand dollars per student to keep them in school. Billions of dollars in incarceration costs might be saved and we might have more productive, tax-paying citizens. Once again, we see the results of "penny wise, pound foolish" public policies in California.

Prison Conditions: The Straw That Broke the Camel's Back

Prison life will never be confused with elegant dining or fancy hotel rooms; austere surroundings are devoid of everyday niceties that most of us take for granted. But for years prisoners have claimed that basic conditions in California facilities are beyond the pale to the point of inhumane. It's difficult to dispute such claims. In fact, for the better part of a decade, state prisons operated at about 185 percent of capacity. Prisoners were assigned sleeping quarters on three-level bunks in libraries, hallways, reception areas, and just about anywhere that beds and bodies would fit.

Periodic lawsuits regarding poor conditions seemed to go nowhere. But in 1990, state prisoner Ralph Coleman sued on the grounds that overcrowded prison conditions caused poor mental health. This, he claimed, constituted "cruel and unusual punishment," a form of treatment banned by the Eighth Amendment of the U.S. Constitution. After hearing the case, a federal judge set guidelines for the state that, for the most part, were ignored for more than a decade. In 2001, Marciano Plata, another state prisoner, sued on the grounds that overcrowding denied him proper medical care. In 2006, these two class action cases, now known as *Coleman v. Schwarzenegger* and *Plata v. Schwarzenegger* were consolidated before a three-judge panel of the U.S. Ninth District Court of Appeals.

After a lengthy hearing, the appeals panel unanimously declared overcrowded conditions, and that such circumstances were unconstitutional. Further, the panel wrote, unless the state built new facilities quickly—and you don't build prisons *quickly*—there would be an order to release enough prisoners to scale back overcrowding to 125 percent of capacity. State authorities appealed to the U.S. Supreme Court. Meanwhile, California began sending some prisoners, about 10,000 in all, to other states to serve their sentences. But the state did too little, too late.

In 2011, the U.S. Supreme Court by a 5-to-4 vote affirmed the ruling of the appeals court and ordered the state prison population to be reduced from 143,000 to 110,000 within two years. The Court had plenty of justification for its decision. Evidence showed that mentally ill prisoners had waited for up to a year without treatment, a single physician was left to attend to as many as 700 prisoners, and the crowded sleeping conditions had been breeding areas for disease and violence. Justice Anthony Kennedy wrote for the Court's majority, "The medical and mental health care provided by California's prisons falls below the standards of decency" afforded by the Eighth Amendment.[59] The ruling was a slap in the face of California's prison infrastructure.

Faced with an order from the Court, Governor Jerry Brown cobbled together a plan to release a few non-violent prisoners outright, while sending most to county jails to serve the rest of their terms. But what seemed relatively simple in concept became difficult upon implementation. For example, the state needed to find at least 30,000 available beds, yet a quick tally showed only 12,000 available.[60] Then there was the question of funding the move. In 2008, the state Legislative Analyst's Office estimated that California counties spend $33,600 per jailed offender.[61] So, if the state funded the costs for offloading prisoners to the counties, the price tag would be close to $1 billion. And given that the state already faced a gaping budget hole of $10 billion for the coming fiscal year, Brown and the legislature had a big problem with few palatable solutions. It goes without saying that satisfying the U.S. Supreme Court order will cost California dearly in the next few years, without doing anything to rehabilitate the prisoners who are released because of overcrowding.

Choosing Penury over Safety

In recent years, the public has found itself caught up between the desire to punish criminals and the costs of doing so. As with so many other values related to revenue raising, the public has opted for less public safety over more taxes. In a 2011 statewide survey, more than 60 percent of the respondents supported reducing life sentences for third-strike prisoners serving time for burglary, auto theft, and shoplifting, while less than one quarter favored raising taxes to build more prisons.[62]

What the public favors here is not much different from opinion on other infrastructure issues: If it costs too much money, we're not in favor. In the case of prisons, Californians now appear to be saying that public safety is not as important as keeping would-be tax dollars in their wallets. Come to think of it, the same theme is playing out in cities and counties, where thousands of police and fire personnel have been laid off in a trade-off for not increasing local taxes.

REBUILDING THE INFRASTRUCTURE ONE BRICK AT A TIME

When it comes to California's infrastructure, two facts are abundantly clear. First, virtually all knowledgeable people agree the infrastructure is in tatters; parts have become downright dysfunctional, others simply ignored. Second, few agree on what should be done, how soon, and by whom. But we know this much: elected officials and the public alike have let the state fall apart at the seams—important seams.

The only way we'll get out of this mess is by committing a sizable portion of resources up front, rather than back-loading so much. That means a willingness to collect more revenues (read taxes) from a state whose leaders and population have been all too reluctant to do so. Whether Californians are prepared to do so now is the question.

Deteriorated roads have not just increased commute times to and from work, they have increased the cost of doing business; that helps to make the state less competitive. Inadequate water systems have placed the state at the mercy of nature's vagaries. While the state gets credit for leading the nation in generating clean energy, transmission capabilities remain suspect at best. Moreover, leaders and the public alike have poured limited resources into a prison system that is both broken and excessively costly, while doing nothing to curb crime. Add to these failures the fact that Californians insist on the most expensive way possible—bonds—to pay for inadequate investments all because we don't want to pay more up front.

As with so many other aspects of the state's failings, there is plenty of blame to go around. Whatever the titles of people elected to office and however the voters have exercised their wills at the polls, together these two political forces have left California's infrastructure in shambles.

With tens of billions of dollars in deferred work and no real urgency to make necessary improvements, the state is less attractive every day, regardless of which political party or leaders are in charge. Time after time, we have taken the easy way out of infrastructure challenges. Yet, the simple fact is there is a price for maintaining elements of the social order, whether it's schools or prisons or roads. The longer we wait to own up to our responsibilities, the more difficult it will be to bring California into the 21st century. That may be true, but for now no one is in a hurry to do otherwise.

ENDNOTES

1. For a discussion of the energy crisis in 2000 and the price paid by Davis, see Larry N. Gerston and Terry Christensen, *Recall!: California's Political Earthquake* (Armonk, NY: M.E. Sharpe, 2004), pp. 16–19.
2. "Voters Express Views on Dealing with the State's Huge Budget Deficit," The Field Poll, Release #2368, March 16, 2011.
3. Kevin Starr, *Golden Dreams: California in an Age of Abundance, 1950-1963* (New York: Oxford University Press, 2009), p. 248.
4. "Rough Roads Ahead," American Association of State Highway and Transportation Officials, Washington, D.C., 2009, pp. 2, 10, 36.
5. These data appear in "Spending for Highways," Tax Education Foundation, Muscatine, IA, 2007.

6. "2011 Ten-Year State Highway Operation and Protection Program Plan," California Department of Transportation, January 2011, pp. v, vi.

7. "19th Annual Report on the Performance of State Highway Stems (1984-2008)," Reason Foundation, September 2010, Policy Study 385, Los Angeles California, 2010, p. 26.

8. "American Idle: On the Road," *Wall Street Journal*, February 2, 2011, pp. D1, D2.

9. "Future Mobility in California," The Road Information Program, Washington, D.C., December 2009, p. 4.

10. California Department of Transportation, State Route 91, http://www.dot.ca.gov/hq/paffairs/about/toll/rt91.htm.

11. "California Toll Road Refunds Excessive Penalties," theNewspaper.com, November 5, 2009, http://www.thenewspaper.com/news/29/2951.asp.

12. "Toll Roads: Ridership Down, Revenues Up," *Orange County Register*, April 12, 2010, http://taxdollars.ocregister.com/2010/04/12/toll-roads-ridership-down-revenues-up/55095/.

13. "Fitch Goes Negative on California Toll Roads," theNewspaper.com, February 10, 2009, http://www.thenewspaper.com/news/26/2683.asp.

14. "Time for L.A. to Pay the Toll?" DailyBreeze.com, November 24, 2010, http://www.dailybreeze.com/ci_16704280.

15. David Carle, *Introduction to Water in California* (Berkeley, CA: University of California Press, 2004), p. 88.

16. See Ellen Hanak and Mark Baldassare, Eds., "California 2025: Taking on the Future," Public Policy Institute of California, San Francisco, CA, 2005, pp. 162–163.

17. Heather Cooley, Juliet Christian-Smith, and Peter H. Gleik, "More With Less: Agricultural Water Conservation and Efficiency in California," The Pacific Institute, Berkeley, CA, 2008, p. 13, and "California's Water Supply and Demand," *Western Farm Press*, February 26, 2010, http://westernfarmpress.com/irrigation/california-s-water-supply-and-demand.

18. "Despair Flows in Water's Absence," *Los Angeles Times*, July 6, 2009, pp. A1, A8.

19. Cooley, et al., op, cit., p. 11.

20. Ibid., p. 7.

21. "Auburn Dam May Really Be Dead This Time," *Los Angeles Times*, November 16, 2008, http://www.latimes.com/news/printedition/california/la-me-dam16-2008nov16,0,4762538,print.story.

22. "Lab Scientist Testifies on California Water Crisis," Lawrence Livermore National Laboratory Newsline, July 25, 2008, www.lnl.gov.

23. Stephanie S. Pincetl, *Transforming California: A Political History of Land Use and Development* (Baltimore, MD: The Johns Hopkins Press, 1999), pp. 206–207.

24. "Delta Ecosystem White Paper," prepared for the Delta Stewardship Council, October 18, 2010, Sacramento, CA, p. 2–18.

25. "Water Flowing to Farms, Not Fish," *San Francisco Chronicle*, October 25, 2005, pp. A15, A16.

26. "Is California Next?" *Civil Engineering Magazine*. November 2005, p. 8.

27. "Central Valley Vulnerable to Flooding," *San Francisco Chronicle*, September 9, 2005, p. A16.

28. "Is California Next?" Op. cit., p. 2.

29. Paul Tullis, "California's Delta Water Blues," *Miller-McCune*, January 3, 2011, http://www.miller-mccune.com/science-environment/californias-delta-water-blues-26552/#.

30. Barry Nelson, quoted in "It Might Be Too Late to Save Delta Fish," *San Francisco Chronicle*, February 16, 2011, p. A1, A8.

31. The facility, Rancho Seco, was owned by a Sacramento municipal utility. After 14 years of troubled existence including a partial meltdown and several rate increases, the electorate voted to shut it down. See Peter Asmus, *Introduction to Energy in California* (Berkeley, CA: University of California Press, 2009), p. 64.

32. Adrienne Kandel, Margaret Sheridan, and Patrick McAuliffe, "A Comparison of per Capita Electricity Consumption in the United States and California," California Energy Commission, unpublished paper, August 2008.

33. "R.L. Polk & Co. Analysis of Hybrid Sales Suggests Segment Affinity Among Hybrid Buyers," Green Car Congress, April 21, 2008, http://www.greencarcongress. com/2008/04/r-l-polk-co-ana.html.

34. "50 Years of Progress toward Clean Air: A Photographic Retrospective," South Coast Air Quality Management District, 1997.

35. "Energy Almanac," California Energy Commission, Sacramento, CA, April 7, 2011, http://energyalmanac.ca.gov/overview/energy_sources.html.

36. "Energy Almanac," Ibid.

37. Margot Roosevelt, "State Acts to Limit Use of Coal Power," *Los Angeles Times*, May 24, 2007, http://articles.latimes.com/2007/may/24/local/me-coal24.

38. "California's Energy Future: The View to 2050," The California Council on Science and Technology, Sacramento, CA, May 2011, p. 1.

39. Asmus, op. cit., p. 293.

40. "A Natural Gas Prices Fall, the Search Turns to Oil," *Wall Street Journal*, May 23, 2011, p. A2.

41. Will McNamara, *The California Energy Crisis: Lessons for a Deregulating Industry* (Tulsa, OK: PennWell Corporation, 2002), pp. 22–23.

42. For an account of this period, see Bethany McClean and Peter Elkind, *The Smartest Guys in the Room: The Amazing Rise and Scandalous Fall of Enron* (New York: Portfolio Publishers, 2003).

43. See "Power Suppliers Accused of Manipulating Prices," *Los Angeles Times*, November 23, 2000.

44. Asmus, op. cit., p. 280.

45. "Employment and Economic Benefits of Transmission Structure Investment in the U.S. and Canada," working group for Investment in Reliable and Economic electric Systems (WIRES) and the Brattle Group, May 2011, p. 8.

46. "Strategic Transmission Investment Plan," California Energy Commission, December 2009, p. 1, http://www.energy.ca.gov/2009publications/CEC-700-2009-011/CEC-700-2009-011-CMF.PDF.

47. "Energy Efficiency and Renewable Energy: State Activities & Partnerships," U.S. Department of Energy, Washington, D.C., June 25, 2008, http://apps1.eere.energy. gov/states/electricity.cfm/state=CA.

48. Southern California Edison derived 19.4 percent from renewables, followed by Pacific Gas and Electric with 17.7percent. San Diego Gas and Electric came in a distant third with only 11.9 percent of its energy produced from renewables.

49. "Renewables Required," *San Francisco Chronicle*, April 13, 2011, pp. D1, D4.

50. Jacqueline Vaughn Switzer with Gary Bryner, *Environmental Politics: Domestic and Global Dimensions*, 2nd ed. (New York: St. Martin's Press, 1998), p. 175.

51. "E.P.A. Says 17 States Can't Set Greenhouse Gas Rules for Cars," *The New York Times*, December 20, 2007, pp. A1, A30.

52. Dave Cook, "Obama Breaks with Bush on the Environment," *Christian Science Monitor*, January 26, 2009, http://www.csmonitor.com/USA/Politics/2009/0126/obama-breaks-with-bush-on-the-environment.

53. "The Economic Impact of AB 32 on California Small Businesses," The Brattle Group, Cambridge, MA, December 2009, p. E1.

54. "Shifting the Problem," Justice Policy Institute, Washington, D.C., 2010, p. 2.

55. "Striking Out: California's 'Three Strikes and You're Out' Law Has Not Reduced Violent Crime—2011 Update," Research Brief, Center on Juvenile and Criminal Justice, San Francisco, CA, April 2011, p. 4.

56. "A Decision Making Framework For Reducing State Correctional Populations," Legislative Analyst Office, Sacramento, CA, p. 2.

57. "Striking Out," op. cit., p. 3.

58. Clive R. Belfield and Henry M. Levin, "The Economic Losses from High School Dropouts in California," California Dropout Research Project #1, August 2007, p. 24.

59. Quoted in "30,000 Inmates Must be Released," *San Francisco Chronicle*, May 24, 2011, pp. A1, A10.

60. "Experts: Prison Plan Full of Holes," *San Jose Mercury News*, May 26, 2011, pp. A1, A9.

61. This number comes from Linh Vuong, Christopher Hartney, Barry Krisberg, and Susan Marchionna, "The Extravagance of Imprisonment Revisited," National Council on Crime and Delinquency, Oakland, CA, January 2010, p. 10.

62. Jack Dolan, "Californians Would Rather Ease Penalties than Pay for More Prisons," *Los Angeles Times*, July 21, 2011 http://www.latimes.com/news/local/la-me-poll-prisons-20110721,0,4309478,print.story.

Section III

The Politics

7

Where's the Party?

I belong to no organized political party. I am a Democrat.

—Will Rogers, social commentator

As a satirist from the Progressive Era to the Great Depression, Will Rogers feasted off the extremes of American politics. Although the quote above refers to his personal political affiliation, the significance of Rogers' observation lies with the impact of his first sentence: American political parties are inherently disorganized, in fact disorganized almost by design. Look around almost anywhere in the United States and you're more likely to see huge conflicts *within* a political party than *between* the parties. Liberal Democrats versus moderate Democrats and social conservative Republicans versus fiscal conservative Republicans are two such examples that readily come to mind. To the casual observer (and most of us are), these fights seem like naked power grabs and little more.

Dismiss them as we may, political parties are vital components of the American political landscape. As organizations, they are depositories of core values and political themes from which candidates seek elective office and, if they win, govern. Of all the influences that contribute to our political decision making as voters, generally speaking none carries more sway than the impact of a political party with which an individual bonds.[1] Of all the influences that guide officeholders, membership in the political party is equally significant.

That sounds reasonable enough, yet we know that candidates-turned-officeholders often behave differently once they hold power. Purists often condemn sometimes wavering behavior as abandonment of "party principles" (whatever they are) for expediency's sake, but the organization of American government makes it difficult for one to adhere consistently to a set of values without yielding to compromise more times than not. The existence of three independent branches makes it all but impossible for the leaders of one party to run the show. In addition, differences over the policy responsibilities of the national and state governments increase the complexity of party governance. Suddenly, it's hard to tell who's doing what, and why.[2] Still, whatever their messiness, American political parties are critical links in the political process and the way we run our representative democracy. Without party organizations, we'd have no mechanism for bonding voters to candidates who ultimately structure governments and shape policies.

Against that cluttered backdrop, we turn to political parties in California, where an incredibly jumbled collection of candidates, professional organizers, and voters make the national party system seem like an award-winning synchronized swimming team. To begin with, the political parties are incredibly fractured within as the state's population. Democrats who live in the Central Valley are likely to have more in common with nearby Republicans than fellow Democrats in San Francisco or Los Angeles. Republicans who live in Marin County are more likely to identify with Democrats than their Republican compatriots in Orange County or San Diego County. Still, "party" matters, although perhaps for many more as a symbol than any sense of organization.

In fact, "dysfunctional" seems to be the best descriptor of California's political parties. Sure, they exist as organizations, their candidates appear at meetings and conventions, and they resonate with most of us in an oblique sense, of sorts. But beyond voting at election time for (or against) party nominees, most of us are at a loss to explain the concept. To that end, one keen state observer has written "in California, for fifty years, party has been of relatively minor importance; politics has been largely personal, built around an individual's capacity to draw voters across party lines."[3] That poignant assessment was written by journalist Mary Ellen Leary in 1977! It could just as easily be written today.

Why, then, do we concern ourselves with political parties in California? Because the themes associated with political parties help us define our own values and who we feel is best able to represent what we want as citizens; because there are substantive differences between Democrats and Republicans, particularly in terms of how their candidates would govern; and because there are consequences from the ability (or inability) of the parties to promote themes as the precursors to public policies such as raising or lowering taxes, spending more or less on public education, and deciding whether undocumented immigrants should or should not be allowed to apply for drivers' licenses.

The strange fact is that, more times than not, our partisan differences do show up at the polls at election time. For example, a statewide exit poll conducted on the day of the November 2, 2010 general election found that 88 percent of all Democrats voted for U.S. Senate incumbent Democrat Barbara Boxer; likewise, 87 percent of all Republicans voted for Republican challenger Carly Fiorina. The same poll showed that 87 percent of those who considered themselves as "liberals" voted for Boxer; meanwhile, 81 percent of those who classified themselves as "conservatives" chose Fiorina.[4] Given that Democrats outnumbered Republicans at the time by a margin of 42 percent to 31 percent, the outcome was understandable. More to the point, exit poll data show that Democrats and Republicans think differently about their candidates. Political party and political values matter more than most of us imagine.

The remaining portions of this chapter wander into the murky world of California political parties. We'll explain how parties are organized here as well as the relationship between candidates and officeholders. We'll examine the power of money and the state's finance laws as they apply to political party campaign efforts. As part of the discussion, we'll attempt to shed light on how campaigns center on candidates rather than parties, even though candidates are quick to attach themselves to political parties. We'll also look at the way minor parties have contributed to California's political demography at crucial moments in history. Finally, we'll return to Mary Ellen Leary's point about personality and politics.

All of these elements are found on the national stage. But in California, as with so many other characteristics, the mystery and weakness of the political party is more extreme than almost anywhere else. The fractured condition of the parties is, in fact, a representation of a state with fractured political values that rarely congeal. It's just one more indication of the extent to which California is so different from the rest of the nation.

WHO BELONGS TO WHAT?

Like so many other aspects of California, political party membership for many is something of an afterthought. Oddly enough, it's incredibly easy to join. There are no formal requirements for membership other than an individual signing up with a county registrar of voters as a member of one party or another. No dues, no loyalty oath, no punishment for contributing time or money to a nominee of a political party other than yours. In other words, it's pretty easy, harmless, and for some, almost ephemeral.

Even at that, many Californians are totally alienated from belonging to any party. A couple of sets of numbers tell the story. According to the California Secretary of State, as of February 2011, 23.6 million citizens in California were eligible to vote. Of that number, only 17.2 million or just under 73 percent bothered to register. But there's more. Of the 17.2 million registered voters, 44 percent claimed membership in the Democratic Party, whereas 30.9 percent declared themselves with the Republican Party. A few Californians, 4.7 percent, chose a minor party—more on that later. Meanwhile, 20.4 percent of all registered voters elected to declare a status officially described as "decline to state," which means they don't affiliate with any party. The short-cut term for these folks is "independents," but that can be problematic because from time to time the state has experienced a political party by the same name.

Why are these data important? The stunning fact is that once you take away those citizens who refrain from registering plus those who opt out of identifying with any party organization, only slightly more than half of the state's eligible voters buy into the value of political parties. So, why is this necessarily a problem? If parties are intended as agents to congeal different political values into manageable alternatives, clearly a substantial minority of Californians have all but washed their hands of a common conduit of political participation. Here, then, we have yet another insight into the fractured nature of California culture.

Sadly, the numbers have worsened over time. An examination of the trends over the past decade reveals three interesting points. First, as of 2011, Democratic Party registration has remained at or very near 44 percent of all registered voters. Second, Republican Party membership has dropped precipitously from 35.2 percent at the beginning of the 21st century to 30.9 percent. Third, the biggest increase in voter registration status has occurred among those who fall into the "decline to state" category, rising from 14.4 percent in 2001 to more than 20 percent today. Combined, these numbers tell us that if present trends continue, a decade or so from now, Republicans may well be outnumbered by political independents. If true, that development will make it all the more difficult for people to understand alternative approaches to governance. Some of these trends, such as a rising number of political independents, are reflected nationally, but as with so many other tendencies, they occur much more sharply in California.

In fact, these findings may be just the beginning of voter disdain about political parties. A statewide survey taken by the Public Policy Institute of California in 2006 found that 56 percent of all respondents thought a third party was needed—up from 46 percent two years earlier.[5] Clearly, Californians are dissatisfied with their political parties and their activities, although in each election more than 90 percent continue to cast their votes for the candidates of the two major parties.

Why don't parties present better-organized campaigns and alternatives for the voters? In fractured California, there are many answers. Three factors (discussed next) include the ongoing presence of factionalism within the parties, the ability of minor parties to siphon energy and control the political debate, and nonpartisan elections.

Factions

The very diversity of California makes it difficult for the political parties to coalesce around pivotal themes. That lack of unity, in turn, leaves party organizations unable to promote successfully key candidates and values to the voters. One such example manifested with the Republicans in the 2010 U.S. Senate race. Early polls showed that former Congressman Tom Campbell, a political moderate, would stand an excellent chance of defeating three-term Democratic incumbent Barbara Boxer *if* Campbell won the party primary.[6] Campbell fared well with moderate Republicans in northern California but trailed eventual nominee Carly Fiorina badly in conservative-dominated southern California. Result: The much more conservative Fiorina won the nomination but lost the November general election to the liberal Boxer who was able to seize the middle. That kind of factionalism has haunted the Republican Party for decades.

Republicans have also been divided on social "wedge" issues such as illegal immigration. The party took a shellacking after passage of an anti-immigrant ballot proposition in 1994 sponsored by then-Republican Governor Pete Wilson. Although the electorate passed the proposition overwhelmingly by a 3-to-2 margin, more than 3 out of 4 Latino voters opposed the measure. From that moment on, Republicans had great difficulty winning Latino support in California elections. Case in point: Republican gubernatorial nominee Meg Whitman won a majority of the non-Hispanic white vote in the 2010 November general election after promising no state benefits for illegal immigrants, but lost because she pulled only about 20 percent of the Latino vote. As the incoming chair of the state Republican Party reflected, "When you deal with immigration, you run into quicksand."[7] That's certainly the case for California Republicans.

But Republicans aren't the only party that has divided over candidates and values; so have the Democrats. Despite their position as the state's largest political party for the past 50 years, Democrats have demonstrated an uncanny ability to shoot themselves in the foot repeatedly. No example of party division is more pronounced than the way Democrats folded over the recall election of Governor Gray Davis. At the leadership level, Davis's Lieutenant Governor Cruz Bustamante feigned support for the governor through his conditional rejection of the recall. But Bustamante also ran with 134 others (including Arnold Schwarzenegger) to succeed Davis, just in case the electorate recalled him. Thus emerged the hypocritical and improbable campaign theme, "No on Recall, Yes on Bustamante." In one fell swoop, Bustamante damaged himself and incumbent Gray Davis. Confused over what to do and who to support, Democrats divided over Davis and Bustamante and Republican Schwarzenegger cruised to victory.

Democrats have also disagreed over key social issues. For example, in November 2008, voters were asked to decide Proposition 8, an initiative that would revise the state constitution to make it illegal for same-sex marriage. In that election, 92 percent of all registered Democrats voted for Democrat Barack Obama, who along with the state Democratic Party, officially opposed Proposition 8. Nevertheless, 30 percent of the Democrats voted for Proposition 8, compared to 70 percent who voted against it. Meanwhile, Republicans were much more unified, with 81 percent voting for Proposition 8 and only 19 percent against it.[8] The proposal carried by the relatively slim margin of 52 percent to 48 percent. In such a close race, there could be many explanations for the outcome one way or another. Nevertheless, the staggering drop off of the Democratic vote was no doubt part—if not the largest part—of the reason that the proposition carried. The lack of party unity shows up repeatedly on both sides of the political ledger.

These are only a few examples of the difficulties of achieving party unity in California. The perpetual presence of factions not only confuses the electorate but also makes it easier for other influences to dominate the political process.

Minor Parties

Over the course of the state's history, California has been witness to the activities of "minor" political parties, organizations with candidates who seek office but usually remain uncompetitive at the voting booth. In the United States, minor parties have tended to be much more ideological than practical, laced with dogma on everything from communism to fascism, from doing away with authority to greening the planet. As such, they're big on abstract themes but weak on any ability to carry out their objectives. Minor parties are often most prominent in times of crisis. That's been every bit the case in California. People sometimes scoff at minor parties, but they play a role in defining key elements of the state's political culture.

The numbers of viable minor parties fluctuate with the times. California today has four minor political parties that are able to place candidates on the ballot by virtue of the fact that they secure at least 1 percent of the vote in a major election: American Independent, Green, Libertarian, and Peace and Freedom. Others exist as platforms for various movements, but they are unable to field candidates on the ballot because of their past inability to meet the minimum voter support threshold. Many approach comedic levels. The Guns and Dope Party is dedicated to—you guessed it—easy access to guns and dope, a version of libertarianism that persists in California. The Humane Liberation Party supports the overthrow of "Amerikan fascism"; its tagline is "no borders, no nations, no flags, no patriots." The California Whig Party supports each state handling its own affairs without interference from the federal government. In all, about a dozen minor parties attempted to qualify candidates for the 2012 elections.

On occasion, minor parties can tilt the state's political direction. During the 20th century, on several occasions minor parties in California stole the political stage, and on at least one occasion government organization as well. The best example occurred with the Progressive Party, part of a reform movement in the early 1900s, which vowed to put strong controls on special interests that had captured de facto control of the state's major parties. The biggest villain of the day was the Southern Pacific Railroad, which literally ran the state through the elective offices of both Democrats and Republicans in the legislative and executive branches.

Led by Hiram Johnson, the Progressives sought to do away with that connection. Temporarily, they succeeded. Johnson not only captured the governorship as a nominee of the fledgling Progressive Party in 1910, but he brought with him Progressive majorities in the state legislature. Many of the Progressive reforms are discussed elsewhere in this book, but the importance here lies in the extent to which those reforms weakened political parties by lessening their ability to control the nominations for state offices and eliminating their roles altogether at the local government levels.

Over the next decade, Progressive majorities in the legislative and executive branches brought a fleet of regulatory bodies to administer policies in place of elected policymakers, ultimately making it easier for regulated interests to influence out of public sight. Ironically, by weakening political parties, the Progressives opened the door for interest groups to exert influence on the political process with more success than ever.[9] For that reason alone, the Progressives failed as a political party, although their dubious legacy lives on to this day via their reforms.

During the 1930s, the socialist movement thrived in Great Depression-riddled California. In 1934, discontent was so great that novelist Upton Sinclair, a Socialist Party nominee for governor in 1930, secured the Democratic nomination for the same office in 1934. Of course, Sinclair lost, but his candidacy showed the extent to which ideas considered well out of the political mainstream found their place in California.

The Vietnam War served as a backdrop for the Peace and Freedom Party, which emerged as a vehicle for expressing opposition to the two major political parties, both of which were committed to prosecuting the conflict over a span of 15 years. Spawned in California, the party ran candidates for office in 1966. No one came close to winning, but the party's opposition stirred resentment that helped to defeat the re-election effort of Democratic Governor Pat Brown by exposing major cracks in the Democratic Party.

Some minor parties have made bold statements about social or environmental conditions. Between 1966 and 1982, the Black Panther Party espoused militancy in response to the state's historic discrimination patterns and, in the eyes of its members, a tepid response to the Civil Rights movement. In recent years, the Green Party has advocated dramatic reforms in the state's environmental practices. In 1999, the party enjoyed brief success in a special election to fill a legislative vacancy by electing a member to the state assembly. The legislator ran as an Independent in 2000 and lost.

Nowadays, even the minor parties that have qualified for elections in recent years find themselves very vulnerable. That's because of California's "Top Two" primary system adopted by the voters in 2010 and effective in 2012. Under the new system, the two candidates with the most votes in the primary face each other in the general election. Given the relatively few votes garnered by the minor party candidates in the past, they're sure to become even more marginalized in the future. More on the "Top Two" primary system later.

Nonpartisan Local Elections

With the exception of the Superintendent of Public Education, candidates campaign for all legislative and executive branches of state government as members of a political party. Oh sure, every once in a while someone runs for partisan office without a party label attached to his or her name, but such efforts rarely produce much more than a small blip on the voters' political radar screen. Still, whatever the drawbacks of political parties at the state level, matters are even worse at the local levels. That's because the California constitution prevents the mention of party alongside a candidate's name, thereby depriving the voter of the ability to link his or her values with the general values sets espoused by the political parties.

Nonpartisan local elections are a product of the Progressives, who wanted to eliminate politics from governance as part of their reform movement.[10] Beginning in the Midwest and extending westward to the Pacific coast states, the movement developed great traction in California. Naively, Progressives believed that if political party affiliations were stripped from the elections and the governing process, powerful interests would be thwarted in their efforts to control those in office. Naively, perhaps, but the electorate bought the concept hook, line, and sinker.

Through a series of ballot propositions, the Progressives convinced the voters to make all local government elected offices nonpartisan—that is, candidates would run for office without the voters officially knowing their political party affiliations. That's been the arrangement since 1913. The offices include city councils and mayors, and at the county level supervisors, assessors, and sheriffs. The outcome of the change is that candidates running for local political offices and judicial positions do so without the official attachment of a political party label. The initial reaction to this change might be a big, "So what? After all, an election is an election, right"?

Wrong.

Inasmuch as political parties provide context on issues and values, the absence of a candidate's political party in a local election campaign leaves the voter without an overarching sense of the candidate's governing objectives. That means that all the organizational distinctions between the political parties stop at the local level. The result is a dismal turnout at the polls, especially when nonpartisan elections are held at times when little else is on the ballot. Case in point: When Los Angeles Mayor Antonio Villaraigosa ran for re-election in 2009, 15 percent of the registered voters went to the polls! Even the first time around, 44 percent turned out in a heated run-off between Villaraigosa and then-incumbent James Hahn for leadership of the nation's second largest city. Without party organizations at work, voters have less reason to participate.[11] That means more influence for those who do participate.

The odd fact is that the candidates themselves usually have strong partisan backgrounds. Fellow activists are clearly aware that Los Angeles Mayor Antonio Villaraigosa, Oakland Mayor Jean Quan, and San Francisco Mayor Ed Lee are Democrats—they commonly frequent the same Democratic circles. Likewise, activists also know that former San Diego Mayor Jerry Sanders and current Fresno Mayor Ashley Swearengin are Republicans for the same reasons.

But most voters are not activists; rather, they are casual observers of the political process. Denied the badge of political party, they make their decisions based on personality, looks, or a variety of factors that leave little knowledge about the candidate's values.[12] With little knowledge, turnout is likely to be depressed.[13] Voters are less informed and fewer races are competitive.[14] That means the poor, minorities, and other occasional voters won't see the call to vote most commonly exhorted by organized political parties,[15] and depressed turnout is most likely to help the status quo interests. In the absence of party guidance, local interests such as developers, major property owners, and large financial interests fill the void. As Chang-Ho C. Ji concludes in his detailed research on local elections, nonpartisan elections favor entrenched interests: "Elected officers and business interests more or less represent one social class (elite), one ethnicity (white), and one ideological community (conservative and pro-developmental)."

There's actually something of a sinister nature that emerged from the reformers: Acting in the name of nonpartisanship, they found a way to discourage ethnic minorities and immigrants while keeping control of government.[16] The Progressives also were less than generous in accommodating organized labor, another indication that political participation had its limits.[17] They used the system to prevent "undesirables" from becoming part of the system. So there you have it, nonpartisan elections are inherently designed to preserve those in power who are likely to be a lot different from those outside the power structure. All this happens under the terribly misleading label of "good government."

POOR ORGANIZATION

To understand fully the ineptitude of California's political parties, you have to begin with their organization, or lack thereof. There is an irony here. The descriptions of party structures are rich in detail, yet there are few vertical connections from top to bottom. That lack of linkage dampens any hope of accountability of the leaders to the followers.

The Missing Links

Both major parties have large governing structures known as central committees. Numbering several hundred, some central committee members exist by virtue of their nomination or election to office; others are appointed by individuals already on the central committee, and others still are elected every two years in elections held in counties. The numbers of county-elected members vary by the sizes of the counties; larger counties are allocated more members. At the top of the "structure" is a chairperson and an executive board.[18] On issues that require public comment, the chairman typically is the "face" of the otherwise faceless party.

If power exists anywhere in the party, and we use the term "power" loosely, it lies with the Chair who is elected every two years at a statewide convention. The chair has an executive committee, which is assisted by regional directors, who work with county committee members. The executive committee recommends policy positions to the larger group at the state convention. All this sounds good "on paper," except that there is no connecting mechanism through which one level exerts any leverage or control over another, save the annual statewide convention where resolutions can lead to some brutal fights often on contentious issues. Furthermore, the party has no way of sanctioning elected policymakers who act in ways contrary to party positions taken at the conventions or other settings. It's smoke, mirrors, and little else.

Management of Nominations

At the beginning of this chapter, we discussed how political parties organized values for voters. Nominees for office are the agents of those values. Upon election, we view them as officials who attempt to represent core party values through the creation of public policies. We expect that most of the time elected officials from the same political party will be on the "same page." That's all well and good, assuming that there is some agreement on major themes, which can only occur through the careful selection of nominees. But it doesn't work that way in California. In fact, anyone can run for a nomination as long as he or she is a registered voter with that party label.

Democrats

For the Democrats, a candidate for statewide office can get the party's official endorsement if he or she captures 60 percent of the vote at the statewide convention. The same threshold exists for offices in other jurisdictions, such as assembly or senate districts, as well as statewide ballot propositions. With the endorsement imprimatur, a notation of party support appears next to the candidate's name on the ballot. Democrats often endorse Democratic incumbents because intra-party challenges are few. When contested party races emerge in cases of non-incumbent offices, endorsement votes usually fail to materialize because of divisions over the candidates seeking open offices. In 2010, for example, there were serious nomination battles for three statewide offices without incumbents—Lieutenant Governor, Attorney General, and Insurance Commissioner. Democrats were only able to muster the 60 percent vote for Insurance Commissioner. The endorsement, perhaps the most important way of separating suitable candidates, rarely appears.

At the local level, the impact of party is unduly weak. Remember, local races don't include party labels, all but eliminating the party's clout. A case in point occurred in 2011 in San Jose, when the overwhelmingly Democratic city council (9 of the 10 council members) voted to place on the ballot a proposal severely curtailing collective bargaining rights of city employees. In response, the Santa Clara County Democratic Central Committee passed a scathing resolution that condemned the Democratic city council members for "violating core Democratic values" with what the Central Committee viewed as an anti-union position.[19] The council members didn't even stop to blink and maintained their positions.

Republicans

What's rare for the Democrats is nonexistent for Republicans. By virtue of their by-laws, Republicans may not endorse any candidates prior to the primary. As a result, the party forfeits one of the few opportunities to develop some control over the nomination process. Republicans do provide for endorsement at the local level offices such as city councils and county boards of supervisors. Moreover, the state central committee has no relationship with county central committees, which "operate under their own bylaws and direction with respect to local election campaigns."[20]

Like Democrats, Republicans may pass various resolutions that they expect elected officials of their party to honor in their positions of office. However, also like Democrats, the resolutions carry no weight other than their brief mention in a news cycle. Again, note the absence of linkage and lack of control. Party organizations extend their values in all directions, yet are impotent beyond imagination. It's another indication of California's dysfunctional political system.

MEANINGLESS PRIMARIES

Without the ability to control nominations, political parties must rely on candidates to reflect the essence of the organization's core values. That's asking a lot inasmuch as one's sense of the party's philosophy is a little like defining "beauty": It lies with the beholder and little more. So, then, how does someone capture a nomination without the assistance of party leadership and funds?

Some states ensure a connection between the party members and the eventual nominee by allowing only individuals who are registered in a given party to vote in primary elections. These "closed" primaries at least guarantee that party adherents will determine their nominee; New York, Florida, and Pennsylvania are examples. Other states have versions of what is known as an "open" primary.[21] In some cases, that means allowing independents to participate; in other cases, people registered in other parties may participate, a situation that can lead to manipulation of the outcome by outsiders. At the open primary extreme are Michigan, Minnesota, and Wisconsin—all Progressive Party-dominated states, by the way—along with a half dozen sparsely populated states.

For most of the past half century, California has operated as a closed primary state, with only party members allowed to determine their nominees. But that process was diluted a bit at the beginning of the last decade when independents were often allowed to vote in the primaries of one or both parties.

Still, voting in the primaries is one side of a two-sided problem. The other side is determining how candidates separate themselves in an environment where the party is not likely to endorse. This is tough in a state like California, where the large populations of assembly and state senate districts discourage candidates from door-to-door voter conversations and other "retail" campaign strategies. Candidates for nomination must rely on their own devices for fundraising, and that often leads to self-financed campaigns. Candidates frequently infuse hundreds of thousands of dollars into their own campaigns. Other times, spending is beyond belief.

Self-funded efforts are often enough to gain traction for a primary victory, although not always. In 1998, Democrat Al Checci invested $40 million—more than $70 per vote—in an effort to gain his party's nomination for governor. Of interest is that Checci had no history of party activism in state Democratic Party circles—only his checkbook. Checci came in third in a three-person race. Ouch.

In the 2010 Republican gubernatorial primary, self-financed campaign records were shattered. Billionaire Meg Whitman spent $91 million on her campaign, easily defeating fellow billionaire Steve Poizner, who spent *only* $24 million on his losing effort.[22] In this case, Whitman's money was just too powerful for Poizner. Still, she had precious little involvement in party politics, which hampered Whitman's effort to mobilize the base in the general election campaign.

Also in 2010, Democratic Attorney General candidate Chris Kelly dumped more than $10 million of his own money into his nomination effort, only to come in a distant second to winner Kamala Harris. Until his decision to run, Kelly had next to no involvement in Democratic Party activities; Harris, however, had extensive involvement in San Francisco Democratic Party politics.

Bottom line: Money can separate the candidates, but it's no guarantee of victory. Moreover, if you build relationships as you go up the political ladder, it's easier to take a support group with you.

The "Top Two" System

In 2010, the voters passed Proposition 14, officially known as "The Top Two Primaries Act" by a margin of 54 percent to 46 percent. A similar proposal was rejected in 2004, but years of legislative gridlock over woeful budget deficits led the voters to do an about-face. Proponents fought for this change because they believed that the "Top Two" system would bring about moderation that is more political from the candidates, rather than the ideologically polarized approaches that have characterized California for decades.[23] Opponents argued that the proposition could very well keep large numbers of voters from having real choice in the general election, especially if the top two came from the same party. Minor parties also saw Proposition 14 as a death knell because of the near certainty that their candidates wouldn't get close to being one of the two candidates with the most votes. But for many, the "Top Two" system offered an end to legislative gridlock. A *San Francisco Chronicle* editorial explained that passage of Proposition 14 would help to weaken party rule: "The parties, of course, hate it. They worry that the proposed system could erode their clout. They may be right—but that is not necessarily bad if the result is legislators who are less beholden to parties and rigid ideologies and more willing to break typecast in search of solutions."[24]

The *Chronicle* was only half right. Yes, passage of Proposition 14 erodes the ability of political parties to influence nominations, but the parties were weak already! Passage means that other, less visible, influences will fill the modest void. Interest groups have long been much more important to the legislative process than political parties have been. For the most part, unions, civil rights groups, and environmental groups back most Democrats; likewise, most of the time businesses, evangelical groups, and agricultural organizations back most Republicans. Moreover, these interests ply legislators with something they don't get from their party organizations—money!

Because of this legislation, effective in 2012, primaries are no longer closed, or even semi-closed for that matter. Wherever there is a primary election for partisan office, the two candidates gaining the most votes will oppose one another in the November general election. Parties can endorse candidates all they want, but no endorsements may appear on the primary ballot. Meanwhile, voters now have lost their most important vehicle for identifying with candidates. And the new system doesn't allow for write-in candidates.

A Repeat of History?

There's no guarantee that the "Top Two" system will produce different candidates, anyway. In 1996, Californians passed an initiative similar to Proposition 14. Officially known as the Open Primary Act, the proposition permitted voters to nominate any candidate from any party. Whoever won the most votes in the primary would serve as the party's nominee in the general election. Representatives from all the state's parties quickly filed suit, alleging that the new system deprived parties from limiting nominations to their own members. In 2000, the U.S. Supreme Court agreed, stating that "Proposition 198 forces political parties to associate with—to have their nominees, and hence their positions, determined by—those who, at best, have refused to affiliate with the party, and, at worst, have expressly affiliated with a rival."[25] In other words, there are differences between the parties, which as institutions exist for their members only. With that decision, the state was forced to abandon the open primary.

Some Californians crossed over the party lines during the primary elections of 1998 and 2000 while the new law was in effect. The question is, did the system produce more candidates who are moderate or less polarization in the legislature? The answer is "no." According to data compiled by the Public Policy Institute of California, "the evidence—much of it from California's experience with the blanket (open) primary—points toward a slight advantage to moderate candidates."[26] What about turnout—did the possibility of moving over to another party's race bring out more voters? Again, the answer is "no," based on a detailed comparison of the two affected primary elections with their predecessors.[27] In other words, changing the nominating process didn't change voter behavior or the types of candidates who emerged from the process, nor did it increase the level of participation.

"Top Two" for Whom?

The "Top Two" nominating system is neither likely to change the legislative divisiveness nor substantially change the make-up of the legislature itself. On the flip side, the "Top Two" system may well reduce the impact of party on an individual's vote decision, making it more likely that the voter will rely on other criteria to make his or her decision. As a result, the connection between elected officials and the public, weak to begin with, is likely to decrease, leaving voters more confused about legislative activity and leaving legislators less tied to party influence and more connected to those interests that care about the process. That's one huge backward step in representation.

LEGISLATORS AND FUNDRAISING

If nothing else, the discussion thus far suggests a sorry record in linking elected officials and voters. California's political parties have been notoriously weak in their abilities to bridge gaps. There is little hierarchy from top to bottom in the state. Finally, a string of recent ballot proposition outcomes from term limits to diluted party primary elections has further diminished the already feeble connection between office holders and voters, while those close to the legislative process—interest groups—have solidified their relationships with policymakers. All this contributes to the fractured nature of California politics.

Taking Advantage of Elective Office

Still, there is one aspect of the state's party apparatus where some of the party leaders show phenomenal success: fundraising. The party organizations are a poor source as originators for this valuable activity because of the lack of hierarchy and inability to control the nomination process, both of which translate into a lack of clout. Over time, however, this task has fallen to elected officials, particularly those in the state legislature. In turn, legislators often give some of the money they raise to the parties for distribution to candidates that have survived the primaries. Convoluted? Yes, but it works in an anything but transparent fashion.

We owe this development to Jesse Unruh, long believed to be the father of California's modern legislature, who once said, "Money is the mother's milk of politics."[28] As Speaker of the state assembly in the early days of the state's full-time legislature, Unruh was among the first legislative leaders to realize that legislators could use lobbyists as much as lobbyists could use legislators. The Democratic leader believed that he could court lobbyists' contributions and address some of their needs in Sacramento while representing his constituency back home in his liberal assembly district.[29] A feat to be sure, but one that has since been emulated again and again by those who succeeded him in office. Unruh became adept at raising huge amounts of money from lobbyists and then distributing the funds to Democratic incumbents and party nominees to protect his Democratic majority.[30] Soon, the Republican leadership in the assembly began to emulate Unruh's fundraising and distribution program. Within a few years, leaders in the state senate began courting lobby money, too.

Funneling Funds

These days, legislative leaders see lobbyists "as conduits for campaign funds, as connectors to interest groups and individual constituencies…"[31] Legislators in less contested districts often redirect campaign funds to candidates facing close races. In 2010, Assembly member Alyson Huber faced such uncertainty, having won election to her seat in a rural northern California district by only 500 votes in 2008. Seeking to reassure her victory, 21 members of the legislature contributed $269,000 to her re-election campaign. Huber outspent her opponent by a 4-to-1 margin and cruised to re-election. In a real sense, then, elected officials in Sacramento are the de facto pulse of the state's fundraising operations, the heart of the party organization even though no official titles come with the job.

The parties play a modest role in general election campaigns. For example, in 2010, the Democratic and Republican state parties contributed $24 million to various campaigns, most of which came from legislators and other elected officials who received contributions. About one-third of that amount went to the 80 assembly and 20 state senate races, with most of the remainder designated for the governor's race. These numbers seem impressive enough, but they paled when compared to self-financed candidate contributions of $207 million, $76 million from organized labor, and $72 million contributed by energy and natural resources interests. All told, of the $717 million spent on the state's political campaigns, 67 percent was donated by interest groups and lobbyists.[32]

WEAK PARTY GOVERNANCE

Disconnected from party supporters in their districts back home and separated from fellow members in the executive branch, legislators live and operate in their own unhinged political worlds. There is no way to punish them for voting in whatever ways they want, whether it stems from expediency, ideology, or personal whim. Add to that sense of independence the difficulties of securing the necessary votes for important legislation and the legislature takes on the look of an unstructured, chaotic body whose members come together only under the most dire and compelling circumstances. Only the threat of withdrawn financial support from leaders can minimize independence, and even then on an ad hoc basis with little guarantee that the withholding of any funds will force errant legislators to fall into line.

Where the Lines Are and Are Not Drawn

On most issues, legislators vote along party lines despite the poor hierarchy. With rare exception, in recent years Democrats have supported legalization of gay marriage, driver's licenses for illegal immigrants, strong environmental protection rules, and physician-assisted right-to-die legislation. Almost to a legislator, Republicans have been on the opposite side of these questions. On these themes, partisanship exists.

On some issues, however, the legislature is rife with intra-party factionalism. This tends to occur more with the Democrats than the Republicans because of their larger numbers, and it often takes place with respect to economic issues. Case in point: In 2009, the legislature considered a bill to ban Bisphenol A (known as BPA), considered by many to be a toxic chemical, from use in the production of plastic cups and bottles for children under three years of age. Even though the Democrats enjoyed a 25-to-15 majority in the senate, the measure failed to obtain a majority because four Democrats voted "no" and two others failed to show up for the vote.[33] By the way, four of the six Democrats who failed to cast "aye" votes received campaign contributions from the American Chemistry Council, which had lobbied hard against passage.[34]

The Curse of the Two-Thirds Vote

A good part of the legislature's dysfunction has nothing to do with the breakdown of party unity per se, but the rules of operation. Particularly problematic is the state constitutional requirement of an absolute two-thirds vote for passage of tax-related legislation. (More on this in Chapter 8.) "Absolute" is not written for emphasis. Rather, it refers to the mandate that approval must come from two thirds of entire legislative bodies—54 of the 80 members in the assembly and 27 of the 40 members in the senate. To put this in context, a vote of 53 to 0 in the assembly or 26 to 0 in the senate fails. The absolute two-thirds requirement gives extraordinary power to the minority party to the point of blocking the will of the majority. How's that for democracy?

Back to our revenue issue: Even though for the past few decades Democrats have held commanding majorities in both houses, they have been just shy of the full two-thirds majority necessary to pass revenue-related bills. As a result, most of the time the state budget has been held hostage by one or two Republicans in each house, forcing the Democrats to make incredible concessions in order to gain passage. The price of these votes can be astounding.

One recent case occurred in 2009, when the Democrat-dominated legislature found itself one vote short of passing emergency legislation to patch a then-$42 billion deficit. The one vote in need was owned by State Senator Abel Maldonado, a Republican, from the central coast. After weeks of wooing by the Democratic leadership, Maldonado finally assented. His price? Legislative retreat from a proposed 12 cent per gallon gasoline tax, a future ballot measure that would freeze state legislators' pay during difficult financial times, removal of $1 million in furniture funding allocated to the state controller's office, and agreement by the legislature to place on the ballot the "Top Two Primaries Act" in 2010.[35] All this for one vote. These negotiations happen all the time in legislative matters, especially when a two-thirds vote is required. How can the parties govern when they are held hostage this way? The answer is they can't. No wonder outcomes are so unpredictable.

Party Rivalry between the Branches

Partisan breakdown occurs not only within the legislature but also between the legislative and executive branches. The lack of cooperation fosters distrust among elected officials even of the same party and conveys confusing messages to the voters, which contributes to the public holding the parties in low esteem.

The drama was played out recently in yet another bruising budget battle. In 2011, with the state facing yet another massive budget deficit, Democratic Governor Jerry Brown attempted to gain the support of four Republican legislators (two in each house) to garner the necessary two-thirds vote to place some temporary tax increases before the voters. The Republicans held their ground. With the budget deadline upon them, Democratic majorities in each house passed a budget without Republican support and awaited the governor's signature. All along, Brown had asked for one of two outcomes—either a budget that included an opportunity to pass the temporary taxes or $10 billion in real cuts that reflected the gap. The Democrats, unable to get any Republican cooperation, passed a budget that maintained many current services without adding the necessary new taxes. How did they manage this? By including billions of dollars worth of gimmicks in the form of deferred maintenance, borrowing, anticipated federal revenues, and other tricks.[36]

Faced with a budget as unrealistic as the budgets of the past decade, Brown vetoed the budget less than 24 hours after it reached his desk. The governor said that the budget "continues the big deficits for years to come and adds billions of dollars in new debt."[37] Furious, Democratic leaders howled that the governor had tricked them. Said one, there was "no excuse for a Democratic governor to blindside a Democratic legislature that was working with him and his staff."[38] So angry was Senate President Pro Tem Darrell Steinberg that he stopped all confirmation hearings on the governor's appointments. Legislative Republicans regaled in the Democrats' disarray. Meanwhile, the voters couldn't help but wonder why the Democrats couldn't get their act together, especially since they controlled both the executive and legislative branches. Such are the perplexities of weak party politics in California. Even people on the same team can't get policies orchestrated very easily or very often.

THE PRICE OF WATERED-DOWN PARTISANSHIP

Let's circle back to the opening pages of this chapter before we move on. Most California residents have little knowledge of the workings of the state. Whatever information they do get comes mostly from television; barely 10 percent turn to newspapers.[39] Their evaluations of state government typically focus on what "the Democrats have done" or what "the Republicans have done," assuming that the party members in positions of political power all move in the same direction, something that political scientists describe as "party government."[40] But party government rarely works at the national level, and works less—if that's possible—in California.

More than ever, political parties in California exist in name only. More than ever, they are candidate-based rather than hierarchical organizations that welcome and help mold candidates in tune with a strong set of values. If the party nerve center is anywhere, it lies with the elected officials and candidates and their ability to run things through funneling campaign funds to other candidates directly and indirectly. It's an awkward way to run a political organization.

We pay a big price for our fractured political parties. The lack of vertical linkage leaves folks at the bottom removed from those at the top. The infighting within and between branches of the same parties confuses the voters even more. The inability to sanction unresponsive members in elected positions of authority allows for interference from outside forces; it also allows for maverick candidates totally outside the structure to insert themselves into the process via huge caches of self-financed campaign cash. Initially, there may be something appealing about a candidate who runs on the platform of being his or her own person independent of the "party machine," but in dysfunctional California a little bit of machinery might go a long way toward making the state run better and its elected officials more responsible to the voters.

Instead, policymakers lumber along, spending large amounts of time arguing with one another and going nowhere fast. When decisions are made, the smallest numbers end up having the greatest power. It's not right, but it's the case more often than not in not-so-golden California, and we all pay the price.

ENDNOTES

1. Marjorie Randon Hershey, *Party Politics in America*, 12th ed. (New York: Pearson Longman, 2007), pp. 101–116.
2. For an in-depth discussion of the American political party system, see William J. Keefe and Marc J. Hetherington, *Parties, Politics, and Public Policy in America*, 9th ed. (Washington, D.C.: CQ Press, 2003).
3. Mary Ellen Leary, *Phantom Politics: Campaigning in California* (Washington, D.C.: Public Affairs Press, 1977), pp. 165–166.
4. "Campaign 2010: California," conducted by CBS News, November 2, 2010, http://www.cbsnews.com/election2010/exit.shtml?state=CA&race=S&jurisdiction=0&tag=contentMain;contentBody.
5. See Mark Baldassare and Cheryl Katz, *The Coming Age of Direct Democracy* (Lanham, MD: Roman and Littlefield, 2006), p. 25.
6. See "Californians and Their Government," Public Policy Institute of California, San Francisco, CA, March 2010, p. 4. Also see Joe Garofoli, "Campbell Fares Best against Boxer in Poll," *San Francisco Chronicle*, May 15, 2010, http://articles.sfgate.com/2010-05-15/bay-area/20899490_1_tom-campbell-poll-head-to-head-matchup.
7. Martin Wisckol, "California GOP's Immigration Problem," *Orange County Register*, January 12, 2011, http://articles.ocregister.com/2011-01-12/news/27029265_1_latino-vote-latino-electorate-latino-community.
8. These exit poll data were prepared by David Binder Research, San Francisco, CA, November 6–10, 2008.
9. George E. Mowry, *The California Progressives* (Berkeley, CA: University of California Press, 1951), p. 268.
10. Ibid., p. 44.
11. Carol A. Cassel demonstrates this point in "The Nonpartisan Ballot in the United States," in Bernard Grofman and Arend Lijphart, Eds., *Electoral Laws and Their Political Consequences* (New York: Agathon Press, 2003), p. 228.
12. H. Eric Schockman makes this point in his op-ed piece, "Nonpartisan Elections Produce a Leaderless Ship," *Los Angeles Times*, November 4, 1990, http://articles.latimes.com/1990-02-04/opinion/op-209_1_los-angeles-city-council/2.
13. See Charles A. Prentiss, "Honolulu's Nonpartisan Elections Are Failing Us," *Honolulu Star Bulletin*, December 18, 2005, http://www.archives.starbulletin.com/2005/12/18/editorial/special.html.
14. Jessica Trounstine, *Political Monopolies in American Cities*, (Chicago, IL: University of Chicago Press, 2008), p. 46.

15. Terry Christensen, *Local Politics: Governing at the Grassroots* (Belmont, CA: Wadsworth Publishing Company, 1995), pp. 132–133.

16. Chang-Ho C. Ji, *Invisible Partisanship* (Lanham, MD: University Press of America, 2008), pp. 14–15.

17. Mowry, op. cit., pp. 291–292.

18. Most of the information in this section comes from the bylaws and rules of the California Democratic Party and the California Republican party.

19. "City Council Vote Creates Intraparty Battle," *San Jose Mercury News*, June 5, 2011, B3.

20. Standing Rules and Bylaws of the California Republican Party, as amended August 22, 2010, p. 2.

21. For an in-depth discussion of political party primary systems and their conse-quences, see Thomas R. Dye and Susan A. McManus, *Politics in States and Local Communities*, 12th ed. (Upper Saddle River, NJ: Pearson Publishing, 2007), pp. 152–153.

22. "Breaking the Bank," California Fair Political Practices Commission, Sacramento, CA, September 2010, p. 27.

23. Robert S. Erikson, Gerald C. Wright, and John P. McIver, *Statehouse Democracy: Public Opinion and Policy in the American Fifty States* (New York: Cambridge University Press, 1993), p. 104.

24. "Proposition 14: Create real competition," *San Francisco Chronicle*, April 25, 2010, http://articles.sfgate.com/2010-04-25/opinion/20865299_1_primary-ballot-party-preference-statewide-offices.

25. The case was *California Democratic Party v. Jones* 530 U.S. 567.

26. Eric McGhee, "Open Primaries," the Public Policy Institute of California, San Francisco, CA, February 2010, p. 8.

27. Wendy K. Tam Cho and Brian J. Gaines, "Candidates, Donors, and Voters in California's Blanket Primary Elections," in Bruce E. Cain and Elizabeth R. Gerber, Eds., *Voting at the Political Fault Line: California's Experiment with the Blanket Primary* (Berkeley, CA: University of California Press, 2002), p. 175.

28. Lou Cannon, *Ronnie and Jesse: A Political Odyssey* (New York: Doubleday, 1969), p. 99.

29. Bill Boyarsky, *Big Daddy: Jesse Unruh and the Art of Power Politics* (Berkeley, CA: University of California Press, 2008), pp. 72–73.

30. Alan Rosenthal, *The Decline of Representative Democracy* (Washington, D.C.: CQ Press, 1998), pp. 180–181.

31. Jay Michael and Dan Walters, with Dan Weintraub, *The Third House: Lobbyists, Money, and Power in Sacramento* (Berkeley, CA: Berkeley Public Policy Press, 2002), p. 3.

32. Follow the Money, California Contributions 2010, http://www.followthemoney.org/database/StateGlance/state_contributors.phtml?s=CA&y=2010.

33. "Consumers Union Disappointed by California Legislature's Failure to Ban Bisphenol A (BPA) in Children's Food Contact Products," ConsumersUnion.org, September 1, 2010, http://www.consumersunion.org/pub/2010/09/016818print.html.

34. See California Secretary of State, http://cal-access.sos.ca.gov/Campaign/Committees/Detail.aspx?id=1011918&session=2009&view=contributions.

35. Kurtis Alexander, "Maldonado's Budget Vote Brings Central Coast Senator Instant Fame," MercuryNews.com, February 20, 2009, http://www.mercurynews.com/centralcoast/ci_11745649.

36. "Budget Passed...But the Gimmicks Are Back," *San Jose Mercury News*, June 16, 2011, pp. A1, A11.

37. Shane Goldmacher and Anthony York, "Gov. Jerry Brown Vetoes 'Unbalanced' State Budget," *Los Angeles Times*, June 17, 2011, http://articles.latimes.com/2011/jun/17/local/la-me-0617-state-budget-20110617.

38. "Democrats Turn Wrath on Brown for Veto," *San Jose Mercury News*, June 18, 2011, pp. A1, A11.

39. "Just the Facts: Californians' News and Information Sources," Public Policy Institute of California, San Francisco, CA, November 2010, p. 2

40. For a discussion on the significance of "party government" and necessary conditions for it to occur, see Angus Campbell, Phillip E. Converse, Warren E. Miller, and Donald E. Stokes, *Elections and the Political Order* (New York: John Wiley and Sons, 1967).

8

Land of Institutional Gridlock

When we have gridlock, the system is working.

—George Will, political commentator

George Will's words might make sense with respect to refining the proper balance between power arrangements in the various branches of the national government, but they certainly don't offer much solace in California. The institutional composition in California is tantamount to the condition of a sailboat on a windless lake—dead in the water and going nowhere fast. In this state, movement toward policy resolution deteriorates into decaying malaise as a matter of course; if you didn't know any better, you would think that change agents are denied entry to the state at the border. Reform is an idle concept left to the whimsical who fail to understand the intractable political cement otherwise known as the status quo.

In California, institutional gridlock is a way of life. It's the Plan "B" for almost everyone in positions of power. Major offices overlap in authority and jurisdiction, with their elected officials perpetually jockeying for power that's almost impossible to exercise. State revenue collection responsibilities are intentionally separated to minimize any abuse of power, with a void of authority as the outcome. The existence of eight separately elected offices within the executive branch guarantees a lack of congruity, often leaving the governor's authority offset by others.

Obstacles abound. Elected public policymakers, particularly in the legislative branch, are constrained by rigorous vote requirement thresholds that approach impossibility. Term limits push out these officials before they ever get the opportunity to understand their prospects and capabilities for action. Since their days are numbered from the minute they take office, elected leaders operate with one eye on current issues and the other on their next possible office. This environment exacerbates an every-official-for-himself mentality, while discouraging cohesion and teambuilding. After all, why dedicate yourself to detailed and potentially painful, long-term policy initiatives on education reform or prison restructuring or streamlined government if you won't be around long enough to see it through? In fact, policymakers have little reason to become masters of their offices.

Unlike most other states, California has a massive "secret" branch of government rarely discussed by anyone but policy wonks. More than 300 independent agencies, boards, and commissions operate as esoteric independent fiefdoms alongside the better-known legislative and executive branches. Don't bother consulting an official organization chart because the offices and their true powers rarely coincide.

Then there's the handiwork of direct democracy. Over the years, the electorate has fulfilled Progressive reformer Hiram Johnson's hope of acting as their own legislatures by passing all kinds of laws, often with little thought and even less understanding of their true meaning. Through the initiative, the voters have placed the legislature in a double bind by repeatedly adding new costly government programs on the one hand while restricting the legislature's ability to fund them on the other. Now that's a combination guaranteed to make you wince. Thankfully, the courts have overturned some of the most confusing and unconstitutional proposals, but enough of these changes have become laws that have tied the hands of elected policymakers. And although the people vote, we know that more times than not, these days most of the proposals are drawn up by narrow interests that simply use the direct democracy tool to obtain benefits they wouldn't collect through the jammed legislative route.

No wonder citizens are confused about the political process. No wonder so little is accomplished by those elected to manage the process. It almost seems as if the state has been set up to fail. In fact, when major policy initiatives do successfully emerge from the ringmaster-less political circus, no one is more surprised than the policymakers are, themselves!

This unhealthy political environment in which the state operates is much more filled with "checks" than "balances," to borrow a concept promoted by the architects of the United States Constitution. At a minimum, these structural impediments have made it very difficult to move the state forward. Then again, maintaining the status quo in political mud may actually translate as brilliant success to others.

The remainder of this chapter is dedicated to discussing California's inability to succeed as a government for its citizens. We begin by discussing the executive branch, which is inherently deformed by virtue of its fractured composition with overlapping responsibilities and power vacuums. The executive branch is not alone, however, as a dysfunctional institution. The legislative branch has just as many problems because of the electorate's penchant for imposing unworkable procedures and enacting unfunded policies, all of which is compounded by the weak political party structure discussed in Chapter 7. We'll also cover the "workings" of the hidden branch, the state's burgeoning collection of agencies, boards, and commissions that, in their totality, make bureaucracy a dirty word. Only the courts escape our attention because they operate efficiently and in a clear, hierarchical manner.

Clearly, the formal institutions of state government were intended as the heart of California's governing structure. But intentions and reality sometimes are far apart. So dysfunctional is the state's governing apparatus that there are moments when it seems that a political "heart" transplant is the only way to save the patient. Until major changes are made to the obstacle-plagued California state government, gridlock will be the state's best-known trait.

THE UNWIELDY EXECUTIVE BRANCH(ES)

Comparing California's executive branch with its national counterpart is like, well, there is no comparison. With the national government, there is a sense of order. Thanks to the 12th Amendment, we're virtually guaranteed that the president and vice president will be members of the same political party. That means there is a great likelihood that the two leaders of the executive branch will share basic political values, which will minimize internal disagreements and assist them substantially in their interaction with the other branches of the government.

There is another difference between the national and California models: the number of moving parts. The president and vice president are the only two executive branch members elected to office. All of the other cabinet members in the executive branch are nominated by the president and confirmed by the U.S. Senate. Here again we see the semblance of tight political organization.

Now we focus on California, which is about 180 degrees removed from its national government counterpart. To begin with, the governor and lieutenant governor run for office independently of each other. That means that they may be from different political parties, and thus may have radically different approaches to running the state. They may even have little in common as members of the same party if they have different political bases. Democratic Governor Jerry Brown and his Democratic Lieutenant Governor Mervyn Dymally barely talked with one another during Brown's first term, 1975–1979. Such political chaos has happened more times than you might imagine. Worse yet, all eight elected members of the executive branch seek their positions independently of each other; that is, there is no party ticket of any kind, period. As a result, usually there are partisan divisions within the executive branch, which can and often do produce some rather ugly battles over interpreting state policies for which two or more executive branch members share power.

This is the backdrop for exercising power and authority in the largest state in the union. As with so many other instances, we see paralysis from top to bottom.

The Governor and His Ragtag Band

Given California's numerous power vacuums, we don't want to trivialize the governor into some kind of politically impotent caricature. The fact is that the state's chief executive has an array of powers that clearly separates him from the rest of the executive branch membership. By the same token, the governor is in the unfortunate position of fending off challenges—often legitimate—from members of his own executive branch as well traditional counterweights such as the legislature, courts, and bureaucracy. Because of this, the power of persuasion becomes a key part of the governor's arsenal, although some are clearly more capable than others are of leveraging it.

The cornerstone of authority lies with the governor setting the tone every year with a proposed budget that must be passed by the legislature, although not necessarily with the same contents. The legislature will spend more time responding to the budget proposal than anything else.

Of course, the state's chief executive has other powers. The governor also nominates people to head various departments in the executive bureaucracy and fills judicial vacancies as they become available. The judicial posts are particularly important; although the judges must run for re-election on a periodic basis, they rarely face serious opposition.[1] The governor also signs executive orders, which can become fairly important policy initiatives. Both Jerry Brown and Arnold Schwarzenegger used the power of the executive order to slice and/or shape state payrolls as part of their efforts to balance state budgets.[2] These are substantial capabilities.

But of all the arrows in the governor's political quiver, oddly enough the governor's greatest clout comes with the power to say "no" in the form of a veto. Over the past quarter century, governors have used this tool increasingly to nudge the legislature in a direction different than its members would choose to go. Republican Governor Arnold Schwarzenegger vetoed more than one-fourth of the bills that landed on his desk, a much higher percentage than his three predecessors, who used the veto about one sixth of the time. This activism is a far cry from the days of Ronald Reagan (1967–1973) and Jerry Brown the first time around (1975–1983),[3] when they used the veto 7.3 percent and 6.3 percent of the time, respectively. Veto power should not be underestimated. Jerry Brown vetoed the entire state budget in 2011 within 24 hours of the bill landing on his desk because it contained "legally questionable maneuvers, costly borrowing, and unrealistic savings."[4] His action stunned the legislature particularly because the budget was passed by Democratic majorities in each house.

The significance of the veto lies in its virtual permanence as a legislative tool. The legislature must obtain an absolute two-thirds vote in both houses to overturn a veto, a threshold that is tied with two other states as the highest in the nation. The last time such an event occurred was in 1979 (that's not a typo), when the Democratic legislature reversed a veto signed by...Democratic Governor Jerry Brown. No veto by a California governor has been overturned since, which shows the extent to which the state's chief executive has the final word.

Usually, but not always. Because the other office holders in the executive branch have their own spheres of constitutional authority, there are occasions when their behavior contradicts the governor's wishes. Sometimes these elected officials prevail, adding more uncertainty over who can do what. For example, in 2005, then-Governor Arnold Schwarzenegger withheld more than $3 billion from public education funding without exercising a veto. Then-Superintendent of Public Education Jack O'Connell viewed the governor's action as an unconstitutional power grab and sued on the grounds that Schwarzenegger violated state law.[5] The case was settled out of court, but not before Schwarzenegger back-pedaled on the issue. On another occasion, Schwarzenegger decided to sell the state-run workers' compensation insurance fund to help balance the state budget. State Insurance Commissioner Steve Poizner sued, arguing that Schwarzenegger exceeded his authority. Again, Schwarzenegger backed off.[6] The bottom line is that the governor is not in complete control of the executive branch by a long shot.

In any other large state, the governorship would be considered a natural jumping off platform for a run at the presidency. That hasn't happened in California since the days of Ronald Reagan and Jerry Brown's first tenure. These days, instead of building proud records of achievement for other governors to emulate, California's chief executives struggle to survive. Perhaps political writer Mark Leibovich assessed the contradictions of the office best when he wrote that "the governorship of California has become an oddly seductive job…, [yet] it has become a graveyard of political aspiration."[7] Recent governors would attest to that whether they were recalled from office or relegated to irrelevancy as they bobbed and weaved through their terms of office.

The Rest of the Cast

The remaining elected members of the executive branch fall into three groups. Only three stand on their own as offices with significant responsibilities or the potential for carrying out major undertakings. The rest have assigned tasks that basically duplicate offices within the governor's domain or overlapping responsibilities that cause havoc in the effort to make policies. Viewed in their entirety, these offices and their staffs contain some of the greatest inefficiencies in the state. Equally important, their competing policies often lead to public confusion and judicial clarification.

Meaningful Members

The position of attorney general clearly is of great value to the state. The holder of this post writes legal opinions for state office holders on potential laws and regulations, may represent California before the state and federal courts in important cases, and oversees all state and local law enforcement activities. Occasionally, the attorney general may even investigate management of local matters if he or she believes the district attorney or other local officeholder is not performing in a manner required by state law. Such responsibilities confer a rather high profile to the holder of the position. This office commands great respect and often serves as the launching pad for more significant jobs such as governor.

The lieutenant governor's office has a history of underutilization, although the occupant is designated as "acting governor" when the governor exits the state. Of course, that assumes some communication between the two offices. When Arnold Schwarzenegger was governor, he travelled outside the state frequently, but rarely told Lieutenant Governor John Garamendi anything, including his whereabouts. Only when Schwarzenegger left the country did he yield the authority of chief executive to his second in command. Potentially, the office could be significant because the lieutenant governor becomes governor should a vacancy occur. That's happened seven times in the state's history, although the transition last occurred in 1953. Otherwise, few responsibilities of importance are assigned to the office. No doubt, trust is an issue, inasmuch as the governor and lieutenant governor run independently of each other. Were the two leaders bonded on the same party ticket, things might be different.

The state superintendent of public instruction is the newest addition to the meaningful members category, thanks to the repositioning of responsibilities by Governor Jerry Brown in 2011. The holder of this office is the highest-ranking education official in the state. As such, the state superintendent of public instruction is "responsible for enforcing education law and regulations; and for continuing to reform and improve public elementary school programs, secondary school programs, adult education, some preschool programs, and child care programs."[8] Until recently, this elected position mirrored a cabinet position within the governor's office, but Jerry Brown eliminated the duplicate functions when he elected not to appoint a secretary of education. Brown's move was opposite the national trend, where 37 states make the head of public education an appointed office because of the expertise required of the person holding the position. Even though the office is elective, the superintendent is still dependent upon the approval of a 10-member state board of education appointed by the governor and a budget provided by the legislature. That said, the office has taken on new significance thanks to Brown's streamlining effort.

Duplication Centers

At least two offices in the executive branches are duplications of administrative functions elsewhere. They include secretary of state and insurance commissioner. The secretary of state is a glorified records keeper. Yes, some in the office have launched initiatives, such as the effort by Debra Bowen to secure safe voting machines.[9] But for the most part, the office collects data on campaign finance, election results, archives, and various forms related to elections. The office has an entire department on political reform, which takes us to the companion agency that overlaps the secretary of state office—the Fair Political Practices Commission. Promoted by reformers in a 1974 ballot proposition known as the Fair Political Practices Act, the Fair Political Practices Commission collects data on candidates, campaign contributions, ethics, and potential campaign finance violations. The commission, a five-member body appointed by the governor and other executive officers,[10] has responsibilities that overlap significantly with those of the secretary of state. In fact, in some respects it's almost impossible to understand the differences between the two. The commission was created as a body to be independent of politics and political influence. Fair enough. Then why keep the secretary of state's office? Clearly, the zeal of reform has overcome clarity of purpose and common sense. We don't need both.

The state insurance commissioner is yet another example of an elected office that simultaneously duplicates and competes with other organizations tucked away in the executive branch. Originally, the California Department of Insurance was created by the state legislature in 1868 to oversee insurance practices, consumer protection, and fraud. But reformers feared that the office was not independent enough of insurance interests. Concern over industry influence led to passage of a ballot proposition in 1988 that set up a separate elective office as part of the executive branch. That would be okay except the office competes with several other government units including the Workers' Compensation Appeals Board, the Commission on Health and Safety and Workers Compensation, and the State Compensation Insurance Fund. In addition, as part of its bureaucracy, the governor's office houses the Office of the Insurance Advisor, which is part of the State and Consumer Services Agency. According to its description, the goal of the office is to "promote public policy that protects consumers while insuring a competitive and financially stable insurance marketplace throughout California."[11]

Wait a minute…Isn't that also the responsibility of the insurance commissioner? The answer is yes. Recently, the insurance commissioner was empowered by the nation's new Patient Protection and Affordable Care Act to require health insurance companies to spend at least 80 percent of their premiums on medical care.[12] That administrative change will add clout to the office. Still, if we are to have an effective insurance commissioner with clear policies, at a minimum the policies associated with its mandate will be more effective if the other elements scattered throughout the executive branch are folded into its responsibilities.

Overlapping Offices

Thus far, we've focused on independent offices that stand on their own and offices that duplicate their services with other components in California's bureaucracy. The third category represents the worst organization elements of California's tangled executive branch. The overlapping components include the controller, treasurer, and five-member Board of Equalization. Ironically, this triad was created in the second Constitutional Convention of 1879 as an attempt to protect the integrity of the state's revenue collection procedures. Instead, the offices that have matured perform overlapping functions and step on one another with regularity.

The controller's office is the most important of the three money-related institutions. Described as the state's "chief fiscal officer,"[13] the controller oversees the California Public Employees Retirement System (PERS) and the California State Teachers Retirement System (STRS), two of the largest public retirement programs in the country. The controller also sits on 78 (yes, 78) state boards and commissions dealing with everything from public hospital construction to coastline protection. Most important, the office is responsible for tax-related receipts and state expenditures in excess of $100 billion annually. In 2011, Controller John Chiang declared that he would withhold salaries of state legislators because of their failure to produce a balanced budget, as required by Proposition 25 in 2010. Whether he was actually empowered to do so remained a point of dispute.[14] Nevertheless, the legislature passed another version two weeks later with Chiang's blessing. All this makes it sound like the controller is the state's "go to" money guru, doesn't it? Maybe so, but there are other players.

The treasurer is described as California's most important "asset manager, banker, and financier." The office uses its resources to finance bonds that are voted on by the public. The office also manages the funding of state and local government public works projects. The treasurer sits on the PERS and STRS boards and 57 other boards of commissions, agencies, and committees. Are you getting a sense of redundancy? If that hasn't hit you yet, read on.

The five-member Board of Equalization is an elected unit. For the purposes of this collective body, the state is divided by population into four districts, each of which elects someone at the time of the other executive branch office elections. The fifth member is the state controller. The agency today is a far cry from its intended purpose when it was established in 1879. For nearly 100 years, the principal job of the Board of Equalization was to make sure that county property tax assessment methods were "equal and uniform throughout the state." But that responsibility ended with the passage of California's Proposition 13 in 1978, which set up strict rules for all property tax assessments. These days, the Board of Equalization totals the collections of various revenues such as sales and property taxes. It also distributes funds for special districts. Perhaps, most important, the board of equalization is an appellate body for franchise and income tax appeals.

Let's remember that these three offices all operate within California's executive branch. The occupants of each will stridently protest that the functions of their institutions are dramatically different from the others, unique in fact. Yet, these offices seem to be one huge employment agency more than anything else. Their responsibilities overlap so much it's difficult to tell where one begins and another ends. As if this isn't enough confusion, the taxes we pay are not sent to the controller, the treasurer, or the board of equalization but to the Franchise Tax Board, which is part of the State and Consumer Services Agency in the executive branch. That bureaucracy actually collects revenues. Moreover, as if to add insult to injury, the members of the Franchise Tax Board are the controller, a member of the Board of Equalization, and the Governor's Director of Finance. More duplication and waste!

The Facts Are the Facts!

The fractured executive branch illustrates the way that Californians have added new offices and roles over the years without considering their purposes, value, or relationships with other elements of government. Some, like the Board of Equalization, have completely lost their original reason for existence and assumed new responsibilities in an attempt to stay relevant. Others, such as the Secretary of State and Fair Political Practices Commission, routinely step on each other with overlapping responsibilities. Especially where duplication exists, the affected offices go to great lengths to justify their existences. Still, at the end of the day, the facts speak for themselves.

Worse yet, these problems are hardly new to the state or its elected officials. Twenty years ago, then-Governor Pete Wilson appointed a distinguished 23-member California Constitution Revision Commission to examine the state's dysfunctional government and make concrete recommendations for improvement. The first three of the commission's 35 recommendations were: place the governor and lieutenant governor on the same ticket; convert the superintendent of public instruction, treasurer, and insurance commissioner into appointed offices much like the director of parks, highways, and other bureaucratic agencies; and convert the responsibilities of the Board of Equalization and the Franchise Tax Board into a single Department of Revenue.[15] The same problems linger to this day.

No wonder Californians are confused and angry with their government. It's been broken and in need of serious repair for decades. But everyone, including us, continues to avoid making the tough decisions, hoping that a band-aid here and a band-aid there will improve our diseased political body. It's a collective state of denial that has become an unfortunate foundation of the state's political culture and the way state government does business. And it's costing us all, one way or another.

GRIDLOCK UNDER THE DOME

Gridlock is every bit as prevalent in the state legislature as it is within California's executive branch. But unlike the executive branch where power is defused because of overlap or contested by various office holders, the legislature struggles to manage in a power vacuum. No self-respecting legislator would admit it, but the legislature's clout has been diminished greatly by outside influences and structural obstacles, many of which have been foisted upon the body by questionable ballot propositions. The most important causes of legislative impotence are high vote thresholds, term limits, redundant houses, and unreasonable constraints courtesy of the voting public. Because of these factors, the legislature has become an increasingly irrelevant policymaking body. This in itself is an irony, given that legislatures are designed as the people's houses.

High Vote Thresholds

Part of the legislature's weakness lies in the rules related to its lawmaking responsibilities. Revenue generation through taxes occurs only with absolute two-thirds majority votes, a near impossibility. Inasmuch as personal income, sales, and corporate taxes comprise more than 90 percent of all state revenues, increases of these taxes fall under the two-thirds rule. Of course, taxes are collected for the state to fund various programs. You can see where this is going: any program or service that is dependent upon state revenues is held hostage to the absolute two-thirds rule. The contentious taxing versus spending argument has produced budget stalemates year after year, including 2008 when the legislature finally coughed up a budget a full 100 days past the constitutional deadline. Prior to that, the gridlock-filled legislature produced on-time budgets only twice in the previous quarter century.

As the state's revenue problems have mounted in recent years, the anti-tax Republican minority in the legislature has won virtually all spending arguments not because of the merits but because of the system's bias for stalemate. In the meantime, lengthy delays in reaching agreement cause havoc for everyone from vendors waiting for payment to schools attempting to determine teacher employment to in-home care providers who must provide services as they await payment. And now the legislature shares in the misery, as the members learned in 2011. After failing to enact a balanced budget, they were denied their salaries until passage. The cost for two weeks of delay? Nearly $5,000 per legislator.

The legislature has attempted to circumvent some of the problems in recent years by increasing "user fees"—revenues that are collected for programs or services by those who use them. Gasoline taxes, state park fees, and court fees are all examples that come to mind. The idea is to attach the cost specifically to the people or businesses that benefit directly from the program or service. At least until recently, the biggest advantage of the concept was that passage required only a majority vote. But even this modest effort may now be thwarted because of the passage of Proposition 26 in 2010, officially titled "Supermajority Vote to Pass New Taxes and Fees."

There is one piece of good news in this otherwise disastrous budget mess. Beginning in 2011, the legislature needs just a simple majority to pass the annual budget or any other commitment of state funds. This comes courtesy of Proposition 25, entitled Majority Vote for Legislature to Pass the Budget, which was passed by the voters in 2010 along with Proposition 26. Of course, there's a hitch—it does no good to pass a budget if it's not funded, which is why Proposition 25 has limited value as long as it is still necessary for the legislature to obtain a two-thirds vote for most revenue increases.

Term Limits

The passage of Proposition 140 in 1990 changed the balance of power in California. By limiting the legislators to three 2-year terms in the state assembly and two 4-year terms in the state senate, the proposition rendered the legislature the status of a second-class policymaking body. To begin with, the legislature lost its desire to challenge the governor and members of the executive branch on policy initiatives. In their lengthy study of the term limits era, Bruce Cain and Thad Kousser conclude, "term limits reduce incentives to devote energy to oversight. If legislators do not foresee a lengthy career in state government, they may choose not to spend precious hours uncovering and fixing its problems. Similarly, they may not wish to sacrifice time and energy to defend the prerogatives of the legislative branch."[16]

A related problem with term limits is the inability of legislators to be in office long enough to gain expertise. Who can expect a recently elected legislator to understand the complexities of a $100 billon business in a year or two? Remember, unlike executives who move up the corporate ladder, in most cases legislators come to office with little exposure to Sacramento. Even if the new legislator is a former city council member or county supervisor, the process and stakes are much greater in Sacramento with virtually no time to get up to speed. The National Conference of State Legislatures confirmed the dilemma of the expertise issue in a survey of 3,500 legislators in states with term limits. The survey found that legislators with little experience "cede more power to and influence to the governor and lobbyists" and become much more deferential to the governors' budgets in term limits environments.[17] This has been the case in California, where the balance of power has swung disproportionately to the governor and interest groups, who are permanently ensconced in Sacramento. The irony is inescapable: We've put limits on people we allow to run for office, while making it easier for those we don't elect to control the process.

Redundant Houses

California's bicameral legislature has become a liability for several reasons. First, like all other states, its organization originally was designed to represent people in the Assembly and land in the Senate. All that was washed away in 1964, when the U.S. Supreme Court ruled that representation by land was unconstitutional.[18] California, like all of the other bicameral states was ordered to organize legislative districts in both houses by population. With that change, the two houses were no longer differentiated in the types of constituents, only the sizes of their districts, which held twice as many residents in the 40-seat Senate as in the 80-seat Assembly.

But the problem is that California has so many people that each district is very populated. State senators now represent almost 1 million people each, a number greater than the district populations for members of the U.S. House of Representatives. There's something out of balance when the largest state in the union has the 35th largest legislature. No other states approach this kind of ratio.

At the same time, the two houses in the state legislature perform almost the same activities. Yes, they are organized slightly differently with the Assembly Speaker leading a more centralized body than his Senate counterpart. Additionally, the Senate has some appointee confirmation responsibilities that do not exist in the Assembly. But fundamentally, the two houses are almost mirror images in terms of legislative responsibilities. Each traditionally has three hearings on bills that are vetted as they wend their way through several committees. Of course, last minute riders and other changes are sneaked into bills, but that kind of chicanery goes on in each house from time to time. Perhaps you see where this is heading.

There is no longer a compelling reason for both houses. The vetting process is thorough twice over. Imagine, however, if the 120 members were part of a single house, as is the case in Nebraska. Now each member would represent a bit more than 300,000 residents, a ratio not enjoyed for decades. As a bonus, the costs of operating the legislature would be reduced considerably because with only one house, the numbers of committees would be reduced by half. A unicameral legislature represents an opportunity to better connect legislators with constituents. And given the redundancies that exist within each house already, there would continue to be multiple opportunities for various parties to make their case. As Harold Meyerson recently wrote, today's California legislature has "two functionally indistinguishable bodies.... Eliminating one house would also eliminate the possibility of behind-closed-doors mischief in the bicameral conference committees that now convene to reconcile the two houses' versions of the same bill."[19] In today's political environment, the two-house legislature is little more than a chamber for obstruction.

Initiatives—The People's Legislative Process

Initiatives have been available as a policymaking route for the electorate since the early 20th century. Over the past 50 years, however, they have assumed an ever-growing prominence in the legislative process. During the 1960s, the voters determined the fate of 10 initiatives; the number grew to 52 during the 1960s and 76 during the first decade of the 21st century.

Campaign costs have ballooned along the way. In a few instances, interested parties have assembled war chests of $150 million or more to make their case before an often-bewildered electorate. Big oil spent over $100 million to defeat a modest tax proposal in 2006, and Indian casino interests spent over $150 million to secure passage of a gaming initiative in 2008, to name a few recent examples. Public utilities, tobacco, agriculture, financial institutions, and labor unions are among the other big interests that stepped into the policymaking process as outsiders, even though they are accountable only to themselves.

All this has turned the legislative process on its head. As discussed earlier, the tools of direct democracy originally were designed to put controls on powerful interests that had disproportionate influence over the state legislature. Instead, over time ballot propositions have often—although not always— co-opted elected officials by the same types of groups they were intended to harness. Today, ballot propositions tend to be "the product of organized interests—not of an unorganized public."[20] They use the process to get around a legislature that is unresponsive, dysfunctional, or both. In the meantime, the legislature has become almost irrelevant when it comes to managing major issues of the day.

In at least one respect, the initiative process actually trumps the legislature's governing ability. That's because as part of the constitutional reform, the Progressives inserted the guarantee that once initiative became law, only the people could amend it through another initiative at a subsequent election.[21] "In effect," in the words of one assessment, "this makes initiatives a higher class of law."[22] This gives a permanent quality to voter-spawned legislation that elected officials don't have.

Initiatives have curbed the ability of the legislature to increase revenues again and again. The most recent example is Proposition 26, which reduces the legislature's ability to enact new fees by requiring an absolute two-thirds vote. At the same time, initiatives have required legislature to spend revenues on specific programs. Consider three such programs, bearing in mind that they are representative of dozens more that have been enacted by the voters over the years.

Proposition 98, officially known as the California Instructional Improvement and Accountability Act (1988), mandates the legislature to allocate a minimum of 40 percent of the state general fund for K–12 public education. Legislators can suspend the allocation with an absolute two-thirds vote, but do so at the peril of voter anger. Most education experts and Californians actually believe that 40 percent is not enough to adequately fund K–12 public education,[23] but the allocation established in Proposition 98 has become a mantra of sorts for legislators. An array of initiatives on other topics—some large, some small—have similarly hamstrung the legislature's ability to create an annual budget.

Proposition 10, the Children and Families First Act (1998), added 50 cents to the cost of a pack of cigarettes. The funds are dedicated to community health care programs for children six years and under. That tax now collects about $750 million annually and cannot be used for any other health care services, regardless of need or the fact that the state has had to cut back health care commitments in other areas such as mental health, shut-in care, and people with severe disabilities. None of this is to deny the value of children's care, but it does show how ballot propositions—even those with the best intentions—tie the hands of California policymakers.

Proposition 63, the Mental Health Services Act, has generated more than $1 billion per year for state coffers since voter approval in 2004, with the funds exclusively dedicated for new mental health programs and clients. The funds may not be used for existing programs or individuals who have been long-term clients of those programs. At the same time that these funds have grown, the legislature has drastically reduced spending for existing mental programs because of budget constraints—nearly $600 million between 2009 and 2011 alone. As a result, the state has two radically different approaches to treating the mentally ill, depending on the category in which they fit: "a Cadillac system for selected new clients, and a dysfunctional, deteriorating system for those already inappropriately served," according to a mental health policy leader closely involved with the program.[24]

All these "earmark propositions," no matter how well intentioned they may be, take a toll on the legislature's ability to organize and pass an annual budget. One recent breakdown of the state budget has mandated spending counting for about two thirds of the general fund—40 percent for K–12 public education and 27 percent for other mandated programs.[25] Other assessments place the figure at closer to 90 percent.[26] When you look at it that way, the legislature has precious room to do anything of importance.

Consequences

When you consider the multiple sources of legislative ineptitude, it's a miracle that the lawmakers get anything accomplished whatsoever. Organizational rules, dysfunctional political parties, term limits, and direct democracy are among the many impediments that slice into the legislature's delicate political fabric. Again and again, obstacles overcome desire to the extent that the most capable legislative steward loses hope. Suddenly, the gridlock becomes understandable, although never acceptable.

Consequently, the legislature plays the role of "second banana" to other power centers, to employ an old Hollywood phrase. Because of so many internal conflicts and external pressures, it has become a body known more for blocking change than effecting meaningful change. The governor, interest groups, and even the bureaucracy each have more clout in the legislative process than the body once designed to represent the people.

ENDLESS INDEPENDENT BOARDS AND COMMISSIONS

Along with the "Big Picture" state institutions, more than 300 independent narrow boards and commissions inundate California. Most have been piled on over the years in response to issues considered by reformers too important for the legislature to manage; the thinking goes that such issues should be removed from "politics." Over the years, few have been deleted, although the need for them no longer exists. In many cases, the policies of these bodies tend to address narrow constituencies, yet some possess considerable regulatory authority.

Other than prominent entities like the California Coastal Commission or Air Resources Board, boards and commissions tend to operate with little public fanfare. Nevertheless, they are participants in the policymaking process, by virtue of their abilities to create and enforce regulations that have the impact of law. The very existence of these entities provides yet another level of confusion for most Californians. Most of all, independent boards and commissions don't necessarily rise above politics as much as they make political decisions from less open arenas.

A few of these agencies are major appointments with sizable salaries, and usually subject to senate confirmation. They sometimes attract attention of the media because of their patronage-like appointments of former legislators to part-time positions. Another group of these offices pays members per diem compensation, nominal amounts that cover expenses associated with meetings. Finally, another category offers no payment whatsoever either because the member serves as a condition of service in another state position or because the group is basically honorary. All of this underscores the simple point that not all boards and commissions are alike; in fact, they're quite different.

One additional point worth mentioning: The areas of policy responsibility and pay frequently do not coincide. For example, members of the California Coastal Commission, a body of great significance to the oversight of coastal development, receive $100 per meeting, or per diem. On the other hand, members of the Public Employment Relations Board, which oversees labor contracts, receive $123,897 annually and meet six times a year—six times! Nice work if you can get it.

Major Boards and Commissions: Some Examples

At least 14 boards and commissions have members in policymaking positions with salaries in excess of $50,000, and often more than $100,000. High-paying boards are frequently laced with former legislators, raising suspicion about qualifications and activities. The California Unemployment Insurance Appeals Board, for example, has seven members, six of whom are former legislators. The "job" pays $128,109 per year; members meet an average of once monthly.

What's so fascinating about many boards and commissions is that many interact with parallel units in the executive branch. It leads one to wonder why there has to be endless duplication. Then again, duplication is a key reason for so much of California's institutional gridlock.

The Agricultural Labor Relations Board (ALRB), for instance, created to keep peace in the fields, has three members; one is Carole Migden, a former state legislator from very urban San Francisco, who earns $128,109 for a few meetings per year. The board is separate from the Department of Labor and Workforce Development that is housed in the governor's office. This is only one example of the redundancy rampant in California state government. If farm worker issues were managed along with all other labor issues, there would be no need for the ALRB. The state also has the Department of Industrial Relations, which is housed under the governor's control as well. Its mandate: "To improve working conditions for California's wage earners, and to advance opportunities for profitable employment in California."[27] Sure, the comparisons are not mirror images, but the overlap is substantial.

Another example exists in the overlap between the five-member California Gambling Commission, created by initiative in 2000 to allow gambling on Native American-owned land, and the California Bureau of Gambling Control. The Bureau is housed within the Department of Justice, which is under the management of the State Attorney General. Its mandate is "to ensure that gambling is conducted honestly, competitively and free from criminal and corruptive elements."[28] Compare that with the California Gambling Commission, whose mission is to foster honest, competitive gambling in California that is free of criminal and corruptive elements.[29] By the way, the Gambling Commission meets about two dozen times each year; its members are paid $123, 897 annually.

The last example covers water resources management in California. Within the governor's office lies the Natural Resources Agency, whose mandate is "to restore and manage the state's natural, historical and cultural resources…," including the coast and wetlands.[30] Competing with the agency is the five-member State Water Resources Control Board, with a mission statement "to preserve, enhance and restore the quality of California's water resources…."[31] Exactly alike? No, but pretty close. Why couldn't these two agencies be merged? Are their responsibilities that much removed from each other? By the way, the board met 22 times in 2011 and held another dozen workshops, and in case you're wondering, each Water Resources Control Board Member earns $132,179 annually.

Other Boards

Not all boards or commissions are redundant with other parts of the state government. Some make perfect sense and should be independent of other government units because of their responsibility. The Commission on Judicial Performance is a case in point. The task of this organization is to investigate claims of judicial misconduct. Given the necessity of an independent judiciary, such work must be done without any redundancy or control elsewhere.

Some commissions or boards deal with vocational specialties and, as such, are populated with people in the field. The Board of Occupational Therapy, the Board of Psychology, the California Architects Board, and the Board of Podiatry come to mind as institutions that seek to maintain standards in the field. Most are blends of practitioners and public members, an approach that makes sense. The members of the various professions board are usually compensated $100 per diem.

Still, even specialty fields are replete with unnecessary and confusing duplication. Why, for example, does California require a Medical Board and Osteopathic Medical Board, when the two units both deal with physicians? Why does the state need a Lottery Commission, Horseracing Board, and Gambling Control Commission, when all of these essentially deal with variations of the same topic? We don't.

The Purpose of Redundancy

These redundant institutions didn't appear by accident. In fact, in many cases, they are creatures of their industries or allies sympathetic to those interests. With boards and commissions, individuals and organizations have yet another way to insinuate themselves into the political influence network. And the best part is that they carry out these roles as "good citizens" rather than purveyors of self-interests.

Examples abound. Consider the fact that the Gambling Control Commission was created as part of the initiative that permitted Indian-owned casinos in California. So far, so good. But the tribes supported the regulatory body, in part, because they were promised approval of at least two of the five commission members.[32] Nothing like having your own people on the inside of the institution that's been created to regulate your organization!

Or take a close look at the California Commission for Economic Development. Created by the legislature in 1971, the 17-member body is chaired by the Lieutenant Governor (one of his few responsibilities) and has 6 members from the legislature and 10 members from the business community. One of its core responsibilities is to "provide a forum for ongoing dialogue on economic issues between state government and the private sector."[33] Never mind that the Governor already has a Secretary of Business, Transportation, and Housing as well as an Office of Economic Development. This organization allows representatives of business interests to connect directly and seamlessly with the state legislature in what is a kind of built-in lobbying conduit.

Good Riddance? Hardly

The boards and commissions underscore the fractured nature of California government. It's also important to remember that these government organizations all have staffs and budgets separate from their counterparts in other state units. That adds up to a lot of people and dollars in some cases working on parallel tracks and in others working at cross-purposes. Either way, it produces messy governance that is often anything but transparent.

It's not that people aren't aware of the boards and commissions problem. In fact, elected governors of both major political parties have sought to rein in the ever-expanding number of independent boards and commissions in California. In 2004, newly elected Republican Governor Arnold Schwarzenegger asked the legislature to eliminate 88 of the panels in an effort to streamline government. The proposal languished in the legislature for a year before the governor saw the futility of his proposal and withdrew the plan.[34] Schwarzenegger did walk away with a small consolation prize, however. In 2009, the legislature did away with the California Integrated Waste Management Board, another traditional soft landing spot for former legislators who met about once each month with a salary of $132,178. One down, 299 to go.

As one of his first reform initiatives in office, Democratic Governor Jerry Brown asked the legislature to do away with 37 independent state boards and commissions in 2011. Brown thought he had a better chance than Schwarzenegger because unlike his Republican predecessor, the new governor enjoyed large Democratic majorities in each house of the legislature.[35] No such luck, despite the state's budget crisis. The legislature clearly signaled its opposition when the State Senate voted down a proposal that would have reduced six-figure salaries of very part-time commissioners to $100 per meeting, as is the case with many state boards and commissions.[36]

Clearly, there is no serious desire for reform among those in elected positions of authority. Despite the overlap of responsibilities, unnecessary if not excessive costs, and absence of transparency, independent boards and commissions continue to make policies in California well underneath the state's political radar.

GRIDLOCK AS THE STATUS QUO

In life, few events are totally random; there's a reason for almost everything, even if we don't always understand it at the time an event or circumstance occurs. It's no different in the case of California's gridlock, which has been more than a century in the making and shows no sign of abating.

Our institutions are unsynchronized and therefore dysfunctional. Elected officials can't do their jobs, which leads to discouragement and distrust; many have great responsibilities but little authority to carry them out. A haphazard collection of independent agencies operates with considerable clout well out of sight of the public eye, despite public meetings attended by few other than the directly affected parties. Our leaders can't lead because of fractured authority and a turnstile approach to governance that discourages the development of expertise. When leadership occurs, it's almost by accident.

Meanwhile, the people are disgusted with it all. Never mind that we share a good deal of blame for the state's gridlock, if for no other reason than because of the impediments we have showered on our leaders and their offices. We want leaders to govern, but not for too long. We expect the process to be productive, but only if those making policies can overcome unreasonably high vote threshold requirements. We desperately need better schools, job training, public safety, and basic social programs, but not if it means taxing the myriad sacred cows that use their skills to avoid paying their share or ourselves. As legislative expert Alan Rosenthal insightfully observes, "It is not surprising that California citizens are dissatisfied with how their governments work. They do not work well at all. Nor is it surprising that California citizens do not acknowledge that they themselves bear major responsibility for the quality of governmental performance."[37] It's always somebody else's fault, never ours. The ironies are endless.

ENDNOTES

1. Superior Court judges run for re-election every six years. Supreme Court and Appeals Courts justices must answer to the voters every 12 years. The question for these posts simply is whether the voters want these justices to continue in their posts.
2. "Gov. Lays Off 10,000 Workers," *Los Angeles Times*, August 1, 2008, pp. A1, A15, and "Brown Puts Freeze on State Hiring," *Los Angeles Times*, February 16, 2011, pp. AA1, AA2.
3. Voters approved lifetime limits of two terms for individuals in the executive branch in 1990. Inasmuch as Brown's first two terms were earlier, he was permitted to seek the governorship in 2010.
4. Shane Goldmacher and Anthony York, "Gov. Jerry Brown Vetoes 'Unbalanced' State Budget," *Los Angeles Times*, http://articles.latimes.com/2011/jun/17/local/la-me-0617-state-budget-20110617.
5. "Superintendent, Union Sue Over Money Pledge, *San Francisco Chronicle*, August 10, 2005, pp. B1, B5.
6. "Plan to Sell Portion of State Fund Collapses," *Los Angeles Times*, December 30, 2009, pp. B1, B5.
7. Mark Leibovich, "Who Can Possibly Govern California," *The New York Times Magazine*, July 3, 2009, http://www.nytimes.com/2009/07/05/magazine/05California-t.html.
8. California Department of Education, "Role and Responsibilities," http://www.cde.ca.gov/eo/mn/rr/.
9. "Touch Vote Machine Ban Hurts Counties," *San Francisco Chronicle*, August 5, 2007, pp. B3.
10. The five members are appointed to single four-year terms as follows: the governor appoints two, with the secretary of state, attorney general, and controller appointing one each.
11. California State and Consumer Services Agency, Office of the Insurance Advisor, http://www.scsa.ca.gov/about_us/oia_info.shtml.
12. "Emergency Regulation Gives California Teeth to Enforce Health Insurance Payouts," *Sacramento Bee*, January 26, 2011, p. B9.
13. Responsibilities of the Controller's Office, http://www.controller.ca.gov/eo_about_resp.html.
14. "Legislature to Forfeit Pay, Chiang Says," *Los Angeles Times*, June 22, 2011, pp. A1, A10.
15. California Constitution Revision Commission, Summary of Recommendations, Sacramento, CA, 1996, p. 7.
16. Bruce Cain and Thad Kousser, "Adapting to Term Limits: Recent Experiences and New Directions," Public Policy Institute of California, San Francisco, CA, 2004, p. 72.
17. Eric Kelderman and Pamela M. Prah, "Report Chronicles Downside of Term Limits," *Stateline*, August 16, 2006, http://www.stateline.org/live/details/story?contentId=134247.
18. The case was *Reynolds v. Sims*, 84 S. Ct 1362 (1964).
19. Harold Meyerson, "Getting the Legislature's Houses in Order," *Los Angeles Times*, August 21, 2009, http://articles.latimes.com/2009/aug/21/opinion/oe-meyerson21.

20. Alan Rosenthal, *The Decline of Representative Democracy* (Washington, D.C.: CQ Press, 1998), p. 40.

21. Elizabeth R. Gerber, Arthur Lupia, Mathew D. McCubbins, and D. Roderick Kiewiet, *Stealing the Initiative: How State Government Responds to Direct Democracy* (Upper Saddle River, NJ: Prentice Hall, 2001), p. 12.

22. "The People's Will: Democracy in California," *The Economist*, April 23, 2011, p. 8.

23. See "Californians and Education," Public Policy Institute of California, San Francisco, CA, April 2010, and Donald Cohen, "California in Crisis," *The American Prospect*, February 1, 2010, http://prospect.org/cs/articles?article=california_in_crisis.

24. "Tax Windfall in State Can't Stop Mental Health Cuts," *San Jose Mercury News*, June 26, 2011, pp. A1, A19.

25. "Perspectives on State Expenditures," 2007-2008, Legislative Analyst Office, Sacramento, CA, http://www.lao.ca.gov/analysis_2007/2007_pandi/pi_04_anl07.aspx.

26. Alan Greenblatt, "California's New Finance Director, Donna Arduin, is bringing Tough-Love Budgeting to a Deficit-Addicted State," *Governing*, January 2004, http://www.governing.com/topics/finance/Calculator.html#.

27. Mission Statement, Department of Industrial Relations, http://www.dir.ca.gov/.

28. Bureau of Gambling Control, Department of Justice, Office of the Attorney General, http://ag.ca.gov/gambling/index.php.

29. Mission statement, California Gambling Control Commission, http://www.cgcc.ca.gov/.

30. Mission Statement, California Natural Resources Agency, http://resources.ca.gov/about.html.

31. Mission Statement, State Water Resources Control Board, http://www.swrcb.ca.gov/about_us/water_boards_structure/mission.shtml.

32. Gregg Jones and Miguel Bustillo, "Davis' Nod to Tribes Criticized," *Los Angeles Times*, August 30, 2003, http://articles.latimes.com/2003/aug/30/local/me-davis30.

33. California Commission for Economic Development, http://www.ced.ca.gov/.

34. "Gov. Pulls Plan to Abolish Panels," *Los Angeles Times*, February 18, 2005, pp. B1, B10.

35. "37 Boards for the Budget Sawmill," *Los Angeles Times*, May 22, 2011, pp. A33, A34.

36. "Bill to Cut State Commissioners' Salaries Is Killed," *Los Angeles Times*, April 26, 2011, http://latimesblogs.latimes.com/california-politics/2011/04/lawmakers-on-tuesday backed-away-froma-proposal-to-eliminate-six-figure-salaries-on-state-commissions-thatserve-assoft-landing.html

37. Rosenthal, op. cit., p. 333.

9

Hijacked! How Powerful Interests Have Taken Over the State

The biggest problem that we have is that California is being run now by special interests.

—Arnold Schwarzenegger

He should know. When Arnold Schwarzenegger was governor of California, special interests made themselves at home in the Capitol like bees in a honeycomb. But unlike bees that produce honey, interest groups and their lobbyists ply elected officials with money and deafening—if one-sided— information. During his years as governor (2003–2010), Schwarzenegger alone received a whopping $143,839,604.[1] Total dollars contributed to state candidates and ballot propositions soared from $61.7 million to $716.7 million, an increase of more than 1,200 percent. Financial contributions from the top 12 special interest categories in California during the same period rocketed from $25.2 million to $131 million.[2] Big money and California seem to go well together. The question is what—or who—does it buy? And what does it mean for the rest of us?

While Schwarzenegger may have been the highest-ranking elected official in California to benefit during this period, he was hardly the only recipient—willing or otherwise, unwittingly or conveniently—of powerful interest group efforts. Along with members of the executive branch, legislators, regulators, and especially the voters have been on the receiving end of specialist interest clout. Nor was he the first California governor to succumb to such pressures. Much like the linkage between automobiles and smog, the profound interdependence between California policymakers and interest groups is an endemic, if unfortunate, characteristic of the state.

"Special interests" is the new description for the powerful influencers who garner cooperation from policymakers for their own needs first, with little concern for others or the public good, for that matter. Years ago, we described these private change agents as "interest groups" or "pressure groups," reflecting their ability to sway legislators to bend specific policies in accommodating directions through campaign contributions and lobbyist connections.

The concept of outside influence has changed over the years. In the state's early days, the Southern Pacific Railroad enjoyed immense influence on matters important to its needs. Indeed, the SP ran the state like a well-oiled engine.[3] But that overwhelming political clout collapsed with the arrival of automobiles and trucking. From the 1920s on, emerging industries and other groups turned to lobbyists as their connections with legislators and other policymakers.

In those days, the legislature met on a part-time basis. With lawmakers earning next to nothing, lobbyists exchanged campaign contributions and other favors for votes and other deals on an as needed basis. Artie Samish, a legislative clerk-turned-lobbyist became the prototype for today's generation of lobbyists.[4] In a rather simple way by today's standards, the job of Samish and his colleagues was to gain legislative acceptance of their ideas through a highly effective combination of money and persuasion. He had files on every important policymaker, taking great care to provide for his whims and seize any weaknesses.

The process remains the same today, although the format is not as crude or direct. Most of the obvious lobbying activity stems from well-organized groups like the Chamber of Commerce, professional associations, and unions. Environmental groups, self-professed public interest groups like Common Cause and single-interest groups like Mothers Against Drunk Driving (MADD) and the California chapter of the National Rifle Association (NRA) also weigh in with their demands. Even local governments lobby the state. Today, thousands of these groups exist in California, but they have been joined by individuals and small collections of people who sometimes can be just as influential in securing attention to their concerns.

Individuals, corporations, and larger groups and trade associations can be laser-like in having their way, whether by convincing policymakers to grant their narrow requests or by thwarting the threatening intentions of others. Most concern themselves with their needs and their needs alone, preferring to slice up the state's policymaking environment with the skills of a pizza baker, with each slice chewed up by its own special interest constituency. Only we're not talking about one political pizza, but a huge kitchen of pizzas sliced and diced in dizzying fashion. The ordinary individual has neither an understanding nor concern for these seemingly arcane activities, which, more times than not, are far removed from public attention. Yet the outcomes, while stunning for those who know how to work the "system," are often very harmful to the well-being of California.

The explosion of special interests is not without reason. Government is a lot more multifaceted these days than in years past. A sophisticated economy, expanded legislative and executive branch responsibilities, and the growth of bureaucracies to carry out thousands of new laws reflecting these changes have transformed the roles of private interests as well. Their reach often extends throughout many sectors of government simultaneously. As a result, there are more potential recipients of political influence and increasing numbers of interests with specialized needs.

There's another almost bizarre twist to this changing relationship: the enduring power of special interests. With no elections or term limits to worry about, they and their minions are permanent fixtures of the state; their spokespeople are always nearby on a virtual 24/7 basis. Elected policymakers are not permanent, thanks to term limits; their temporary presence increases the difficulty of gaining political traction and sufficient expertise to better judge the demands of special interests. That unbalanced political equation gives special interests the upper hand in policymaking. So powerful are these forces that they are often referred to as the "Third House" of the state legislature alongside the senate and assembly. How's that for an eye-opener?

These days special interests have new powerful weapons in their influence arsenal. Money and arm-twisting are as important as ever, but the ever-growing transparency of such efforts can sometimes cause embarrassment and temporary setbacks. Yet, new rules and technologies have more than offset awkward situations. The Internet has phenomenal capabilities for special interests in areas from fundraising to messaging. In addition, the ability of special interests to manipulate the voters through the well-intentioned tools of direct democracy has further tilted the political process in the direction of the powerful, not always but on enough occasions to dramatically alter public policies as well as important revenue-raising and spending arrangements. Add these two capabilities to the already well-financed positions of special interests and an often-ignorant electorate and you have the makings of a state that often benefits the desires of the few while ignoring the needs of the many. That's vintage California.

Special interests don't always get their way. Sometimes two or more with conflicting objectives battle each other for the attention of public policy-makers, with the legislature or other public authorities refusing to referee the contest. On other occasions, the national government prevents a powerful private interest from having its way because its objective clashes with the national interest. There are also times when the public sees through an effort of an individual or group to have its way via direct democracy. And every once in a while, a group or individual is actually caught going beyond traditional activities in the form of illegal behavior. All these instances occur in California, although the collective power of special interests remains substantial.

In the remaining sections of this chapter, we delve into the intricate web of special interests at work in California. Like the often-elaborate mesh-work of their eight-legged friends, interest group webs are deceivingly sticky and adept at disarming their unsuspecting prey. We will see that while California's framers formed three co-equal branches to govern the state, their relationships are often inconsequential because of the ability of non-elected lobbyists and other communication specialists to control the political system with greater success than those who are in "official" positions of authority.

A POROUS POLICYMAKING ENVIRONMENT

Think of those water-filled bowls at county fairs, each housing a goldfish. They're likely to go absolutely nowhere because of the far distance from which the individual tossing the ping pong ball attempts to capture the prize. But imagine if that person was hovering right over the bowl prior to dropping his ball; absent a strong gust of wind, he'd have a pretty good shot at walking away with his coveted goldfish. That's what happens with special interests in California. The best-organized and influential interests fulfill their objectives with great regularity in the form of favorable legislative and regulatory policy outcomes. Why? Because they hover over the policymakers without hesitation, always keeping their eyes on the prize.

California is a perfect target for special interests. State government is a seemingly endless array of overlapping, redundant centers of power that rarely function in a complementary fashion. This collective means of "organization" distributes responsibilities for policymaking in so many hands that the institutions are easily penetrated by outside forces for their own uses. In fact, the nature of the system is a virtual invitation for interest groups' intervention from beyond the official walls of the policymaking arena. What makes it also so inviting are the multiple entry points, any one of which may be exploited by the special interest for promotion of its agenda, particularly if it is focused on prevention of legislative activity.

Overlap in the Legislature

The legislature is a good place to begin. During any given two-year session, each house operates with about two dozen "standing," or permanent committees, with each member assigned to three or four. A few of these committees are divided into subcommittees to delve into specialized topics within the general responsibilities of the committee. In addition, each house has about 40 "select committees" that conduct research on issues and follow up with recommendations to the standing committees. Although they're intended to be temporary, most of the select committees assume a near-permanent status. With more than 60 policy-framing units in each house, the result is incredible fragmentation and overlap at the same time.

Here's a real illustration from the 2011–2012 organization of the California state assembly. To begin with, of the 24 standing committees, three focus on various aspects of health care: the Committee on Aging and Long-Term Care, the Committee on Health, and the Committee on Human Services. Each committee has a staff dedicated to supporting its research and policy-recommending responsibilities. In addition, three select committees deal with several properties of health care: the Select Committee on Disabilities, the Select Committee on Healthcare Workforce and Access to Care, and the Select Committee on State Hospital Safety. As if these jurisdictional overlaps aren't confusing enough, the Assembly Budget Committee has six subcommittees, one of which is the Subcommittee on Health and Human Services. Matters are only slightly better in the state Senate, which assigns responsibilities for health-related issues to three separate committees, two select committees, and one subcommittee of the Budget and Fiscal Review Committee.

All told, 13 different legislative units deal with health care, each with its own staff, competing objectives, and overlapping responsibilities, and each with its own turf to protect. Each of the many interests associated with health care—physicians, nurses, insurance companies, hospital organizations, elder care providers, AARP, and disabilities groups, to name a few—attach themselves to the committees or subcommittees where they feel the most kinship. The same complexity exists with other policy areas such as public education, transportation, business development, labor, and environmental resources management. It's a circus, with special interests often playing the role of ringmaster.

The legislative intersection between interest groups can lead to some interesting outcomes, often at the expense of the public. Case in point: Current state law separates eye examination clinics from facilities that manufacture eyeglasses. The law exists to prevent any possible collusion between eye health professionals (optometrists and ophthalmologists) and eyeglass providers. In February 2011, Assembly member Toni Atkins introduced AB 778, a bill that would allow optical manufacturing companies to have a doctor on site to provide eye examinations and prescriptions—a sort of one-stop shopping facility for eye care. Atkins offered the legislation to make it easier "to help people get the eye care they deserve."[5] Really?

Over the next three months, Luxotica, the world's largest eyewear company and its well-known subsidiary, LensCrafters, spent more than $60,000 on lobbying for AB 778—as much money as the company had spent on lobbying during the previous four years.[6] Recipients of Luxotica contributions included the chairs of three Assembly committees through which the bill traveled. Assembly Speaker John Perez also received a handsome contribution; it never hurts to attend to the speaker, generally viewed as the most powerful person in the legislature. The bill passed all three committees before sailing through the Assembly by a vote of 55 to 5 in May. But the story didn't end there.

Opponents to the legislation included the California Optometric Association (COA), which argued that the policy change would compromise the independence of optometrists. During the first sixth months of 2011, COA spent $120,000 on lobbying activities, including campaign donations to the chair of the Senate Business, Professions, Economic Development Committee and three members of the Health Committee—both of which were slated to hold hearings on AB 778.[7] For reasons never disclosed, the bill was withdrawn from Senate consideration.

Often, interest group lobbyists make their cases to committee staff members, who may have considerable influence with legislators. It goes without saying that legislators depend upon staff for substantive knowledge as well as their understanding of the political process. The problem is that in the post-Proposition 140 (term limits) environment, staffers are much less seasoned than they were years ago.[8] Many of the best and brightest have become lobbyists themselves, leaving those remaining little more than political putty for the special interests. Nevertheless, staffers frequently interact with lobbyists. As one account by a California Nurses Association lobbyist explains, "Strong relationships with the legislators, their staff and other lobbyists are really the key. This is how you share information, this is how you stay on top of things."[9]

For their part, inexperienced legislators—a staple in the term limits era—welcome interest group assistance. One newly elected legislator recently recalled how a lobbyist approached him about a bill in his committee before the legislature even knew he was assigned to that committee![10] Another new legislator added, "We rely on input from the Third House in sponsoring bills because they have so much experience."[11] Multiply that kind of interaction by more than 1,000 lobbyists and you get a sense of the questionable frenetic activity that takes place.

In fact, interest groups don't only prey on inexperienced legislators; sometimes they go straight to the top, virtually bypassing the legislative process altogether except for the final outcome. That's what happened in 2011. In the midst of a horrible state budget mess that drastically reduced state funding for public schools, the California Teachers Association persuaded state Senate President Pro Tem Darrell Steinberg to enact a law that barred any teacher layoffs for the coming fiscal year because of reduced funding. The new law was passed without a single committee hearing in either house. And how would strapped districts be able to maintain all of their teachers with less money? The same law permitted districts to reduce the school year by a full week, if necessary.[12] That was the trade-off: teacher security for fewer school days. Who wins there?

With so many pressure points in California's legislative process, special interests don't have to plug all or even most vulnerable areas. All they have to do is probe for the weakest link—a few members of single committees or their staffers to fall into line with an interest group's policy objectives— and the rest is likely to be history. It's a part of the policymaking process that few even know about, and fewer know how to manipulate.

Overlap in the Governor's Office

Earlier we lamented that California was more a state of executive *branches* than a simple executive branch. That's because each office has its own election separate from the others. State law doesn't allow for voters to select a "straight party" ticket, the same political party for each executive branch nominee. And nowadays, the "Top Two" primary system further undermines any sense of party cohesion. In the general election, the governor and lieutenant governor run independently, a circumstance found only in 18 other states. As an indicator of even more confusion, the three money offices in the executive branch divide responsibilities among the controller, treasurer, and Board of Equalization. No wonder so many people cringe at the thought of voting. Because of these rules and outcomes, the lack of policy coordination is almost a given.

That's bad enough, but there's another level of confusion, and that's the many layers of power and influence within the governor's office. In all, the governor's office contains 93 different state agencies and departments—93 pressure points. To no one's surprise, many of these overlap with one another, similarly to the problems in the legislature. For example, somehow the Environmental Protection Agency (EPA) operates independently of the Natural Resources Agency. Within the EPA is the Office of Environmental Health Hazard Assessment, and within the Natural Resources Agency is the Department of Resources and Recovery. More duplication and more opportunities for leverage. And so it goes with many other service areas such as the Department of Managed Health Care, found in the Business, Transportation and Housing Agency, and the Department of Health Care Services, located in the Health and Human Services Agency. Dozens of other duplicative offices exist as well.

Of course, ask any of the department heads in these and the other executive branch units, and they will describe at tedious length the many circumstances and responsibilities that justify their existence. Some of these offices deserve to remain in place, but surely others are unnecessary or at least could be folded into what appear to be duplicative bodies of authority. But such discussion is really beside the point. The overlap in responsibilities and power is what counts. For special interests, this fragmented authority gives them the numerous openings they need to have their way. They tend to seek out rulings or interpretations of laws from those agencies that seem closest to their own values, often setting up conflicts within the state's executive branch.

Getting Someone on the Inside

Examples abound. In 2004, shortly after Arnold Schwarzenegger was elected governor, lobbyists for the California Restaurant Association (CRA) approached administration officials about re-writing a regulation requiring restaurant employers to provide two breaks and a meal for workers during their shifts. These breaks were cutting into their profits. The business interest group had contributed substantially to Schwarzenegger's gubernatorial campaign in 2003, and now wanted a return on its investment.

Where to go for relief? They might have appealed to the Office of Administrative Law, the executive branch agency responsible for reviewing administrative regulations, but they had no allies there. Instead, the restaurant industry petitioners sought relief from the Labor and Workforce Development Agency, where a former CRA lobbyist had been appointed to an administrative post and now lobbied for the change from the inside. Even that effort met resistance. The agency's chief counsel, a 15-year employee, balked at the request to water down the break provision, contending that it would be deleterious to the well-being of the employees. But the CRA persisted. Within a few months, the obstructionist bureaucrat was removed from his post and an emergency regulation eliminating the rule was put into place.[13] Score one for the CRA working its will via the bureaucracy.

Redefining Regulations

Sometimes, it's a matter of redefining existing rules rather than replacing them. During his run for the governorship, Arnold Schwarzenegger received substantial campaign contributions from developers and other industries related to land use. In April 2005, three business groups, the California Building Industry, the California Business Properties Association, and the California Chamber of Commerce, wrote to the governor requesting major changes in the California Environmental Quality Act, whose regulations they considered an obstacle to economic growth because of onerous regulations that led to costly construction delays.[14]

Schwarzenegger, himself, had expressed similar concerns in his 2005 State of the State address earlier in the year. Environmental groups such as the Sierra Club and the Planning and Conservation League fretted over possible changes but took comfort knowing that they had allies in the legislature.[15] Of course, that assumes that changes would come through the legislature. They did not.

In December 2009, the California Natural Resources Agency redefined a series of regulations in an effort "to reduce the costs of environmental review."[16] Environmentalists were aghast, referring to the new regulations as "a willy-nilly approach to environmental review [that] offers favors to those with political or financial clout, and shrouds the process in secrecy."[17] They had supporters elsewhere in the administration, particularly in the Environmental Protection Agency, but that was not the route taken by friends of the developers. Ironically, these changes occurred in the shadow of AB 32, said to be the most forward-looking environmental legislation of its time.

Cluttered Bureaucracy Equals Chaotic Policymaking

Bureaucracies exist to carry out specific functions of government. But with so many overlapping agencies in the governor's office, there often are numerous paths to making rules and regulations on the same issue. Special interests understand the maze better than anyone does. They not only know what battles to pick, but also the best routes to take en route to victory.

Independent Agencies, Boards, and Regulatory Commissions

As mentioned earlier, California has more than 300 independent agencies, boards, and regulatory commissions. Some examples include the California Horse Racing Board, the California State Athletic Commission, and the California Fish and Game Commission. Typically, the commissioners are appointed by the governor and serve without the need for senate confirmation. These regulators are generally appointed because of their expertise, passion, and commitment to their specific industries. Most of these government units are assigned narrow responsibilities, meet on a sporadic basis, and are governed by members who receive token honoraria of $50 or $100 per meeting. If they're doing it for the money, they had better be keeping their day jobs, that's for sure.

But there are about a dozen or so boards and commissions in California with major policymaking responsibilities that affect large swaths of the public. These organizations have been created to manage controversial policy areas free of politics. Over the years, however, they have become employment centers for ex-legislators, prominent individuals, and generous campaign contributors. Often they bring little expertise to their appointments, which casts even more doubt on the value of their appointments.

The members of these prominent boards and commissions are nominated to four-year terms by the governor and serve only with confirmation of the state senate. Their organizations often have large staffs; members receive annual salaries in excess of $100,000, and often meet only two or three times per month. For example, the Agricultural Labor Relations Board, a five-member body, oversees employment practices in the fields; typically, the board schedules one meeting per month. Appointees are paid $128,907 annually. The California State Water Resources Control Board, another public agency directed by appointed members, oversees the allocation of water to various public purchasing units and monitors the quality of California water. Appointees to this five-member body receive $132,179 annually. This organization schedules two public meetings per month but has an extensive record of cancelations.

As independent policymaking bodies, these units are intended to be "above politics" and removed from legislative control. Yet, despite their appearance of isolation, major boards and commissions are targets for interest group activity. Add to that the combination of few meetings and high pay, and you can see why some elements of California fail to pass the "smell" test.

Turnabout of the PUC

One organization with wide-ranging policy responsibilities is the five-member California Public Utilities Commission (PUC). Originally created as the California Railroad Commission in 1879 to regulate the out-of-control railroad industry, the commission was quickly overrun by railroad-friendly appointees. Although the railroad's domination was relatively brief, for the 30 years following creation of the commission, the transportation entity secured commission approval on virtually every rate request.[18] The regulatory environment changed dramatically after the elections of 1910, when Hiram Johnson and the Progressives were ushered into power. The Progressives broadened the commission's responsibilities to include services such as electricity and water and renamed the body the Public Utilities Commission. Today, it is one of the state's most important independent agencies with responsibilities for regulating privately owned electric, natural gas, telecommunications, water, railroad, rail transit, and passenger transportation companies—all in ways that protect consumers with reasonable rates and reliable service.

The commission has five members, each appointed to six-year terms at annual salaries of $128,109. The commission meets on an average of once every three weeks. As of 2011, three of the five members had extensive backgrounds as utilities executives—a cause of concern to those who worry about independence from the industry.

Because the PUC regulates so many avenues of commerce and business behavior, businesses and consumer groups that are impacted by the PUC's decisions constantly attempt to make themselves heard in the hope of receiving favorable treatment. One recent skirmish occurred over cell phone policies. In 2004, the consumer-friendly PUC whose members were appointed by former governor Gray Davis developed a "Bill of Rights" for cell phone users on issues including service contracts, marketing practices, billing, and late payments.[19] The action set off a war between interest groups. The Consumers Union heralded the change as a "victory for consumers." Governor Schwarzenegger chastised the PUC for overreaching its regulatory responsibilities and threatening California's jobs environment.[20] The industry had spent millions on the Schwarzenegger campaign, but the PUC remained unfriendly because of its composition. Soon that would change.

Over time, Schwarzenegger was able to replace outgoing PUC commissioners with his own appointments. The organization's values underwent a transformation. By 2005, the PUC had a majority friendly to Schwarzenegger's pro-business ideas. The commissioners suspended the new rules and adopted a new set concerning termination of contracts, contract transfers to different carriers, and protocols for disputes over bills "more palatable to the [telecommunications] industry."[21] Consumer groups complained that the industry was irresponsible; industry representatives argued that the newness of the field demanded "responsible" regulations. Within another 18 months, the Commission deregulated all aspects of cell phone service.

The California Gambling Control Commission and Building from the Bottom Up

California has a great record of periodically adding more commissions to the state's governing structure, while rarely eliminating any. These new units reflect the state's growing complexity and the unwillingness or inability of the legislature to govern the new activities. This in itself is a sad commentary on the political capacity limitations of California's lawmakers.

The California Gambling Control Commission is the most recent addition to the state's regulatory bodies. The voters created the commission as part of an agreement to permit Indian casinos in California. Indian gaming came into its own in 2000 after years of disputes between the tribes and state and national government leaders over whether "sovereign" Indian nations in California could offer gaming without government intervention,[22] with an agreement between then-Governor Gray Davis and several dozen Native American tribes. The tribes had been very generous to Davis' gubernatorial campaign in 1998 and Davis, following the leadership of previous Governor Pete Wilson, negotiated a gaming compact. The state's voters approved the deal on two occasions, in 2000 and 2002. Under the terms of the compact, Indian tribes are allocated about 65,000 slot machines throughout the state as well as other table games in casinos located in rural areas. The state receives little money from the $7 billion annually generated, except a couple of hundred million dollars designated as state gambling addiction funds. Courtesy of Indian gaming, California now has 30 percent of the nation's receipts, with next to no taxes to show for it.

But the most intriguing element of the compact is the "regulatory environment" that oversees tribal gaming activity. Created as part of the agreement, the California Gambling Control Commission is intended to oversee casino activities and assure operations devoid of manipulation or criminal elements. As with other major state regulatory organizations, the commission members are nominated by the governor and confirmed by a majority of the state senate. So far, so good.

But here's where things got murky with Davis. As part of the arrangement to guarantee sympathetic regulation, Davis agreed to give representatives of Indian tribes the right to choose at least two commission members. That's like allowing drug makers to determine the safety of their products or tobacco companies to decide the extent to which their goods are harmful to smokers. In the words of a political reform authority, "it's beyond the perception of propriety...It's an incredible sellout."[23] Not so, according to a tribes representative, who responded (with a straight face!), "I think it's an excellent idea. Nobody understands the issues better than the tribes themselves."[24] And that's exactly the problem: Indian representatives regulating Indian gaming is the political counterpart to the fox guarding the chicken coop. Only in this case, no feathers are ruffled.

Independent Regulatory Units: Not So Independent After All

Beginning with the Railroad Commission in 1879, Californians have viewed designed regulatory bodies as policymaking units above politics. But that's often not the case. As soon as the Railroad Commission was created, individuals from the industry were appointed to serve on the board, putting a quick end to its independence.[25] Conditions are not much different today with many "independent" boards and commissions inasmuch as many appointees are from the industries they are supposed to regulate. Nevertheless, commissioners make decisions that often escape public scrutiny. And because they are appointees, these policymakers are not accountable to voters or anyone else. That doesn't seem right.

There's another problem with the commission arrangement: The most important objective of this "hands off" arrangement has been for regulators to consider issues for the public good in a manner beyond the reach of those industries or services they regulate. But special interests don't subscribe to this separation. As far as they are concerned, anyone or any institution that has the capability to exercise power over their domain is fair game. As a result, much of the time special interests have their way, leading to a "win" for private interests and a "loss" for the general public.

SPECIAL INTERESTS AND THEIR TOOLS

In the never-ending struggles between private interests and the public good, those with targeted objectives for their members rely upon an assorted arsenal of political weapons to secure success. Among their instruments are the effective uses of money, utilization of expertise, manipulation of the policymaking body by someone on the inside, maneuvering via the Internet, and promotion of direct democracy. Rarely do these forces seeking to protect their beneficiaries employ one tool exclusively over all the others. Instead, special interests commonly rely upon a combination of these ingredients to achieve their objectives, whether to make policy or to block it. The costs of failure are too great to bear.

To be sure, some groups have many more weapons of persuasion at their disposal than others. Although their apparent advantage doesn't always translate into victory, it's typically better than not to have such advantages at a group's disposal.

Money

In politics, it's hard to overestimate the value of currency. That's because money is a versatile political tool that can be used for everything from the hiring of staff to the promotion of a message. Regarding personnel alone, money provides campaign directors, organizers on the ground, fundraisers, speechwriters, and pollsters; it also covers communications equipment, voter contact lists, and general day-to-day expenses.

Money also lubricates the flow of ideas between interest groups and policymakers. Legislators, particularly, are dependent upon interest group campaign contributions and advice—the two usually go together. It's also contributed to a legislature whose members are guided more by direct campaign contributions than by party philosophy, which makes policymaking outcomes difficult to manage. With this divide-and-conquer mentality, special interests have greatly reduced the importance of party leaders, who find it difficult for them to compete for attention. Organized agriculture has learned this lesson well. With farmers comprising a very small, if vital portion of an increasingly urban state, farm interest groups have shown an uncanny ability to cobble together legislative relationships that cross party lines.[26]

There are other ways to influence other than going directly to an elected official or staff member. Conferences and other getaways are particularly valuable because they give lobbyists and policymakers the opportunity to bond in a focused way.[27] During a recent three-year period, lobbyists spent $700,000 to be with policymakers at conferences.[28] Then there's the abstract, yet politically useful tool of general support. From the days of former Governor George Deukmejian to current Governor Jerry Brown, state chief executives have benefitted from the California State Protocol Foundation, a privately funded organization with a fancy name that funds housing, travel, and other expenses not funded by the state.[29] Countless other groups attempt to influence through donations that extend from legislators' favorite charities to "educational trips."

Usually, these donations are routinely reported, lest donors find themselves running afoul of the law. But it really doesn't matter because few observers ever pay close attention, thanks to the glut of data, the cumbersome reporting systems divided between the Secretary of State's office and Fair Political Practices Commission, and short attention span of the public. Sure, once in a while a dedicated reporter will spend an inordinate amount of time digging into obscure records that most people never heard of for possibly questionable relationships between interest groups or powerful individuals and government officials, but such efforts are rare and the impact unfortunately brief. Otherwise, the result is a policymaking environment guided by clout first, and values a distant second, further diminishing the ability of elected officials to act in the name of the public good.

Money is critical to special interests during political campaigns, whether in terms of candidates' campaigns or statewide ballot propositions. Groups impacted by the state's revenue collection and spending practices spend voluminous amounts that most individuals can't get close to matching. During 2010 alone, electric utilities spent close to $52 million, followed by public sector unions, which spent almost $46 million, and general trade unions, which added another $46 million. Insurance groups, environmental groups, oil and gas associations, securities interests, public education groups, television and movie interests, real estate, and high technology representatives all added to the mix.[30] Anyone who has direct interest in the state's policies mobilizes to make their case; if they fail to do so, they're likely to lose out to others who do.

Besides campaigns, interest group money goes to places that might influence voters as well as elected officials. A single full-page campaign ad in the *Los Angeles Times* will cost $70,000 or more.[31] A single week of television ads up and down the state will cost at least $3 million.[32] With controversial campaigns often lasting several months, you can see how the money adds up fast, and the simple fact is that some groups are much better at generating the necessary funds than others. In California politics, the squeaky wheel may not always get the oil, but it can generate enough noise to easily drown out the competition.

Expertise

Money goes a long way for special interests, but other resources can be very important to their influence arsenal as well. Of course, many organizations have stables of experts who conduct research for their causes. Such individuals provide a certain amount of clout, although their very employment often implies bias. Special interests know this, so many have rounded out their capabilities by bringing in former legislators, former bureaucrats, and former journalists to help promote credibility.

Former Legislators

Term limits guarantee that legislative and executive office careers in California are relatively short. Sure, a few politicians have made a career of hopping from one elected office to another—Gray Davis was such an example through successive elections to the state assembly, controller, lieutenant governor, and ultimately governor over a span of more than 20 years. But few leaders at the state level are able to last so long for a variety of reasons. Given their relatively short lives in public office, many termed out elected officials continue their careers in politics by becoming lobbyists or spokespersons for organized interests. Now, just a small step from official centers of power, legislators-turned-lobbyists are able to get through barriers encountered by others to make their case before legislators and relevant staff members.

California law requires ex-legislators to wait one year before becoming lobbyists. After that, they are free to do as wish. And they do, frequently hooking up with trade associations or other special interests with concerns parallel to the legislators' expertise. For example, in 2006 a state senator cast a key vote against physician-assisted suicide, reflecting the position taken by the California Medical Association (CMA). Three months after he retired, the now ex-legislator joined the CMA as its executive director. Another legislator specializing in entertainment-related issues joined the world's largest talent agency upon his "retirement." Moreover, this turnstile behavior is not restricted to former legislators. Inside the governor's office, the legislative affairs secretary—the key individual for monitoring all sensitive bills going through the legislative process—left to join a law firm whose members constantly interact with the legislature.[33] Another former deputy chief of staff for former governor Gray Davis left to quarterback government relations for PG&E, only to return as a top staffer for Governor Jerry Brown. Now that's moving! A recent study by the Center for Public Integrity found that in 2005, a typical year, 35 former state legislators were registered lobbyists.[34] And that number doesn't count the dozens of others who joined interest groups in other capacities.

Former Bureaucrats

In their capacity as policy researchers and implementers, bureaucrats learn a lot about the ins and outs of making policies work. Much of their work borders on the arcane, but it's important work nonetheless. All this occurs in what Anthony Downs refers to as the effort to "achieve the formal goals of the organization,"[35] whether its objectives have been established by the legislature, executive branch, or other policymaking authority. Along the way, many bureaucrats amass considerable expertise in their efforts to do their jobs. That expertise has value not only to those who expect the work to be carried out, but also to those who would thwart it, all of which leads to the intersection between bureaucrats and special interests.

On occasion, bureaucrats leave state employment to work for the "other side," where they can earn more money under better working conditions. Changing sides can help opponents immensely. In the late 1990s and early years of the 21st century, a major chemical pesticide consulting firm, Jellinek, Schwartz and Connolly, beefed up its practice by hiring several national and state environmental experts, one of whom was head of regulation for the California Department of Pesticide Regulation.[36] That hire allowed for the transfer of knowledge as well as the ability of the ex-bureaucrat to lobby former co-workers.

One recent example of a bureaucrat-turned-special interest advocate occurred in 2005 when the former chief enforcement officer of the California Department of Corporations joined the California Certified Financial Planner Board, an industry group. Said the CEO, the former administrator's "experience as a policy, enforcement and administrative leader in California state government will serve her well at CFB Board...."[37]

Industry groups love to pick the brains of former bureaucrats. Who better to know how the state will execute the laws?

Former Staffers

Unlike bureaucrats, staffers are temporary employees; they serve at the pleasure of the legislators who hire them. Whether working for a specific legislator or committee, these employees are dedicated to the objectives of those who employ them. Their loyalties notwithstanding, staffers often know a good deal about the policymaking process and policy areas where they toil. They are valuable agents of support with great reservoirs of knowledge. Unlike legislators who must wait a year before they take up lobbying activities, staffers have no interval restraint.

In recent years, the uncertainty of employment because of term limits has exacerbated this "brain drain."[38] When former staffers move to the private sector, they not only transfer allegiance but also bring immense amounts of knowledge about what they do and how such efforts can be stopped. Such changes also leave the legislature with reduced depth.

For their part, interest groups routinely boast of their access to the legislative process via former staffers and others. As one organization puts it, "Our experienced lobbyists have decades of service in the State Legislature as both elected officials and top staff...." Adds another, "After years of working in state politics and alongside many administrations, [the special interest] has developed relationships with numerous department agencies."

Between their knowledge and immediate availability, ex-staffers can be extremely valuable to those who hire them. For example, a few years ago, the chief policy aide for a Republican speaker of the Assembly left to head political operations for the California Dental Association without missing a beat. Similarly, the press secretary for a Democratic senate president pro tem joined the California Professional Firefighters as its legislative director. The list goes on. Interest groups know that the best way to tap into the system is by working with people from the system.

Former Journalists

Retired news reporters are also important resources to interest groups. As people who have mined all kinds of sources for their stories, journalists develop an expertise in connecting the policymaking dots. These communication specialists don't always lobby, but their experiences in the field contribute to the overall preparation of interest groups in their efforts to communicate issues either to key policymakers or larger audiences. As wordsmiths, former journalists know how to tell their stories in the most compelling ways. In short, former journalists can add a valuable dimension to the ability of an organization to influence the policymaking process.

Most former journalists prepare interest group representatives through backgrounders or media training, but a few actually operate on the front lines of lobbying. One former newspaper reporter-turned-lobbyist has become a legend of sorts. For his public policy influencing successes, Sam Singer was described as "The Fixer" by the *San Jose Mercury News*. Another paper, the *San Francisco Chronicle*, called the lobbyist a "Top Gun for Hire." These descriptions may not be complimentary, but they scream success to interest groups that want their cases made in the most powerful way.

The Internet

Now for a fast-moving story: the Internet. It's "fast-moving" because in a relatively short period, the Internet has exploded on the scene as a major means of communication, but in more ways than you think. Millions of Californians are online every day, using email, paying bills, and instant messaging with their friends and colleagues. Maybe you connect on a regular basis with some of the more than 1 billion Facebook users the world over. Yes, the Internet has become a ubiquitous communications instrument for modern society.

What you may not know is the extent to which the Internet has emerged as a cornerstone of political activity here and elsewhere. In today's world, the Internet is critical both from the standpoints of communicating themes and collecting campaign contributions.

Getting the Word Out

With just about everyone having access to a computer or smart phone, the Internet allows for mass communication on the reader's schedule. Unlike TV ads, which are shown at specific times, or newspapers ads, which have huge costs and inattentive audiences, the Internet is an inexpensive tool with an incredible reach. Bloggers, candidates, government agencies, and interest groups are among the many users who clog the Internet with political information. In 2010, Democrat Jerry Brown declared his candidacy for the governorship via the Internet, rather than the traditional press conference. Increasingly, political statements are made on such sites as Facebook, Twitter, and You Tube. Of course, filtering out the truth can be difficult at times. Much of what appears online is inaccurate, or worse yet untrue, but it doesn't keep people from logging on and reading interesting entries.

Perhaps the most dramatic use of the Internet in California occurred with the successful recall effort of Governor Gray Davis in 2003. Of the previous 31 efforts to recall a California governor, none had come close to being successful, and for good reason. Under the state's recall formula, recall sponsors were required to collect petition signatures from 897,158 registered voters in 160 days, 12 percent of the number who voted in the 2002 gubernatorial effort, an awfully big nut even in California. When the recall campaign against Davis began in March 2003, proponents had energy but little traction. Sure, a few conservative talk show hosts had been complaining long before Davis was re-elected in 2002, but they appeared more as gadflies than political revolutionaries. The Internet gave Davis's enemies the voice they needed to make their case, and make it they did.

Early into the campaign, two anti-Davis websites were created. One website (www.davisrecall.com) was the work of Ted Costa, head of the People's Advocate, an anti-tax organization originally founded by Howard Jarvis ally Paul Gann. The other (www.recallgraydavis.com) was set up by Sal Russo and Howard Kaloogian, two conservative Republican consultants who later became prominent members of the Tea Party movement. Both organizations called people to action and put recall petitions on their sites. Costa claimed that within weeks 1 million people downloaded recall petitions.[39] Russo reported 450,000 petition downloads as well as 20 million Internet hits to his organization's site.[40] Assuming both accounts are close to accurate, about 1.5 million petitions reached the public, and while we'll never know how many were signed through the Internet route, it's reasonable to believe that the websites had considerable impact on the recall campaign. From such public exposure came additional contributions, $2 million alone from conservative Republican Congressman Darrell Issa. But make no mistake about it, the Internet was crucial to disseminating recall information and petitions for pennies on the dollar, compared to traditional signature-gathering at shopping malls or neighborhood signature collection drives.

Messaging for Dollars

Prior to the Internet, candidates and campaign organizations spent sizable percentages of their resources raising funds at campaign events such as dinners or rallies. When they reached out to potential contributors for campaign funds, the candidates' phone banking teams would "dial for dollars." These efforts remain staples for campaigns but they have been joined by Internet solicitations.

As of 2009, 8 percent of all Internet users received political information online.[41] That percentage has grown over time and has led candidates to invest in online solicitations. In 2010, Internet experts estimated that candidates for various elected offices in California would spend about $50 million on Internet advertising, or about 2 percent of all of their campaign expenses.[42] The question is, how much did they get back in return? Jerry Brown alone raised at least $1 million via the Internet.[43] ActBlue, a Democratic online fundraising company, raised even more, $1.2 million for Barbara Boxer's re-election bid, as well as more than $600,000 in Russ Warner's unsuccessful bid to unseat Republican Congressman David Dreier. For California Democratic congressional candidates alone, ActBlue raised more than $1.5 million in online contributions.[44] While Republicans didn't have the same online organizational presence, they had their moments. U.S. Senate candidate Carly Fiorina led the way with $5 million raised online to get her through a difficult primary and on to a general election defeat against Barbara Boxer, according to an online fundraising company.[45]

The Internet is not likely to replace television in the near future as the major center for campaign activity. That's because in 2010, candidates spent 35 times as much on television as the Internet to get out their messages.[46] Still, as Internet use grows by leaps and bounds, this means of communications is only likely to grow in stature in the years to come.

Direct Democracy

Direct democracy is part of the political bedrock of California. Poll after poll shows that Californians revere this concept of citizen participation in the policymaking process, whether through the initiative, referendum, or recall.[47] At the same time, surveys show that Californians are almost equally divided about the merits of what comes out of the process.[48] But whereas Californians may be of two minds, interest groups clearly have found benefits from direct democracy, particularly with either supporting or opposing initiatives.

Special interests appreciate the three links associated with direct democracy: the drafting stage, the qualification stage, and the campaigning stage.[49] Whereas the average voter knows little about these ballot measures other than the noise on television or the campaign ads taken out in the local newspaper, interest groups attempt to influence the process in one, two, or all three of these political moments, depending upon the nature of the issue. And they often succeed, particularly when it comes to generating defeat of a proposal that threatens their well-being.

The Drafting Stage

The actual drafting of an initiative is an esoteric experience far removed from the public realm. It's when sponsors present the official language of the proposal to the state attorney general. If the proposed initiative has no glaring unconstitutional elements or is not overtly misleading, the attorney general usually certifies the proposed initiative for signature circulation.

Esoteric or not, this stage is hardly a benign or antiseptic moment. Special interests often work very hard to label their proposals with titles far from their intent. For example, in 2010, major oil interests presented to the attorney general a proposed initiative called "California Jobs Initiative," which sought to suspend AB 32, California's historic energy reduction law until the unemployment rate in California dropped to 5.5 percent for an entire year. The proposal was incredibly unrealistic, given that unemployment at the time hovered at 12 percent. But here's the most important point: far from any concern about jobs, proponents were worried about the costs to them associated with California's new strict emissions reduction law.[50] In a rare moment of public awareness, the voters defeated the measure.

The Qualification Stage

The qualification stage is also distant from most voters, although the participation of some is critical to assure success. During this period, sponsors of the initiative must collect enough valid signatures over a 150-day period to qualify the proposal for the next election—5 percent of the voters in the previous gubernatorial election for a simple law and 8 percent if the sponsors are promoting a constitutional amendment. Most proposals fail to qualify because of the difficulty in collecting enough signatures.

But powerful interests can carry sway at this point by paying people to do the job. Chances are when you see someone at the shopping mall collecting signatures, that individual will be paid anywhere between $3 and $10 for each signature. Payment amounts depend on the seriousness of the issue and the supporters behind it. The organizations behind proposed initiatives are too smart to hire signature gatherers directly, so they rely upon petition specialist companies to do the job for them. These companies specialize in "quality petition management." In the words of one signature-gathering company, "We deliver measurably higher quality signatures and bill for valid signatures only." These days, the price for gathering enough signatures hovers around $2.5 to $3 million dollars. In 2010, electricity provider PG&E gave more than $6 million to signature-gathering companies to qualify an initiative that would have made it much more difficult for municipal utilities to expand their electricity programs. (By the way, $46 million later, the initiative failed.) Simply, put, the signature-gathering deck is stacked in favor of those with the big bucks. The days of volunteers going from door to door—the original intent of direct democracy—are long gone.[51]

The Campaign Stage

The campaign stage is the most visible stage of the initiative process. That's because campaigning begins in earnest relatively close to the election, when voters are more attuned to the issues. It's the time when interest groups saturate the airwaves with commercials for, or in some cases against, a particular ballot proposal.

In recent years, some groups have spent $100 million or more on a ballot proposal to convince the voters, often with campaign messages that greatly distort the issue. The idea is very simple: take up so much space with a negative campaign that the "yes" side is simply drowned out. Tobacco, big oil, health insurance, and unions have all enjoyed the benefits of raising obscene amounts of money in turning back various revenue-collecting or reform efforts. In 2006, for example, health groups placed on the ballot Proposition 86, which would have added $2.60 to each pack of cigarettes with the funds going to hospital services, cancer treatments and tobacco prevention programs, and children's health care. Initially, the voters favored the proposition, but the tobacco companies argued *ad nauseum* and without merit that the money would go to nameless bureaucrats instead of health care.[52] The voters bought the bogus claim and defeated the initiative. Moral of the story: It's much easier to get the public to say "no" than "yes," especially when it comes to the powerful combination of initiatives and big money.

The Perils of Direct Democracy

In theory, direct democracy is terrific. Of course, when they enacted it, the Progressives assumed an enlightened electorate. Yet, today's voters are amazingly disconnected from the process only until the time to vote, when they listen to the claims of the loudest voices.

OF THE PEOPLE, BY THE PEOPLE, BUT ULTIMATELY FOR THE SPECIAL INTERESTS

The rules of governance and public policy outcomes don't square very well in California. On the one hand, at first blush the state's political arena seems open to all as a place of fairness and an enabler of public participation. On the other hand, few people care and even fewer understand the extent that the lack of public involvement allows manipulation by special interests, often at great cost to the state's citizens. As seen elsewhere, California is not the entrepreneurial "anyone can make it" environment that so many mistakenly believe. In fact, the state's political deck is stacked.

But let's be clear about one fact: Special interests aren't necessarily inherently bad or evil; at their cores, they are organizations seeking to advance the goals of their members. Fair enough. There's nothing new about that. In fact, James Madison, considered by many the father of the U.S. Constitution, wrote about the presence of special interests, described in those times as "factions," shortly after participating in the creation of the famous governing instrument.[53] Of course, while Madison worried that factions would divide us, he praised the new model at Philadelphia that would allow factions to express themselves in an environment where they would be countered or offset by others.

That's part of the problem in California. Here we simply don't have the filter or counterweight to control excesses of special interests. More times than not, the power of special interests overshadow the ability of elected leaders and regulators to act in the public good, however that may be defined. Because the policymaking environment is so weak, porous, and inefficient, some groups forge privileged positions that place them and their needs far above the rest of us.

Other institutions of government share culpability, too. When it comes to tracking campaign contributions, the synonym for futility is "California Secretary of State's Office," where the most seasoned researcher can become discouraged by a maze of unconnected materials. Such shoddy record keeping goes a long way toward obscuring any sense of record keeping transparency, regardless of any official intent.

But our problems don't begin and end only with people in official positions of authority. We are responsible for unchallenged special interests, as well. We're responsible because we don't invest the time and energy to see what's going on; instead, we blindly accept the instruction of 30-second campaign commercials as gospel, rather than sorting out the issues. We're also responsible because at the same time we turn over all responsibility to elected officials, we deny them the ability to gain expertise and act responsibility by limiting their stay in office. Would anyone limit a successful CEO to six or eight years? We duck responsibility as citizens and then criticize policymakers for not acting wisely or fairly. For these reasons, real change in California will not depend upon a new law or limitation of power. It will depend upon people—regular people like us—investing in the process. But in an environment that discourages education and public participation, it's difficult to imagine such a change.

ENDNOTES

1. "Special Interest Contributions," ArnoldWatch, http://www.arnoldwatch.org/special_interests/index.html.
2. National Institute on Money in State Politics, http://www.followthemoney.org/press/ReportView.phtml?r=452&ext=1#tableid1.
3. For a fictional account of the extent of the railroad's domination, see Frank Norris, *The Octopus: A Story of California* (New York: Doubleday & Co.), 1901.

4. Samish, who served time in prison for not reporting incomes from individual contributors and various interest groups, boasts of his success in his autobiography. See Arthur H. Samish and Bob Thomas, *The Secret Boss of California* (New York: Crown Publishers, 1971).

5. "Patient Access and Choice—AB 778," A Note from Toni, eNewsletter, Assemblywoman Toni Atkins, June 2011, Volume I, Issue 3, http://legplcms01.lc.ca.gov/PublicLCMS/images/AD76/images/June2011/Atkins_eNewsletter_06092011.htm.

6. "Eyewear Legislation Comes Into Focus, Under Scrutiny," *San Jose Mercury News*, May 16, 2011, pp. B1, B4.

7. Source: California Secretary of State, Campaign Finance: Committees, Parties, Major Donors, and Slate Mailers, http://cal-access.sos.ca.gov/Campaign/Committees/list.aspx?view=majorDonors.

8. Bruce Cain and Thad Kousser, "Adapting to Term Limits: Recent Experiences and New Directions," Public Policy Institute of California, San Francisco, CA, 2004, p. 39.

9. "Capitol Clout," *NurseWeek*, November 11, 2003.

10. "Why Lobbyists Rule the Capitol," *San Jose Mercury News*, July 19, 2010, pp. A1, A6, A7.

11. Ibid.

12. "Teacher Layoff Law Is Assailed," *Los Angeles Times*, July 10, 2011, pp. A27, A34.

13. "Documents Show Clout of Lobbyists with Governor," *San Francisco Chronicle*, September 7, 2005, pp. A1, A4.

14. "Developers See Opportunity at Gov.'s Table," *Los Angeles Times*, May 15, 2005, pp. A1, A23.

15. Ibid.

16. California Natural Resources Agency, "Final Statement of Reasons for Regulatory Action," Sacramento, CA, December 2009, p. 18.

17. Brian Leubitz, "Chipping Away at CEQA," *California Progress Report*, March 3, 2010, http://www.californiaprogressreport.com/site/?q=node/7509.

18. George E. Mowry, *The California Progressives* (Berkeley, CA: The University of California Press, 1951).

19. "PUC Sets Protection Rules for Consumers through Telecommunications Bill of Rights," press release, California Public Utilities Commission, May 27, 2004.

20. "Schwarzenegger, Wireless Industry Criticize California Telecom Rules Designed to Protect Consumers," *vision2mobile* electronic newsletter, May 28, 2004, http://www.vision2mobile.com/news/2004/05/schwarzenegger-wireless-industry-criticize-califo.aspx.

21. "Cell Phone Lobby Thwarts Reform Efforts," *San Jose Mercury News*, September 18, 2007, pp. 1A, 15A.

22. For a history of the long-simmering dispute over gambling autonomy between Native American tribes and government leaders, see Jay Michael and Dan Walters with Dan Weintraub, *The Third House: Lobbyists, Money, and Power in Sacramento* (Berkeley, CA: Berkeley Public Policy Press, 2002), pp. 66–70.

23. Gregg Jones and Miguel Bustillo, "Davis' Nod to Tribes Criticized," *Los Angeles Times*, August 30, 2003, http://articles.latimes.com/2003/aug/30/local/me-davis30.

24. Ibid.

25. Mowry, op. cit., p. 18.

26. "Bumper Crop of Clout," *Los Angeles Times*, September 22, 2004, pp. A1, A22.

27. "Donor Money Often Talks in a Whisper," *Los Angeles Times*, December 27, 2007, pp. A1, A22.

28. "Watchdog Targets Lawmaker Junkets," *San Francisco Chronicle*, February 11, 2008, pp. A1, A6.

29. Shane Goldmacher, "Private Donors Run Second Nonprofit for Brown," *Los Angeles Times*, June 25, 2011, http://articles.latimes.com/print/2011/jun/25/local/la-me-jerry-brown-20110625.

30. "Follow the Money," National Institute on Money in State Politics, http://www.followthemoney.org/database/state_overview.phtml?y=2010&s=CA.

31. "How Much Does It Cost to Advertise in Newspapers, Gaebler.com, http://www.gaebler.com/Newspaper-Advertising-Costs.htm.

32. "She's Everywhere: Whitman Blankets Calif. with Ads," msnbc.com, October 28, 2010, http://www.msnbc.msn.com/cleanprint/CleanPrintProxy.aspx?unique=1312239521624.

33. Dan Morain and Evan Halper, "Elective Office Improves a Resume," *Los Angeles Times*, November 24, 2006, http://articles.latimes.com/print/2006/nov/24/local/me-jobs24.

34. "Ex-Legislators Registered to Lobby, 2005," The Center for Public Integrity, Washington, D.C. October 12, 2006, http://projects.publicintegrity.org/hiredguns/reg.aspx.

35. Anthony Downs, *Inside Bureaucracy* (Santa Monica, CA: The Rand Corporation, 1966), p. 133.

36. "From Bureaucrats to Fat Cats: EPA Pesticide Program is a 'Farm Team' for the Pesticide Lobby," Environmental Working Group, Washington, D.C., June 30, 1999, p. 2.

37. "Former Regulator Joins CFP Board," *Financial Advisor Magazine*, June 28, 2005, http://www.fa-mag.com/fa-news/2251.html.

38. Jordan Rau, "Term Limits Add Up to Brain Drain," *Los Angeles Times*, July 23, 2006, http://articles.latimes.com/print/2006/jul/23/local/me-lobby23.

39. "'Nutballs' No More, Talk Radio Jocks Bask in Their Recall Role," *San Francisco Chronicle*, October 9, 2003, p. A15.

40. "The Rise of the Voters," *California Journal,* September 2003, p. 25.

41. "Civic Engagement Online: Politics as Usual," Pew Internet & American Life Project, September 2009, Pew Research Center, Washington, D.C.

42. "For Ads, Campaigns Play It Old-Media Safe," *Los Angeles Times*, October 29, 2010, pp. A1, A20.

43. Steve Lopez, "Jerry Brown, His Wife and that Weird Fundraising Challenge, *Los Angeles Times*, September 4, 2010, http://latimesblogs.latimes.com/lanow/2010/09/steve-lopez-jerry-brown-his-wife-and-that-weird-fundraising-challenge/comments/page/1/ .

44. https://secure.actblue.com/.

45. "Two Rising Stars on Our Team," Campaign Solutions, June 13, 2011, http://www.campaignsolutions.com/2011/06/two-rising-stars-on-our-team/.

46. "For Ads, Campaigns Play It Old-Media Safe," op. cit.

47. Mark Baldassare and Cheryl Katz, *The Coming Age of Direct Democracy* (Landham, MD: Rowman and Littlefield, 2008), p. 31.

48. "Special Survey on Californians and the Initiative Process: Bad Time for the Ballot Box; Californians Disapprove of Special Election, Schwarzenegger, and State Government," Press Release, Public Policy Institute of California, San Francisco, CA, August 25, 2005.

49. Elizabeth R. Gerber, Arthur Lupia, Mathew D. McCubbins, and D. Roderick Kiewiet, *Stealing the Initiative* (Upper Saddle River, NJ: Prentice Hall, 2001), p. 9.

50. Michael Hiltzik, "Oil Industry Is Driving Force behind Proposition 23's Attack on California's New Greenhouse Gas Regulation," *Los Angeles Times*, July 27, 2010, http://articles.latimes.com/print/2010/jul/27/business/la-fi-hiltzik-20100727.

51. *Democracy by Initiative: Shaping California's Fourth Branch of Government*, 2nd ed. (Los Angeles, CA: Center for Governmental Studies, 2008), p. 168.

52. A detailed analysis by the California League of Women Voters prior to the November 2006 election clearly refuted Big Tobacco's claims. See "Tax on Cigarettes," http://ca.lwv.org/lwvc/edfund/elections/2006nov/id/prop86.html.

53. Madison is the author of Federalist 10, one of the Federalist Papers. See Alexander Hamilton, John Jay, and James Madison, *The Federalist*, originally published in 1787.

10

Bankrupt State

From its politics to its economy to its environment and way of life, California is like a patient on life support.

—Paul Harris, reporter for *The Guardian*

The problem with life support is that artificial medical intervention often is a temporary fix until it, too, loses its capacity to restore the patient's well-being. Most of the time, the response is the final desperate life-saving effort before the patient expires.

Whether California is on life support is a matter for debate, but it's hard to imagine a moment in its history when the state's economic health has been more threatened than now. At the same time when the state faces almost overwhelming obligations, public policymakers and the public alike have shown little willingness to rescue us from ourselves. The successive accumulations of incredibly unrealistic and underfunded state budgets years after year have brought California to the point where the state is expiring from collective public penury and governmental programmatic neglect. It's a poisonous combination that is hurling California to Third World status.

California is bankrupt, maybe not in a technical sense but in virtually every other imaginable context. The state has lost its ability to produce reliable annual balanced budgets that meet the public's needs. For years, members of the state legislature and the governor have seized every possible sleazy accounting gimmick to make the budgets appear balanced by or near the June 30th deadline of each fiscal year, only to see them fall apart within months, sometimes weeks, because of overly optimistic assumptions, inflated expectations of federal government help, court decisions negating unconstitutional short-cuts, and silly accounting tricks. Legislators have borrowed from dedicated funds, deferred payments to schools and local governments, and assumed huge federal bailouts that have never arrived and were never promised. Perhaps the most blatant example of bookkeeping chicanery occurred in 2009, when the legislature "balanced" the budget in part by shifting the monthly pay of state employees from June 30, 2010 to July 1, 2010 so that the fiscal year would have only eleven payments and a one-time savings of $1.2 billion. Come on!

Of course, it's not just the legislature that's done us in. Year after year, governors—Democrats and Republicans alike—have blithely gone along, denying any budget sleight of hand magic and thanking the legislature for an "honest" budget at the end of tough negotiations. Some governors have sliced state commitments to federally mandated commitments, only to see the courts slap them down for it.[1] Who are they kidding, anyway?

Some would argue that state's public policymakers have been patently dishonest in their budgetary efforts. That may be true for a few such individuals, but in all likelihood, it's probably something so simple as wanting to avoid a confrontation with the public that has shown a steadfast resistance to raising taxes. Telling the voters that California's budget is out of balance is hardly the best way to incur favor, even if it's the truth. No one likes to share bad news, especially if it might cost them re-election, and so the state's leaders have looked for ways to ease the pain through temporary fixes year after year, decade after decade. Now, the last-ditch life support efforts are failing us.

A budget isn't just another document. In a technical sense, a budget is a government's bookkeeping tool that designs revenue collections and spending commitments. That's as much the case for California's $85 billion annual state budget as it is for your own budget. You generally know where the money is coming from and how you intend to spend it.

But a budget has another sweeping purpose in that it explains the values of a polity, specifically what is important to fund and what is not, how, and why, as well as the means to getting the necessary money. Budgets are anything but neutral documents, and there are always more demands than resources. Still, there are basic choices. A government that keeps taxes low accepts the trade-off between minimal revenues and minimal services to its citizens. Conversely, a government that commits to collecting more revenues honors the value of better programs and services for its citizens. In a very real sense, then, a budget reflects "the general public consensus about what kinds of services governments should provide and what citizens are entitled to as citizens of society."[2]

Of course, there are instances when policymakers make decisions that differ greatly from public values, such as the commitment to move 30,000 state prisoners to local jails in 2011 per a federal court order. But most of the time, the two universes are fairly well aligned. The reason is simple: The more that policymakers drift away from issues with a general public consensus, the more those elected officials risk losing their jobs.

This brings us back full circle to our discussion of California's miserable fiscal condition. Ever since the days of Proposition 13 in 1978, state public policymakers have refused to make difficult budget decisions in terms of raising enough revenues to meet the state's needs. The problem centers on a public that expects more from government than it is willing to pay and a collective state leadership that has been divided about what to do.

Fiscal conservatives have had it the easiest, for they believe in low taxes and little government. If people want more than the bare minimum services, they should pay for them on their own, whether it's for private schools, gated communities, or any number of services they choose to embrace beyond the state minimum. Fiscal liberals have been the most pained because they have wanted to raise new revenues to meet what they perceive as growing public needs in the very same areas. The voting public has brokered the deadlock by reluctantly accepting fewer services as a tradeoff for paying less. But there's a growing hitch in that increasingly the *voting* public is not the same constituency as the *entire* public. Therein lies the great conundrum of modern California—a state where the declining percentage of the "haves" still exercise control over the growing percentage of "have-nots," although those days may be numbered.

The rest of this chapter centers on California budget making in terms of process and the long-term costs to Californians. It's not a pretty picture, particularly because of the ability of the minority to stifle the needs of the majority through uncaring, suffocating budget decisions. The process tells as much about the values of the state's policy influencers as it does about the growing chasm between the few who are well to do and the rest who are not. The story is anything but flattering, but it's a story that must be told.

INADEQUATE REVENUE COLLECTION

How can a state with a gross domestic product equal to that of the eighth-largest nation in the world constantly be on the verge of financial disaster? That's the painful dilemma California faces year in and year out. The short answer lies with how much we take in and how much we spend. By most accounts, California suffers an annual structural deficit in excess of $20 billion. More significantly, projections by the state's legislative analyst point to growing annual deficits for the near future.[3] This predicament occurs because our obligations created by state and federal commitments exceed our revenues. Critics argue about whether the problem stems from the state failing to collect enough revenues or spending too much. When he was governor, Arnold Schwarzenegger persistently complained that California had a spending problem, not a revenue problem. Yet, after several years of drastic cuts in the annual state budget, even Schwarzenegger reluctantly conceded that California had a spending problem *and* a revenue problem.[4]

But it's the "long" answer that is particularly problematic for anyone who wants to see California return to grandeur. The simple fact is that as much as most Californians want greatness whether in terms of first-rate public education, a network of manicured parks, sleek highways, preventive health care for our children, world-class research centers, or any sign of prowess, we don't want to pay for it. Public opinion surveys repeatedly show that the public supports all of these elements and is often willing in the abstract to pay more taxes for them, but once presented with proposals for specific tax increases, public support disappears in a flash.[5] This shameless hypocrisy has become a cornerstone of the state's political culture. And given the persistent erosion of the state over the past quarter century, it shows no sign of abating. Rhetoric notwithstanding, most Californians accept mediocrity over more taxes. Meanwhile, we're left with a patchwork quilt-like, uneven revenue network that extracts a disproportionately high price from some sectors, modest amounts from others, and exempts several sectors from responsibility altogether.

High Taxes

Personal income taxes and sales taxes raise the lion's share of revenue for California's general fund. Because they dominate the means of revenue collection, these sources are vulnerable to gyrations, particularly in uncertain economic times.

Personal Income

Among California's revenue streams, personal income taxes provide more than half of the state's taxes for the general fund. Reliance on this revenue source has grown dramatically over a short period. Twenty-five years ago, personal income taxes and sales taxes each accounted for about 35 percent of the take, suggesting more of a balance, but that's no longer the case. Because it is a "progressive" tax—obligation percentages increase with incomes—today the personal income tax rates vary between 1 percent and 10.3 percent, depending upon income level. The rates are lower than the 15 percent maximum when the legislature first enacted the tax in 1935, but higher than the 6 percent maximum put into place during the years Earl Warren served as governor.

Compared to other states, California has the third highest personal income tax requirement. That's not an issue for most people because of the nature of the tax, which is the most progressive in the nation, according to the conservative Tax Foundation.[6] In fact, during most years, the top 1 percent of the most affluent residents account for about half of all personal income taxes.[7] Clearly, these folks are paying their share. The major problem, however, lies in the volatility connected with the state's economy. As noted in *Stateline*, a nonpartisan news service of the Pew Center of the States, "Rather than having a steady flow of money from several sources as many states do, California experiences wild swings in revenue because of its dependence on a small group of people: its wealthiest taxpayers."[8] When employment is robust and incomes are high, personal income tax revenues tumble into the state like water flowing through an opened dam. When unemployment soars, California is denied the bounty of its largest revenue producer.

Sales

California also has a high sales tax and is among the top half dozen states, depending upon add-ons of as much as 1.25 percent in different local jurisdictions. Like the personal income tax, the genesis of this revenue source goes back to the Great Depression, when the state legislature established the rate at 2.5 percent. While the sales tax percentage is high, it's applied only to about 40 percent of all purchases of goods. Groceries, repair services, and fee-charging visits to physicians, attorneys, and other specialists are exempt from sales taxes. Even with exemptions, sales tax collections can dive when the economy tires. With the onset of the recession in 2008, for examples, sales tax revenues dropped by more than 10 percent, or about $3 billion.[9]

Critics call the sales tax "regressive" because the poor pay the same percentage as the wealthy. Inasmuch as the poor don't have as much discretionary income as people of means, the tax will hurt the poor more, particularly in tough times. That takes us to the concern with the sales tax, namely that, like the personal income tax, the volume generated for the government rises and drops with the general condition of the economy.

The Biggest Slices of the Revenue Pie

Whatever your concern about the volatility of the personal income and sales taxes, the most important point to remember is that combined, they account for about three-fourths of all taxes collected in California. That dependence puts California in a big bind every time the economy sputters. So, while people may differ on whether these taxes are too high or unfair, the larger issue is that these sources are not balanced by other revenue streams for the states.

Low Taxes

Several state revenue sources resemble trickles more than streams. These include property taxes, sin taxes on purchases such as alcohol and tobacco, and taxes on corporations.

Property

While property taxes are collected by counties primarily for programs and services, they are very much a part of the state's overall fiscal revenue structure. That's because the changes precipitated by Proposition 13 drastically reduced the ability of local governments to collect revenues and placed them at the mercy of the state. Today, California is tied for 48th in property tax rates.[10] No wonder why it seems local governments don't have two nickels to rub together.

Proposition 13 has been a game changer in California politics and the state's governmental hierarchy. Since the enactment of this initiative, California property owners have saved more than $500 billion on local property taxes.[11] That's the good news. The bad news is that local governments have lost $500 billion in local revenues. Let's remember that historically local governments have been responsible for providing public education, police and fire protection, roads, libraries, emergency health care, and a host of other programs and services. But Proposition 13 reduced their revenues by 57 percent, and local governments have never recovered. Think back to earlier discussions in this book about poor services at local government levels and you begin to get a sense of long-term costs to Californians from Proposition 13. It's "penny wise, pound foolish" in real time.

Low local property tax rates in the post-Proposition 13 era have forced local governments to ask the state for relief. These annual requests for assistance, in turn, have put tremendous pressure on state legislators, who have found it increasingly difficult to meet general statewide obligations and make up some of the funds lost through reduced property taxes simultaneously.

Some reformers have advocated applying the property tax to businesses with a higher formula, perhaps 1.5 percent of market value, compared to the 1 percent paid by homeowners. The thinking is that businesses change hands or move much less frequently than homeowners do, resulting in artificially low values and taxes. Such a shift would generate anywhere between $3 billion and $7 billion in new revenues, easing local government revenue shortfalls.[12] A version of this proposal appeared as a statewide ballot initiative in 1992, but a fierce battle waged by business groups and the Howard Jarvis Taxpayers Association assured its demise.

"Sin" Taxes

Sin taxes refer to taxes collected on discretionary services such as tobacco, alcohol, and gaming. The tax rates for all three of these services are incredibly low and have remained so for years. In each case, you can credit the affected industry for successfully stifling legislative change and campaigning against occasional ballot propositions that would intrude on their obscene profits.

Let's begin with tobacco. California's cigarette tobacco tax of 87 cents per pack ranks 33rd among the 50 states. Comparable urban states like New York, Massachusetts, and Connecticut tax cigarettes at three and four times as much as California. More significantly, since California last raised tobacco taxes by 25 cents per pack in 1998, 48 states have raised their taxes on this product.[13] There have been efforts, if ill-fated, to correct this problem. The last occurred in 2006, when anti-tobacco sponsors qualified an initiative for the ballot that would have added $2.60 per pack to the cost of cigarettes. But the tobacco industry raised $65 million for a campaign loaded with distortions, and the proposition was defeated. And here's why: As of 2011, 11.9 percent of California adults were smokers.[14] Assuming that each adult burns through one pack of cigarettes per day, the revenue from an additional levy of $1 per pack would amount to $1.25 billion annually. Even at that, California would rank 16th in tobacco taxes. Clearly, tobacco is an under-taxed commodity.

We turn next to alcohol, another California industry with under-taxed products and huge revenue losses. California last increased taxes on alcohol in 1991. Inflation alone over a period of more than 20 years would suggest some kind of upward adjustment, but none has occurred. As a result, California has one of the lowest set of industry-wide alcohol taxes in the nation. 2010 data compiled by the Tax Foundation ranks California 46th in table wine taxes and 35th in hard liquor taxes; only in the case of beer does California approach average, where the state is tied with three others for 23rd place.[15] The taxes paid have been miniscule. For the wine industry alone, the sector generated $18.5 billion worth of sales in 2008, yet total state and local taxes amount to $3.3 billion.[16] Remove the local sales tax portion, and the amount paid to the state approximated $1.6 billion, or 8.6 percent. No matter how you cut it, this is hardly an over-taxed industry.

Since 1991, there have been efforts to increase the industry's responsibility, but all have been futile because of industry opposition. In 2009, even Governor Arnold Schwarzenegger—generally a vigorous opponent of tax increases—proposed a modest tax increase of 5 cents per drink on beer, wine, and spirits, which would have raised more than $750 million to offset the state's budget deficit. The proposed legislation never got out of committee.

Ironically, the public gets the problem, even if legislators don't or are unwilling to. In 2010, a statewide poll jointly administered by the Pew Center on the States and the Public Policy Institute of California asked respondents how they felt about raising taxes on alcohol and cigarettes as a way to close the state's deficit. Nearly three-quarters of the respondents said "yes," compared to 25 percent who said "no."[17] Clearly, the public sees the need to make fundamental change in sin tax rates.

Corporations

Two issues exist with respect to the state taxes paid by corporations. First, while the tax rate has hovered around 10 percent over the past third of a century, the amount paid by banks and corporations as a percentage of revenues collected has declined from 14.6 percent of the take in 1980–1981 to 10.9 percent in 2006–2007.[18] That leads to a second point, which is the extent to which corporations have become adroit at avoiding corporate taxes altogether. One recent study for 2001 found that over half of the profitable corporations in California paid no more than the $800 minimum. Worse yet, for the same year, 46 corporations with more than $1 billion in receipts paid only the $800 minimum. Simply put, corporations are not paying their share.

How have they managed this? Over the years, the legislature has enacted oodles of loopholes for corporations, amounting to more than $4 billion in state corporate tax breaks in 2011 alone, according to research conducted by the California Public Research Group (CalPirg).[19] The list of write-offs is lengthy. Data provided by the California Franchise Tax Board for the 2010 year shows credits, deductions, and exemptions for dozens of corporate activities including Enterprise Zone hiring, research activities, business activities conducted within military areas, hiring of prison inmate labor, and use of ultra-low sulfur diesel fuel, to name a few. Some of these write-offs may be noble, others not, but at a time when the state is hurting for every lost tax dollar, corporations doing business in California are doing fine, thank you—irrespective of what they may say.

All of this is carried out in relative secrecy, which is somewhat amazing given the computer know-how in a state like California and growing demands for political transparency. Nevertheless, a study of the 50 states by the nonpartisan CalPirg Education Fund in 2011 gave California a D+ (tied for 31st place) on access to government spending data, including corporate tax breaks.[20] Even some state policymakers have begun to feel a bit squeamish about the disconnect between empty state coffers and huge corporate tax breaks. In 2010, the legislature passed a bill calling for the state to disclose corporate tax breaks as well as to whom, how much, and for what purpose. Then-Governor Arnold Schwarzenegger vetoed the bill on the grounds that corporate tax data is published by the Franchise Tax Board and Department of Finance—but it's not!

The Costs of Low-Taxed Industries

It doesn't take a rocket scientist to see that California pays dearly for affording special treatment to low-taxed industries. By simply adjusting business property taxes, adding $1 per pack to tobacco taxes, tacking on a nickel per tax to alcoholic drinks, and removing corporate tax breaks, the state could add close to $10 billion annually, thereby cutting in half the $20 billion structural deficit. Of course, powerful interests have and will continue to oppose any and all of these changes. While these sectors may take pleasure in reinforcing the pro-business status quo, Californians will continue to pay a high price for the state's deteriorating infrastructure.

No Taxes

In addition to high- and low-taxed sectors, a few industries in California pay no state income taxes on state-related operations. The most outrageous candidate is California's oil industry, followed by out-of-state Internet businesses.

California Oil

Most people think of Texas and Alaska as the nation's premier oil-producing states, and they're right. But what most people don't know is that California is the nation's third largest oil-producing state at 240,000 barrels per day, just ahead of Louisiana (4th), New Mexico (5th), and Oklahoma (6th). At $100 per barrel, California oil extracted from the ground has a retail value of $8.76 billion per year. How much of that is taxed? None! In fact, California is the only oil-producing state that does not tax oil severed from the ground. The other 21 oil-producing states have oil severance taxes ranging from 2 percent to 15 percent.[21]

Over the years, various attempts have been made in the state legislature to lay a severance tax on oil but all have either languished or died in committee hearings—a traditional industry ploy. In 2010, industry lobbyists persuaded legislators to abandon two bills. In 2011, a bill calling for a

12.5 percent severance tax also died after an oil-industry supported group decreed tens of thousands of jobs would be lost. Lost in the discussion was an independent study by faculty at the University of California, Berkeley, who predicted an oil severance tax would cost no more than 300 jobs, while providing major financial benefits for the state.[22]

Outside the legislature, reformers have turned to the ballot proposition process in hopes of passing an oil severance law, to no avail. The last initiative effort in 2006 would have taxed oil companies between 1 and 6 percent of the oil value (depending upon the volume extracted) over a 10-year period, with the funds dedicated to alternative energy research. Estimated revenues for the state amounted to $4 billion over the entire period. Compare that figure with $8.76 billion earned by the industry *per year*. At first, public opinion supported the tax; a Field poll in July 2006 showed the "yes" vote trouncing the "no" vote by a margin of 63 percent to 32 percent.[23] Then the oil industry went to work, spending more than $100 million on a campaign to secure defeat. Predictably, the proposition lost by ten points.

Taxing Out-of-State-Based Internet Businesses: A Rare Victory

In recent years, the issue of Internet taxation has taken center stage in California as well as in several other states. In 1992, the U.S. Supreme Court ruled that states could compel companies to collect sales tax from Internet-facilitated commerce only if the companies had a physical presence—a store or a warehouse, for example—in the state. Otherwise, Internet-facilitated companies would not be required to pay state sales taxes. How much is that worth? As much as $1.1 billion in lost sales tax revenues in California alone, according to some studies.[24] Of course, 1992 is ancient history in terms of Internet use; so much has happened with commerce patterns since then.

The protection of "etailers" like Amazon from sales taxes places them at a competitive advantage over traditional brick-and-mortar outlets that are required to collect sales taxes. Even huge retail corporations like Wal-Mart have suffered at the hands of Amazon because of Wal-Mart's presence in every state and, therefore, the requirement to collect sales taxes on its online sales.[25]

Over time, some state governments have concluded that the 1992 Supreme Court decision may be out of date, given the now-pervasive flow of ecommerce via the Internet. By 2011, 11 states had legislated that etailers such as Amazon should pay sales tax along with brick-and-mortar stores. For its part, Amazon has had a two-pronged strategy. It has succumbed to collecting sales taxes in states where it has warehouses (Washington, Kansas, Kentucky, and North Dakota). However, in other states, Amazon has refused to pay, citing the 1992 Supreme Court decision.

In 2011, the California legislature, in a move dictated more by desperation for revenue than any political courage, enacted legislation requiring all etailers, including Amazon, to attach sales taxes to the prices of their products. It's estimated that the new online sales tax may generate more than $300 million in the first year alone, if not more.[26] Amazon initially refused, claiming the state had no right to order the collection of such funds. The massive corporation threatened to fight the new law by qualifying a referendum to overturn the legislature's new law. After a few weeks of tussling through the press, Amazon negotiated a deal with California that would exempt Internet tax collection until 2012, unless Congress passed a national law prior to that time.

Some might argue that the outcome reflected courage of the state legislature to take on the mammoth etailer. In fact, Wal-Mart and other companies had become so incensed over Amazon's advantage that the legislature had little choice. As the head of the California Retailers Association complained, "Amazon is killing our business in bricks-and-mortar stores."[27] Regardless, the new law represents a rare victory of the state's public policymakers over a private interest, even if others in the private sector helped along the process.

An Out-of-Whack Revenue System

We've long heard what has become the classic debate about whether California has a spending problem or a revenue problem. It turns out that neither claim is correct. In fact, California has a "missing revenues" problem. If the tax system were arranged to collect revenues from all important parties rather than balancing on the backs of citizens, the structural deficit would all but go away—this without adding a dime to personal income or sales taxes, which do a pretty good job collecting revenues from all segments of society. But with so many sacred cows in California's potentially lucrative revenue pasture, the collection of taxes takes place in a very uneven political environment dominated by a few powerful interests. Until we address those missing pieces, the state will suffer.

SPENDING IN A STRAITJACKET

Thus far, in this chapter we've focused on the money coming in to state and local government treasuries, or the lack thereof. What about the money going out? Beyond the primary concern of insufficient revenues to meet basic needs, spending is a problem in California for two critical reasons: mandated programs and constitutional restraints. Either one of these might be manageable, but combined they leave California in a fiscal straitjacket.

Mandated Programs

Over the past few decades, the state has assumed responsibility for several expensive programs and services. Some are guarantees that have been added in the state Constitution as amendments; others are statutes that have been adopted by the legislature; others still have been voted in by the people either as statutes or as constitutional amendments. Regardless, what unites these changes is that by their design, they mandate, or require, spending in specific policy areas regardless of other needs or issues.

Mandated spending is hardly a trivial activity, although it seems that many decisions to do so are made without serious considerations of the long-term implications. Every time a new program or service is mandated in perpetuity (or until it is changed by a different mandate), public policymakers lose ability to address changing needs, whether in the form of responding to lingering issues or sudden emergencies. That's because the more that sizable portions of the budget are pre-committed, the less that state policymakers are able to distribute funds to other areas. In fact, mandated spending has become the dominant portion of the state budget. It's hard to give a precise figure, but in all likelihood it's somewhere around 70 percent of all state spending.

Unfunded Programs

Some mandated categories stand out like a sore thumb, not only for their largess but also for the lack of revenue to fulfill the program's objective. Consider public education, a particularly vulnerable category in the wake of Proposition 13, which you may recall, decimated the ability of local governments to collect property taxes for public education and other uses. Proposition 13 forced public education leaders to turn to the state, but funding was always questionable. That uncertainty led to the passage of Proposition 98 in 1988, otherwise known as the "Classroom Instructional Improvement and Accountability Act," which mandates 40 percent of the state budget general fund for K–12 public education; in terms of the 2011–2012 budget, that amounts to about $38 billion—the largest, but by no means the only, example of mandated spending.

There are dozens of other cases of mandates without revenues, albeit on a less grandiose scale than Proposition 98. Proposition 184, California's famous (or maybe infamous, nowadays) "Three Strikes" initiative passed by the voters in 1984, requires a prison sentence of 25 years to life without parole for a two-time felon who is convicted of a third crime. Today, about 7,500 prisoners fall into that category; at about $50,000 per convict per year, that mandate adds about $3.75 billion in pre-committed funds.

Perhaps the most convoluted of all mandated programs without designated funding is Proposition 49, the After School and Safety Act, passed by the voters in 2002. The brainchild of then-soon-to-be Governor Arnold Schwarzenegger, the law mandates $550 million for after-school programs. After-school programs are wonderful in theory, but how can we even think about funding them in the face of incredibly low public education allocations by the state legislature? That half billion dollars could be put to use quickly in our dilapidated, crowded, poorly performing public school classrooms, but the mandated requirements of Proposition 49 make no allowances. Instead, the money must be allocated to after-school programs only—even if the schools lack necessary supplies or personnel for educational instruction. There's something wrong here, that's for sure.

In summary, neither Proposition 98, nor Proposition 184, nor Proposition 49 included provisions for raising the money committed to their targets. Rather, these propositions only established new spending categories that the legislature is required to fund. That concept may be naive or simplistic, but it happens repeatedly.

Funded Mandates

Other examples are only slightly better in that they direct specific taxes or fees for specific purposes. Proposition 42, the Transportation Congestion

Act of 2002, requires that all gasoline- and automobile-related sales taxes be spent for public transit, and state highway and local repairs. In 2011, those taxes amounted to $2 billion. Proposition 63, the Mental Health Services Act of 2004, adds 1 percent to the income taxes of all Californians who earn $1 million annually or more, with the proceeds directed at selected state and local mental health programs. The amount allocated in 2011? $713 million. Then there's Proposition 10, officially called the California Children and First Families Act of 1998, which added a 50-cent tax to the price of a pack of cigarettes and similar tobacco products, with the $600 million raised annually awarded to counties for community healthcare and children's healthcare education.

Problems with Mandated Spending

All of these ballot initiatives direct resources to worthy causes, but they tie up the state budget in pre-determined knots irrespective of anything else going on, including emergent issues that no one may have expected. Simply put, they rob the state's policymakers of any budget flexibility. The six examples just cited account for well over half of the state general fund.

Thankfully, all mandated spending could be suspended on a temporary basis if the legislature obtains a two-thirds vote. That's happened more often than you might imagine. State revenues under the present system have been so weak that the legislature reduced mandated payments of 50 programs in 2011 alone. In some cases, notably K–12 public education, suspensions have been in place for a decade or more.[28]

But suspension leads to its own problem, namely legislative credibility. Most voters naively believe that when they authorize funding for a specific program, the money will be there. They don't make the connection between revenue raising and revenue spending, and the sponsors of unfunded initiatives aren't about to say otherwise, lest they generate voter disapproval.[29] Sure, California law requires a "fiscal impact statement" included as part of the description of a proposition, but the language is often oblique and buried among a bunch of other equally confusing material. As a result, large numbers of voters understand more about the proposed spending than any sources of money for the program.[30] In the end, not only are many mandated programs dysfunctional because of absent state funds, but voters are angry because they feel misled.

Constitutional Restraints

In addition to a history of the legislature and voters establishing a series of unsustainable programs, the voters have passed several constitutional amendments designed to restrain the state's ability from collecting revenues for budget distribution. Just as Proposition 13 has drastically reduced the opportunity for local governments to generate revenue, for the most part passage of these propositions has choked off many revenue-producing opportunities at the state level and reduced California's ability to meet its growing needs. Not surprisingly, California has fallen behind almost all other states in virtually every public policy category, leaving its residents without the tools to compete or succeed. To this day, most voters don't realize the extent to which their actions in the ballot booth have wrought such harm. Some of the most damaging changes are discussed next.

Limits on Moving Local Revenues to the State

Even though local governments are technically appendages of the state (remember, they are not mentioned in the U.S. Constitution), recent ballot propositions have been promoted to keep the state from taking locally collected taxes. This a curious attitude, given the incredible funding burden placed on the state via Proposition 13 and other changes, but it's the case nonetheless. More to the point, it's another example of just how out of touch—or uncaring—the voters are regarding California's unmet needs whether in terms of infrastructure of basic education or social welfare programs.

Recent efforts to minimize state extraction of local revenues recently emerged first with Proposition 1A, Protection of Local Government Revenues Act, in 2004. Under the terms of this constitutional amendment, the state is prohibited from seizing locally collected taxes and fees for statewide use. Preservation of local finances was the theme again in 2010, when the voters approved Proposition 22. Officially titled the Local Taxpayer, Public Safety, and Transportation Protection Act, this constitutional amendment prevents the state from seizing special district, local redevelopment agency, and local transportation funds made available through sales taxes.

With the passage of these two ballot propositions, local governments have gone a considerable distance toward inoculating themselves from state intrusion. That might not be so problematic if the state had other means of raising revenues, but as noted previously, those have been closed as well.

Increasing the Vote Threshold for State Fees

For tax opponents, warding off the state is part of the process of minimizing government activity. But from their perspective, that's not enough to weaken, if not kill the state revenue-sucking "beast." In 2010, Californians passed Proposition 26, the Supermajority to Pass New Taxes and Fees Act. Even prior to this initiative, local governments had been required to obtain two-thirds vote approvals on parcel taxes and other special district legislation, thanks to Proposition 13. But with Proposition 26, any new taxes, levies, new regulatory fees, or user fees proposed by the state or local government could take place only with a two-thirds vote of the legislature for state matters, or voters in the case of local proposals. In other words, henceforth, any new revenues at the state or local level can be adopted only with a two-thirds vote.

As with the case of the two-thirds requirement for Proposition 13, the irony here was hard to ignore because of the majority vote requirement to set up a two-thirds rule. As a result, the majority has become hostage to the minority at least when it comes to raising revenues in California.

Lowering the Legislative Spending Vote Requirement: A Minor Victory

One shred of hope for reversing the tide of restraint has emerged with a reduced requirement for legislative passage of the state budget. Since the days of the Great Depression, state law required an absolute two-thirds vote in each house to pass the budget. "Absolute" referred to two thirds of the seats (54 of 80 in the assembly and 27 of 40 in the senate), not merely two thirds of the legislators present at the time of the vote. Over that long time span, rarely has one political party captured enough seats in both houses to control the budget outcome. More times than not, gridlock ensued, with budgets passed sometimes as late as three months after the constitutional deadline. And when budgets finally emerged, they revealed the characteristics and values of the powerful minority much more than the majority.

This changed in 2010, when the voters enacted Proposition 25, a constitutional amendment entitled "The Majority Vote for the Legislature to Pass the Budget Act." Now, with the new provision in place, passage of the state budget occurs with a simple majority, paving the way to end legislative stalemate. Proposition 25 did end the stalemate, and the 2011–2012 state budget was passed on time. But in an important sense the measure is hollow because the two-thirds provision for raising taxes remains in place. Simply put, it doesn't really matter much that a simple vote is necessary to enact a state budget if the document lacks the necessary funding to do what needs to be done. For this reason, Californians remain hostages of minority rule to this day.

Impact of Minimalism on California

For the most part, the forces of minimalism have prevailed in California, particularly in recent decades. Yes, there was the building period during the 1950s and 1960s when Californians yearned to make the state a model environment—a place where their children would attend top-notch schools, where residents would travel on a fabulous highway network, and where other first-rate infrastructure elements would complement the state's idyllic physical setting. But from the days of Proposition 13 forward, the state has stumbled in the opposite direction. Deterioration has overcome determination, individual struggles have replaced shared hopes, and political rigidity has asphyxiated political elasticity. The state's unofficial attitude has morphed from "we can do it" to "no way."

Collective penury has increased in recent years. Even during the current decade, when the state has been in the greatest need of new revenues to remain competitive and successful, opponents of new revenues have roiled against them. Repeatedly the "haves," fearing deterioration of their standing and, more specifically, the extraction of their own resources, have resisted ballot proposals designed to benefit the public good, including the "have-nots." Bear in mind that the voters have not been representative of the state population as a whole; students and immigrants who aren't citizens—documented or otherwise—can't vote at all, and many first- and second-generation minorities have not voted in great numbers. It's in this unique environment that the anti-tax, anti-government influences have enjoyed their finest hour, and an elongated one at that.

BONDED TO BONDS

In 21st century California, the state policymaking process is squeezed between limited revenue sources and strict spending limitations. Combined, these powerful forces have crushed the state's ability to provide for its people. But beyond California's rules of governance, the voters have relied on bonds disproportionately to finance many long-term projects and a few short-term crises.

With bonds, governments commit to long-term borrowing over a period of 30 or sometimes 40 years in exchange for having costly projects built right away. This commitment takes place if a statewide vote approves the proposal by a simple majority. Some of the categories include natural resources development, K–12 public education construction, UC and CSU building construction, and public transportation networks. In addition to meeting public infrastructure needs, these projects put thousands of people to work in good jobs to build dams, roads, prisons, or other long-lasting facilities. Not all state infrastructure projects are financed through bonds, but Californians rely on this financing method much more so than most other states. Increasingly, voters look to state bonds to pick up the infrastructure slack because of the simple majority element; bonds at the local level require a two-thirds majority, making passage very unlikely. And, of course, paying for things over time seems much more desirable than coughing up the dough now.

Extent of the Crisis

Getting right to work on projects rather than waiting for all the funds to accrue has its benefits, but at a steep price. The projects can cost an awful lot by the time their bonds are paid off—sometimes twice as much or more as the original estimated cost. Another point: Californians have a history of approving bonds at rates faster than interest on older projects is paid off. As a result, over time these accumulated debts can play havoc with a government's budget as interest set aside to pay off the bonds eats into the revenues that could go to other programs or services. The public and policymakers alike would rather ignore that long-term picture.

In fact, the public is pretty much removed from how bonds work altogether, even though reliance upon the funding mechanism has put the state deep into long-term debt. A statewide public opinion survey taken in 2004 found that only 8 percent of the voters knew "a lot" about the interest costs associated with bonds,[31] which shows how detached most people are from a process that commits huge sums of public funds to various projects. Massive ignorance notwithstanding, survey respondents continued to support state bonds on a regular basis. The public's confusion may be typical, but it's also irresponsible, given that bonds increase the state's obligations without ever attaching revenue sources. People just think that the legislature will "figure it out." It's pass the buck (literally) California style, but in fact it's the public that winds up holding the empty bag and ultimately paying for it several times over.

And the money adds up. As of October 2010, Californians were paying interest on $89.98 billion worth of bonds, an amount close to the general fund state budget for the entire year. In addition, the voters had approved another $52.72 billion of bonds that the state had not yet issued to financial houses for purchase. That's a total of $142.70 billion worth of bonds.[32] It's also a lot of debt. On a per capita basis, the state's debt is $2,362. In other words, if all the bond debt was divided by the state's population, each resident would owe $2,362. When state and local bond commitments are combined with public pension obligations, per capita debt swells to $9,228. As of 2010, California ranks as the 11th most bond-dependent state in the nation.[33] As bad as that is, three years earlier, the state ranked 23rd in bond debt,[34] another sign that California is mortgaging its future big time.

Increased reliance on bonds for various projects has reframed the way the legislature organizes the annual state budget. In 2011–2012, about 6.5 percent of the state budget, or $5.5 billion, was dedicated to bond interest. By 2012–2013, the annual payment on bond debt is scheduled to rise to 11 percent of the state budget, leveling off to 9 percent in the near future.[35] Out of a $100 billion state budget, that would equal $9 billion, almost as much as the state commits to higher education. That might not seem like a large portion of the budget, but in a state where most of the dollars are pre-committed through various mandates, bonds suck up a huge proportion of the few dollars that are not yet spoken for. As a result, areas such as higher education or social services—policy areas without official mandates—go without (or without nearly enough) because so much of the budget is siphoned off to pay for previous commitments and bond payments. It's a vicious cycle that won't go away.

All this comes at a cost in terms of California's credit worthiness. These days California has the lowest credit rating of the 50 states. The poor evaluation was caused by the state's annual inability to balance its budget in a timely fashion and the large ratio of debt to the size of the budget. The problem takes a toll in hard dollars as well as financial reputation. State Treasurer Bill Lockyer explains that the state is paying 40.2 percent more interest simply by having the lowest rating instead of the highest rating; that amounts to billions of extra dollars in interest every year.[36] That's the penalty for being irresponsible.

Bond Abuse

Bond votes are placed on the ballot most often by the state legislature, although supporters can also qualify proposals by gathering enough initiative signatures. Either way, these proposals sometimes can be a bit devious to the extent that they are padded with unnecessary expenditures.

Misleading Proposals

One recent example occurred with a proposed $11.4 billion bond in 2010, called the Safe, Clean and Reliable Water Supply Act. Opponents criticized the bond for containing at least $2 billion in projects that were either poorly designed or provided state funds for private water companies. In addition, it also contained at least $3 billion in previously passed water bonds that had not been spent on previously approved water projects, undermining the sponsors' claims of "crisis."[37] The condemnation was so strong from environmentalists and taxpayer groups that Governor Schwarzenegger and the legislature removed the proposal from the ballot, with the hope of submitting a streamlined, less controversial version in 2012.[38]

Schwarzenegger's Dubious Legacy

The most egregious abuse of bonds occurred in 2004 shortly after Arnold Schwarzenegger won the governorship in the recall election of Gray Davis. Immediately upon assuming office, he assigned an executive order to eliminate a motor vehicle tax that brought in revenues of $4 billion annually. In the next breath, he warned the public of a $15 billion budget deficit, and he asked the voters to pass a $15 billion bond to balance the budget: "We can slough our problems into the future or we can honestly and squarely confront our budget problems in a way that shares our burdens fairly and strengthens our state for the future," he said at a campaign rally shortly before the election.[39] How preposterous! You don't "balance" a budget by going into more debt, yet that's what Schwarzenegger proposed and that's what the voters bought. Like so many others in government, he kicked the state's finance can down the road, rather than tell the voters directly about California's shaky budget situation. Meanwhile, it will cost the state $28.6 billion to pay off the $15 billion bond, with nothing built to show for it.[40]

Bonds in Perspective

So, are bonds a bad financing tool? Not necessarily, assuming the projects are worthy and the state has the money to pay off the bonds down the road. The problem we have in California is that the state has committed to an ambitious bond-financed schedule of state projects with limited means to support the efforts. Between roller coaster-like state revenue cycles and large percentages of a relatively bare bones state budget committed to bond interest payments, California doesn't have much wiggle room. That's why the state has the worst credit rating of the 50 states, which leads to higher interest rates. That's also yet another reason why California has no room for programs beyond mandated commitments and bond interest payments. Worse yet, projections show only more pressure on the state's financial structure in coming years.

―――――――――――

NO WAY OUT?

California's precarious financial condition is not the result of one bad revenue year or a sudden crisis or corruption. Any one of those predicaments might be dealt with through a mid-course correction or housecleaning of those responsible for malicious activities. Sadly, our issues are both historical and complex.

It's clear that for some time large numbers of residents have been willing to accept budgetary mediocrity. Sure, many complain about poor services and underfunded programs, but the complaints grow silent when the same people are asked to pony up more money to better those programs.

The reluctance of elected policymakers to move in bold directions is routinely reinforced by special interests that have carved out close relationships with key legislators as well as consistently bombarded the airwaves at election time with distorted messages. There are plenty of untapped and underutilized revenue sources commonly collected in other states, only to be given a "free pass" from obligation in California. Meanwhile, an electorate more concerned with the bottom line now than any impacts down the road has not been enthusiastic about accepting any calls to enact new revenues, particularly when they believe that their pockets will be picked. What a combination.

The state's inertia is all but guaranteed by a policymaking environment framed by a series of voter-passed constitutional constraints that effectively leave control to legislative minorities, much to the chagrin of the state's overlooked and under-served majority. Consequently, annual state budgets are woefully underfunded to meet the state's burgeoning needs. When it comes to budget making in California, both hands are tied—the inability to raise money as well as constraints with respect to spending it. That's not the way to run the eighth-largest economy in the world.

Incredibly, poorly funded public education programs, an untrained workforce, a decaying state infrastructure, reduced state services, and increasingly unresponsive local governments somehow have failed to convince people of their enveloping peril and equally discouraging futures. Instead, a curious, yet harmful alliance of self-centered individuals and powerful interest groups, bolstered by a legion of uninformed voters and a cumbersome policymaking process, have embraced mediocrity as a noble cause. Such a scheme may work for a few Californians in the short term, but it's hurting most of us in the end. Unfortunately, by the time most of us figure out the true costs of these bad decisions, the state's miserable condition may be well beyond our ability to fix it.

ENDNOTES

1. For example, see "Courts Add to Budget Woes," *San Francisco Chronicle*, May 22, 2010, pp. A1, A8.
2. Irene S. Rubin, *The Politics of Public Budgeting: Getting and Spending*, 5th ed. (Washington, D.C.: CQ Press, 2006), p. 1

3. "The 2011-2012 Budget: California's Fiscal Outlook," November 2010, Legislative Analyst's Office, Sacramento, CA, p. 1.

4. Press Conference, Sacramento, CA, November 6, 2008.

5. For a recent example of these contrasting themes, see "Californians & Their Government," Public Policy Institute of California, San Francisco, CA, May 2011.

6. "Tax Data: California," The Tax Foundation, Washington, D.C., March 3, 2011, http://www.taxfoundation.org/taxdata/show/228.html.

7. Pamela M. Prah, "The Path to California's Fiscal Crisis," *Stateline*, May 15, 2009, http://www.stateline.org/live/printable/story?contentId=400337.

8. Ibid.

9. "California's Tax System," The California Budget Project, Sacramento, CA, February 2009, p. 4.

10. "State-by-State Property Tax Rates," *The New York Times*, April 10, 2007, http://www.nytimes.com/2007/04/10/business/11leonhardt-avgproptaxrates.html.

11. Howard Jarvis Taxpayers Association, 2009, www.hjta.org/index.php.

12. "Democrats' Proposed Split-Roll Tax Would Devastate California Economy," *Capitol Weekly*, February 21, 2008.

13. "State of Tobacco Control 2010," American Lung Association, Washington, D.C., 2011, pp. 23–24.

14. "Smoking Rate Hits New Low," *San Jose Mercury News*, July 14, 2011, B1, B8.

15. Tax Foundation, www.taxfoundation.org. These data reflect rates as of February 1, 2010.

16. "California Wine Has $51.8 Billion Economic Impact on State and $125.3 Billion on the U.S. Economy," Stonebridge Research, report prepared for the California Wine Institute, December 2008.

17. "Facing Facts: Public Attitudes and Fiscal Realities in Five Stressed States," Pew Center of the States, Washington, D.C. and Public Policy Institute of California, San Francisco, CA, October 2010, p. 19.

18. "Sunshine for California: Shining Light on Corporate Tax Secrecy for Healthier State Budgets, Investments and Markets," California Public Interest Research Group (CalPirg), Sacramento, CA, Summer 2006, p. 2.

19. "Corporations Exempt from State Budget Uncertainties," press release, CalPirg, Sacramento, CA, August 6, 2010.

20. See "Following the Money in 2011: How the 50 States Rate in Providing Online Access to Government Spending," CalPirg, Sacramento, CA, March 2011, p. 5.

21. "Oil Severance Tax Gets Close Look at the Capitol, *Capitol Weekly*, January 15, 2009.

22. Ken Jacobs, T. Laurel Lester, and Laurel Tan, "Budget Solutions and Jobs," Center for Labor Research and Education, University of California, Berkeley, March 2010, p. 2.

23. "Drop in Support for Propositions 86 (Tax on Cigarettes) and 87 (Alternative Energy/Oil Tax)," Field Poll, release #2215, October 4, 2006.

24. Michael Hiltzik, "Internet Sales Tax Scofflaws Cheat State," *Los Angeles Times*, December 24, 2009, http://articles.latimes.com/print/2009/dec/24/business/la-fi-hiltzik24-2009dec24.

25. "Walmart Struggles with Online Presence," *San Francisco Chronicle*, July 25, 2011, pp. D1, D3.

26. Marc Lifsher, "California Tells Online Retailers to start Collecting Sales Taxes from Customers," http://articles.latimes.com/2011/jun/30/business/la-fi-amazon-tax-2011 0630.

27. "Amazon Pushes Hard To Kill a Tax," *The New York Times*, September 5, 2011, pp. B1, B4.

28. "2001 Cal Facts: California's Economy and Budget in Perspective," Legislative Analyst's Office, Sacramento, CA, January 5, 2011, http://www.lao.ca.gov/reports/2011/cal-facts/calfacts_010511.aspx.

29. "Initiative and Referendum in the 21st Century," National Conference of State Legislatures, Denver, CO, July 2002, p. 27.

30. "Public Ignorance Bites California in the Wallet," *Los Angeles Times*, January 31, 2010, pp. A31, A35.

31. Mark Baldassare and Cheryl Katz, *The Coming Age of Direct Democracy* (Lanham, MD: Rowman and Littlefield, 2008), p. 104.

32. "Debt Affordability Report," California State Treasurer, October 2010, p. 5.

33. "The Best and Worst Run States in America: A Survey of All Fifty," *24/7 Wall Street*, October 4, 2010, http://247wallst.com/2010/10/04/the-best-and-worst-run-states-in-america-a-survey-of-all-fifty/.

34. Judith Lohman, OLR Research Report, January 2, 2009, http://www.cga.ct.gov/2009/rpt/2009-R-0009.htm.

35. "Debt Line," California Debt and Advisory Commission, Sacramento, CA, 29(1), 4, 2010.

36. "California's Increasing Debt Burden Threatens State's Ability to Fund Vital Infrastructure Projects," December 2009, p. 5, Kerstenscommunication.com.

37. Juliet Christian-Smith, Lucy Allen, Eli Moore, and Peter H. Gleick, "The 2010 California Water Bond: What Does It Say and Do?" Pacific Institute, Oakland, CA, August 2010, p. 27.

38. See Patrick McGreevy, "California Water Bond Pushed Back to 2012," *Los Angeles Times*, August 10, 2010, http://articles.latimes.com/print/2010/aug/10/local/la-me-water-bond-20100810, and "Lawmaker Backs 25% Cut in Bond," *San Francisco Chronicle*, January 21, 2011, p. C3.

39. Joe Mathews, "Props. 57, 58 in Final Drive," *Los Angeles Times*, February 28, 2004, http://articles.latimes.com/2004/feb/28/local/me-arnold28.

40. George Skelton, "Arnold was Unfaithful to Us," *Los Angeles Times*, May 19, 2011, p. A2.

Section IV

Restoring the Dream

11

Can This Patient Be Saved?

All the king's horses and all the king's men
Couldn't put Humpty together again.

—Humpty Dumpty poem

Or can we?

With 38 million residents, California is a single political jurisdiction constructed on a multi-faceted, uneven foundation. It is home to people with roots in more than 100 countries and all of the nation's states. Some are first-generation stakeholders, others go back hundreds of years, but now all are Californians. Many have assimilated; others have not. Ethnic enclaves within the state abound—some voluntarily, others not— whether they are Latinos in Los Angeles, Armenians in the Central Valley, Indians in Fremont, or Vietnamese in Westminster.

There are other differences. Wealth spans the state financial status ladder from the extremely rich at the top to the very poor at the bottom. To give you an idea, California has 90 billionaires, far more than second-place New York (70) or third-place Texas (40).[1] And yet, California ranks 4th of the 50 states in the per capita number of homeless people.[2] There is also the matter of the state's economy, which runs the gamut from agriculture to nanotechnology, from self-employed push cart operators to multinational corporations. Few state economies have so many components.

Diversity has produced a state rich in competing values, yet these days those same attributes often fail to blend in a healthy way that strengthens the loose weave. Their dissonance has yielded not one California but many Californias. There's entrepreneurial California, racially divided California, agriculturally productive California, patent-rich California, corporate California, anti-tax California, the California of hope, and the

California of despair. We are anything but one California, and in this very uneven state some parts suffer much more than others.

There's so much potential here—incredibly rich farm land, brilliant scholars and researchers, companies that begin with unique ideas one day that mushroom into multi-billion dollar corporate giants the next. When you look at these indicators, it's hard to believe that California is in decay. But not all indicators point in an upward direction; just look at the state's dysfunctional public education system, segregated housing patterns, dilapidated infrastructure, and the unwillingness of the public to support a revenue collection process that provides for those who are to infirm, too young, or too poor to provide for themselves. Just look at the inability of the state's leaders to govern sensibly and rationally in a political system that discourages governing. These indicators more than offset the upward tendencies, leaving most Californians gasping for hope.

Some astute observers have been ahead of the downward sloping curve in forecasting the state's troubles. More than a decade ago, Peter Schrag lamented California's downward drift when he wrote, "If California seemed to be a national model of high civic investment and engagement in the 1950s and 1960s, so it has become the lodestar of tax reduction and public disinvestment of the 1980s and 1990s."[3] That slippage has escalated into a free fall. Today, obstructionism and the status quo are the informal laws of the land. Substantial numbers threatened by the possibilities of change are virulently anti-tax, anti-government, anti-public anything, particularly if there is a cost to their status or well-being. More than ever, those who have resources roil against committing anything more than minimally necessary to government, whereas those who do not are left to cope on their own.

We are stuck in neutral, metaphorically speaking, if not reverse. Historical events, demographic conditions, economic clout, and politics have produced a "business as usual" arrangement that protects the privileged and ignores the powerless. To that end, increasingly the political process is manipulated by those with the most financial resources, leaving those without at a distinct disadvantage and destined to be left behind in a society. Worse yet, in all probability their children will never catch up. Meanwhile, the rules of governance discourage expertise among those in official positions of power through archaic processes and needless duplications of public authority—further successes for private interests at the public's expense. No wonder the state is struggling.

It's patently obvious that the California of today is a much different place than the California of 50 years ago. Ethnic minorities, once a small share of the population, are now the state's majority. Some may not like to admit it, but this development has left large numbers of whites uncomfortable, so much so that many are no longer willing to fund public institutions that provide social services disproportionately to less affluent nonwhites. At the same time, whites are losing their political base. Slowly but surely, nonwhites are voting in percentages closer to their actual population in the state. They have become increasingly restless from the largely white-led power structure that has not responded to their needs. In 1992, as southern California exploded after six Los Angeles police officers were acquitted for the unprovoked brutal beating of Rodney King—clearly videotaped—King pleaded on television, "Can we all get along?" There may not be riots today, but a quarter century later the question remains in California. Can we all get along? Can we collectively succeed in making California great again?

The intent of this chapter is to tie together the strands of information and insights about California presented in the foregoing pages. Looking back at California's colorful history and subsequent political development, we need to know how this once-open, vibrant environment has left so many without hope and the state's future in jeopardy. We need to understand what can be done to reverse this unacceptable trend, and why it is vital to do so. We also need to identify the most egregious obstacles in the state's governmental apparatus that thwart promotion of the public good at a time when so many individuals and interest groups have retreated from participating in the process.

But the book doesn't end with a critical diagnosis alone, for this "patient" is anything but dead. California still has a pulse, albeit a weak one. There is hope, even if it is hard to see in these very trying times. Toward the end of this chapter, we focus on positive steps that can make California successful again. As we have noted, this state is not without assets; in fact, it abounds with all kinds of wealth from precious natural resources to great minds and creative geniuses. Our task is to unlock the state's capabilities so that we all may move forward, but to do that will take both cooperation and sacrifice in a state where such commodities have been in short supply. Whether we are prepared to move forward in enough numbers with a shared vision is another matter.

A LACK OF DIRECTION

Inconsistency is everywhere in California when it comes to ideas for rescuing the state from both its financial difficulties and social ills. In fact, the two are intrinsically connected. Nearly everyone wants the state to move forward, yet few want to make the tough choices to ensure success. Many of the same leaders of corporations who desperately need highly trained employees resist paying their share of taxes necessary to educate those employees and provide for the public services they use. Many of the same residents who fret over rising crime and poor safety protest contributing more revenues to assure sufficient law enforcement and other local services. Many of the same people who suffer from poor air quality don't understand why the state needs to spend money regulating pollution rules. These claims are not without merit; in fact, they are demonstrated repeatedly through decisions we make at the voting booth and the actions of those we elect to office.

We suffer from a lack of commitment to make California great again. Some of the resistance to investment is philosophically based. There are among us those who believe the best government is the least government. These people have their share of success and leave it to others to get theirs, whether they are long-term Californians or new residents. Close by are those folks in the "middle class," many of whom have witnessed their standard of living slide with the state's faltering economy. That slippage has been accompanied by rampant fear—fear that these millions are losing forever the dream they once viewed as an inherent right and permanent part of their lives. Mistakenly, they see those below them on the economic ladder as a threat to their prosperity, rather than the big picture of an under-invested, perk-driven political environment in which the status quo guided by the few denies almost all of us prosperity.

For others, the resistance to commitment stems from profound ignorance about California's policymaking process and their rush to escape responsibility for understanding unattended issues and their consequences. In increasing numbers, these people choose to opt out rather than dig in. They know that the state is in a mess and throw their hands in the air hopelessly in disgust. By leaving responsibility to others, they add to their own peril as well as the peril of the rest of us.

In some ways, the first group can be forgiven more than the second can, for at least they are engaged in the political process albeit in a self-centered manner. As for the second group, their concoction of apathy and alienation are particularly threatening to a society that's lost its way.

While most Californians agree that the state is stuck in neutral, if not falling behind, there is little agreement on how to proceed. It seems much easier to point fingers of blame than to develop and follow through with any meaningful plan for systemic change. The fact is California has no direction because few want to pay the price to move forward. Such protectionism may succeed in the short term on an individual basis, but will surely fail down the road.

If a chain is only as strong as its weakest link, the few strong links in California surely will be pulled apart sooner or later from the many that are broken. Businesses require the elements of a sophisticated infrastructure to succeed, cities need to provide safety for their citizens, and individuals must have training and education to fulfill their potential. These ingredients make a polity successful, but they don't emerge out of thin air. Rather, they must be nurtured by basic government-sponsored programs and services that serve as critical building blocks. Those things can't be done without sufficient revenues gathered from all able to pay their fair share and be real partners.

POLICIES DETERMINED BY THE FEW

As demonstrated throughout this volume, California has an unusually varied demography, diverse population, and multi-faceted economy. Yet, a relatively small cadre of people in and out of government dominates the state. Their mastery lies in that these groups rarely tangle with one another. Instead, they have skillfully carved up the state for their own purposes and benefits, helping to disintegrate the whole into hapless, disconnected parts. Harmon Zeigler describes this phenomenon as "the triumph of many interests."[4] It's also the triumph of the powerful over the powerless.

The people who drive these power centers have had help both from a legislature frustrated by minority rule and from the voters who often find that they are casting ballots for or against proposals designed by the powerful for the powerful. It's not always the case, of course. There are those rare instances when private interests lose a fight, such as when PG&E suffered a bitter and embarrassing defeat at the polls in 2010. Nevertheless, more times than not, moneyed interests prevail in California with policies crafted to their benefit.

The legislature has been little help in stopping the powerful. With an absolute two-thirds vote requirement in each house to enact taxes, perpetuation of the status quo is practically guaranteed—except in cases when the powerful persuade legislators to provide special tax breaks or other benefits. That's what happened in 2009, when in the midst of attempting to close a whopping $42 billion state budget gap, corporate lobbyists persuaded the legislature to reduce their state income tax obligations by as much as $2 billion—this as programs and services were slashed to the bone to make ends meet. Term limits help promote the status quo to the extent that legislators are never in office long enough to grasp the issues in anything but superficial terms. Instead, they depend upon interest groups to help them "understand" what's going on, including preparation of proposed legislation ready for approval. Besides, with limited time in any elected position, the legislator is more likely to plot his or her next race than worry about the issues at hand.

Things aren't much better in the executive branch, which is replete with overlapping offices that add another level to citizen confusion, while allowing knowledgeable people to insinuate themselves in any one of multiple centers of authority. Add to these problems the more than 300 state boards and commissions and, well, you've got the makings of one confusing governing structure that offers little transparency.

As to the voters, it can only be said that Californians are a sorry lot when it comes to owning responsibility for their often thoughtless roles in public policymaking, particularly with respect to the management of ballot propositions. Most of us do little research on the issues, other than watching one-sided campaign commercials, the overwhelming proportions of which are aired by moneyed interests with skin in the game. It's a dismal exercise of citizenship. Voters are "prepared" in part by the public education system, which does a poor job teaching youngsters about their future citizenship roles. It's hard to blame educators, however, given a short academic year of overcrowded classrooms filled with outrageous expectations and few resources to meet them.

Rather than accept responsibility, the public points fingers at policymakers. After all, it's much easier to look elsewhere than do the spade work necessary to be active players in the process. So incensed is the public with the state legislature, for example, that nearly two-thirds support turning the institution into a part-time body,[5] as if meeting less frequently would result in more thoughtful policies. In their rush to make legislators more responsible through high vote thresholds and term limits, the voters fail to realize that full-time lobbyists and full-time bureaucrats—neither of whom are elected—would fill the policy gap with even more narrow perspectives than legislators, who at least are responsible to the voters who send them to office. The easy way out is rarely the best way out.

For the curious who dare to gather the facts by going to public agencies such as the secretary of state's office, good luck. Although the secretary of state's office is the state's chief record keeping unit, the material available there is almost impossible for the user to gather without an enormous amount of work. Such difficulty in extracting information is pervasive throughout the system. When the state legislature released the financial details of separate office budgets in 2011 after months of prodding by the press, the obfuscation of categories was so confusing that the exercise only incensed an already angry public.[6] It's almost as if the keepers of public information believe that if they inundate their sites with volumes of documents, the public will be satisfied that the information is "there" without ever mining it. Perhaps these information-gathering impediments exist as yet another example of an underfunded bureaucracy. If so, we've done ourselves a great disservice in the "penny wise, pound foolish" category.

WHAT SHOULD BE DONE?

Enough tearing down the not-so-Golden State; criticism is the easy part of describing the state's precarious condition. The question is what should be done? How can we make California golden again? Following are some ideas on what we shouldn't do was well as what we should do in the coming years to rescue our state.

A Constitutional Convention?

Many observers have asked these questions in recent years as the state has spiraled into disrepair. Often, their answer is to call a constitutional convention, wipe the state's slate clean of thousands of archaic laws and regulations, and begin anew. After all, the last constitutional convention was in 1879, a time when the state was rural, people communicated by telegraph and traveled by horse. How can we compare that era to the 21st century in a state that now houses 38 million people with instant information, ever-changing online technological applications, and mass transit?

On the surface, this suggestion makes a lot of sense. The number of issues at stake seems without end and the times certainly are different. Further consideration invites all kinds of nagging questions with few satisfactory answers. What topics would be considered at a constitutional convention, and how would they be determined? Who would be the attendees? What process would be used for selection of the attendees? Would the convention be open to the public or closed to participants only? How would the entire process be managed to give people the feeling that they have been heard? What processes would be in place for the voters to amend the decisions of the convention? Would the proposed constitution be sent to the legislature for consideration and possible changes before submission to the voters for final approval? And what assurances would there be that the very interests that already have special influence in state politics and policies would not be just as influential at the convention? After all, didn't the Southern Pacific Railroad hijack the outcome of the last constitutional convention in 1879, which attempted to place strict controls on the special interest giant?[7]

The call for a constitutional convention may sound simple and direct, but it's likely to precipitate many more problems than solutions. Instead, we need to address California's issues with a step-by-step, incremental basis much as we have in recent years by adopting a Citizens Redistricting Commission in place of legislative apportionment and changing the state budget adoption process to a simple majority instead of a two-thirds vote. In each case, the voters were given a specific proposal and responded with constitutional change. In the case of the Redistricting Commission, the voters rejected seven previous state ballot initiatives before saying "yes," but they did. We have templates for change, even if they don't move at the speed some would like.

So, how do we get there? How do we make California golden again? The remaining pages focus on specific changes such as infrastructure investment, better revenue streams, and the removal of unnecessary bottlenecks in the policymaking process. If undertaken one at a time and with sound voter education and public discussion, we may be able to work our way out of the mess we're in.

We Must Invest

For decades, Californians have not invested enough in our state to stay competitive with others in the national and international arenas. By not committing to first-class transportation networks, an up-to-date power grid, and a more efficient and safe water delivery system, we have made it more expensive to do business here. By not providing first-class public education and training, we have left businesses without an adequate workforce and denied our children the skills to thrive. By not embracing immigrants (to the extent that federal law allows) to assist in the fields as well as other areas of the workplace, we have jeopardized billions of dollars in crop harvests and harmed various aspects of the economy. In short, we have operated the state economy with one hand tied behind our backs.

Investments such as these cost money, but what shortsighted elected officials, self-centered special interests, and uninformed voters fail to realize is that they offer returns. We already know that thousands of jobs in technology companies and green industries go begging right here because we don't have the people with the right skills to take them. Is it better for California companies to bring in H-1B workers while California residents are unemployed? What makes more sense—to educate and train people or distribute social welfare funds to them? Surely, whatever the costs, the funds will be returned several-fold in the form of more tax-paying individuals and fewer state welfare dollars. But it starts with providing the necessary training to bring hundreds of thousands of Californians in the workplace. Raising tuition at local universities and colleges and tolerating high numbers of high school dropouts increase the costs of investments long-term rather than lowering them.

We Must Increase Revenues for Those Investments

Okay, take a deep breath before you continue. Initially, investing in the future will cost much more money than most Californians have been willing to spend, but we should be prepared to make the necessary sacrifices today to secure a healthy, stronger California tomorrow. There's no other way out of our mess. To those who want less government, this proposal may seem counter-intuitive. However, by increasing investment now, we actually can lower many government costs downstream as well as reduce state income tax and sales tax burdens for many Californians. Of course, any time you call for more revenues, you're stepping on some big toes. Yet, if we don't step now, we surely will be stepped on by other states and nations down the road.

To begin with, the legislature should reconsider every special interest tax break it has handed out to the tune of more than $4 billion in lost taxes annually. What benefit is there for the entire state when businesses are allowed to forego sales taxes when purchasing high-tech equipment? Why should farmers be able to write off their equipment expenditures when teachers and firefighters can't do the same with their new cars that take them to and from work? And why should yacht and RV owners be forgiven their sales tax charges if they keep their expensive toys outside California for at least 90 days after purchase before bringing them in state? None of these is fair to the rest of us. Surely, there are more examples of special interest treatment; it must stop. Beyond this general overhaul, following are some specific areas worthy of serious reform.

Spread Out the Sales Tax Structure

We can begin by spreading out the sales tax structure. Currently, we apply sales taxes only to about 40 percent of all items and services. We leave out all services such as attorney fees and car repairs; we exempt livestock, farm supplies, alternative energy equipment, technology purchases by businesses, and, of course, groceries. Whether we should add sales tax to all of these areas is a reasonable question for debate, but clearly we need to broaden the sales tax to many of these categories. Billions of dollars in sales tax are at stake. Some people would argue that the sales tax is "regressive" in that the poor would be hurt more than the rest of us because they have less disposable money and more sales tax-related needs. No argument. But, as noted previously, for California to obtain enough necessary revenues, everyone must sacrifice, even the poor.

Bring "Sin" Taxes into the 21st Century

Additional taxes on tobacco and alcohol are long overdue. They have not been changed in decades only because of the power of these industries to influence policy in their sectors. Unfortunately, when we think of the costs of alcoholism and tobacco-related illnesses to the state, the revenues we collect don't come close to covering the expenses. These taxes "hurt" only those who use the products. It's high time that the consumers of these products pay their fair share. An additional nickel per drink, for example, would bring in $600 million per year, and $1 per pack added to the cost of cigarettes would raise another $1.25 billion. In both cases, California taxes would remain far below sin taxes in the highest states.

Tax Those Who Have Not Been Taxed

Clearly, the oil industry is the poster child in this category. Thanks to incredible lobbying and manipulation of the voters, this industry has escaped paying a severance tax, leaving California the dubious honor of being the only oil-producing state that does not have such a revenue source. There might be an argument to the contrary if the oil industry was in financial trouble, but this sector of commerce has thrived and continues to amass enormous profits. Even anti-tax Republican Governor Arnold Schwarzenegger conceded the need for oil revenues in 2009 when he asked the legislature to pass a 9.9 percent severance tax, which would have brought in $855 million annually. Of course, the industry cried "poor" and that the proposal really would be a "pass through" tax on drivers. Of course, as with so many other instances, the legislature wimped out. The state can no longer afford a free ride for this industry or any other sacred cows. Revenues from the oil industry are long overdue.

Reform Proposition 13

No single change in California's tax system has been as harmful to revenue collection as Proposition 13, the property tax reduction ballot measure enacted by the voters in 1978. There were good reasons for taking action at the time, although the action steps were flawed. For several years prior to the proposition, local country assessors increased assessed property values at rapid rates, placing many citizens in jeopardy of losing their homes simply because of unacceptably high property taxes. The 57 percent reduction to 1 percent of the value of property at the time of purchase— and forever more during the period of ownership—guaranteed protection for homeowners as well as all other property owners. Of course, facilities like assembly plants, shopping malls, and amusement parks, to name a few, don't move locations as often as people who buy and sell homes, and therefore begin anew with the 1 percent property tax assessment on their changed places of residence. Therein lays the greatest inequity associated with Proposition 13. Commercial property owners have been suspended in 1978 ever since. For them, things have never been better. For the rest of the state, others now bear their burden.

It's time to correct this mistake. We can keep homeowner property taxes in place and let Howard Jarvis rest in peace. But taxes must be adjusted upward for commercial interests. As noted earlier, even a slight upward tick to 1.5 percent of market value would bring between $3 billion and $7 billion annually to local governments, depending upon the details of the formula, and remove the rescue burden from the state. State legislators, then, would be free to address other issues. Business interests are likely to whine that the change will make the local environment sufficiently uncompetitive to force them elsewhere. Yet we know that such claims are puffery and little more. A recent comprehensive study by the Public Policy Institute of California demonstrates beyond doubt that local taxes have little to do with the decisions of businesses to move from California elsewhere.[8] It's time to put that myth to rest and make businesses pay their share of property taxes.

We Must Remove Bottlenecks to Public Policymaking

We can make California governable again by removing several obstacles to the policymaking process. Along the way, we can provide long-overdue transparency that will help the public feel confident about our state and become more respectful of our leaders, rather than depressed and distrustful.

Streamline Commissions and Boards

We should start with elimination of most of the state's more than 300 commissions and boards. Created over the past 125 years, these entities have been given responsibilities for managing specific programs, services, and industries. Their members, once appointed, have virtually no accountability to anyone. Some appointments, particularly those boards with full-time salaries for part-time employees, are paybacks to former legislators or wealthy supporters of elected policymakers. In other cases, boards with part-time members have responsibility for major policy areas such as coastal management (California Coastal Commission) or transportation policy (State Transportation Commission). But many more are little more than examples of industry puffery that could easily be managed within the state's full-time bureaucracy. Do we really need an Off-Highway Motor Vehicle Commission? A Board of Forestry and Fire Protection? A California Apprenticeship Council?

These appointments might be nice perks for governors and legislators to distribute to political allies and contributors, but they do little to streamline the policymaking process. Most should be eliminated, and almost all with substantive responsibilities overlap with similar agencies in the state bureaucracy. In the past, some governors have tried to reduce the numbers of boards and commissions, including Arnold Schwarzenegger, who asked for the legislature to eliminate 88 such appointments, but had to settle for only one after lawmakers in both political parties and special interests loudly decried the proposal. In 2011, Governor Jerry Brown proposed eliminating 43 boards and commissions, and again was rejected by the legislature. We can do much better.[9]

Merge Overlapping Elected Offices and Agencies

We discuss this section with the recognition that the topic covers a pasture of sacred political cows, which makes the proposed changes all the more important. The executive branch is replete with overlapping offices that should be either eliminated or combined. A good place to begin is the lieutenant governor's office where, in reality, the most important responsibility for the officeholder is to learn whether the governor awakens each day. Once that's determined, his or her job is mostly done. The lieutenant governor replaces the governor if he or she dies or leaves office. That last happened in 1953 when then-Governor Earl Warren was appointed chief justice of the United States Supreme Court. Perhaps the only significant responsibility of the lieutenant governor is that he or she breaks a 20–20 tie in the state senate where he or she "presides" as president. But such outcomes hardly ever happen. Otherwise, the lieutenant governor is acting governor when the chief executive leaves the state. That might have been significant in the days of the Pony Express and telegraph, but that era is long gone and this office should disappear with it.

Nor do we need the treasurer, controller, and board of equalization offices; merger of these elected positions is long overdue. All of these offices deal with the collection, dissemination, and oversight of state revenues, most of which are sent to the Franchise Tax Board. It's only logical that these tasks would be better managed in a single office; at a minimum, there would be better organization and less confusion. Think of all the jobs that would go away with the elimination of overlap and duplication.

With respect to other independently elected offices in the executive branch, the insurance commissioner is a glorified record-keeping institution with little authority other than to monitor insurance practices; it has no ability to force companies to reduce rates. In function, its responsibilities greatly overlap the Consumer Services Agency, which is housed in the governor's office. A similar argument could be made for the awkward arrangement between the Superintendent of Public Instruction, an elected executive branch official, and the state Department of Education and state Board of Education. These three offices easily could be swept into the existing California Department of Education, with the head appointed by the governor.

Why such concentration of authority? The fact is that Californians know little about most elected offices in the executive branch. Routinely, we tend to vote for candidates who are best known for their previous positions in government or who have spent vast sums of money to gain recognition, rather than support someone who has expertise associated with the office. If we clean house and reduce the number of elected offices, we'll be doing the voters a big favor—even if it means eliminating California's version of the "Full Employment Act for Elected Officials."

These changes would not be without their share of controversy. You can only imagine the screams of outrage from elected officials, their staffs, and the interest groups that curry their favor. Such resistance only underscores the value of the suggestion.

On a less self-serving level, the argument can be made that these reorganization efforts will strengthen the governor's powers. Why not? This is the state's highest elected office. If we consolidate the governor's powers, that will enable him or her to govern more effectively, with voters in a better position to endorse or reject his or her policies through the ballot. And if we strengthen the legislature's powers as well (see next), the concept of checks and balances in California will be stronger than ever.

Eliminate Legislative Term Limits

Other than Proposition 13, legislative term limits may be California's biggest self-inflicted wound. Oddly enough, we enacted both of these changes as simple efforts to correct seriously dysfunctional governments. That's the problem—the changes were simplistic as well as simple. Neither has worked because the diseases were much more toxic than the prescriptions and few voters were interested in understanding the complete diagnosis. Californians enacted term limits in 1990 because of their frustration with the governing process and the people in charge of it. Naively, the voters believed that if we just keep turning people out of office, they won't have the opportunities to abuse them.

Of course, abuse can occur any time, and the fact is that with respect to corruption or malfeasance, California is one of the cleanest states in the nation.[10] On the other hand, studies show that term limits have backfired in California. The legislature is less independent as a policymaking body, both in terms of deference to outside interest and the governor. Effective leadership is inhibited by inexperience associated with the turnstile arrangement and members have little opportunity to develop the expertise required for their committee assignments.[11] Whatever the intentions of term limits, the artificial restraint on the lengths of elected service has wrought serious consequences for the institution, its members, and the state. Checks and balances have been tossed out the Capitol window.

Beyond the tilting of power, term limits are inherently undemocratic. Use of the practice almost assumes that the voters aren't capable of determining where or when to replace poorly performing legislators with their challengers. What an insult. Perhaps the argument could be made of the need for term limits in the days when the legislature redistricted itself every 10 years to assure safe districts for incumbents. But that's no longer the case, now that California has an independent Citizens Redistricting Commission. It's time to give back to the voters the capability to make decisions on who they want to serve and for how long. If nothing else, this will empower the voting public to take responsibility for its role in the political process.

Time for a Unicameral Legislature

Before *Reynolds v. Sims*, the 1964 U.S. Supreme Court case on malapportionment, there were reasons for bicameral bodies. Prior to that decision in California and most other states, the assembly represented people, while the senate represented land. Since *Reynolds*, however, the districts of both houses are organized by population. Meanwhile, California's population has grown so large that each state senate district contains more people than a congressional seat. Consequently, people are detached from their elected state legislators.

But imagine if the 120 seats of the assembly and senate were combined into one house. Now each district would be much smaller, about 315,000 people in terms of today's state population. Such reorganization could go a long way toward restoring the connection between the people and their elected officials. Districts will be smaller and more compact, making it easier for people to petition their elected officials.

There will be those who argue that two houses prevent bad legislation because legislators in one house can stop bad bills in the first house. That's a head scratcher, given the rash of bad legislation that emerges from both houses these days! Besides, with virtually every bill heard usually in two or three committees, if not more, there are plenty of opportunities to kill bad bills. In addition, the more we look into the issue of moving from a bicameral to unicameral legislature, we learn that the reasons for bicameralism are based more on tradition than contemporary political realism.[12] Simply put, this issue begs for serious examination, even if it is ultimately rejected. At a minimum, the concept of unicameralism should be considered as one approach to improving representation and closing the gap between the voters and elected public officials.

Restructure Direct Democracy

Once viewed as the mechanism for the voters to keep special interests from overpowering the state, the initiative and referendum have become the tools of wealthy private interests. These days, the formula is pretty simple: anyone with $2 million or $3 million can pay for campaign organizations to gather enough signatures to place a proposal on the ballot. That puts those without resources at a distinct disadvantage to those who have resources. The fact is that affluent interests have hijacked direct democracy, whether they are wealthy individuals, businesses associations, or organized labor. As a result, increasingly the ballot is stacked disproportionately with proposed laws designed by those with means. The Progressive reformers from more than a century ago are no doubt rolling in their graves.

We can change the proposition process by ratcheting up the requirements for ballot qualification. Instead of requiring 5 percent of the number of voters from the previous gubernatorial election to sign the necessary petition, we should increase the requirement to 10 or 15 percent. Larger percentages should be required for qualifying a constitutional amendment, which currently requires signatures from 8 percent of the voters. The idea here is that any change in the law should be the desire of a wide swath of the population, not the few. A higher signature threshold will increase the costs for affluent elements that seek to stack the political deck.

Along these lines, we should require that the legislature have the opportunity to respond to a ballot proposal before it goes before voters burdened with nonstop campaign messages. If the legislature doesn't respond to a qualified ballot measure within a specific time period, perhaps 120 days, then the measure would go before the voters at the next scheduled election. This would make the legislature accountable and relieve the public from any unnecessary burdens. That's the way it works in Washington State and a few other states and, as a result, many issues are resolved before they appear before the voters.

Happily, the legislature is finally beginning to consider some reforms, powerful opposition notwithstanding. In 2011, several legislators introduced bills to restrict placement of initiatives only in November elections, the time of the highest voter turnout. Legislators also proposed to raise filing fees as part of an effort to reduce frivolous initiative efforts, to permit the legislature to act on proposed initiatives prior to their presence on the ballot, and increase transparency regarding those who fund these efforts.[13] These early efforts have met with resistance, even from Governor Jerry Brown, who vetoed a bill that would have outlawed payments to signature gatherers on the grounds that the consequences might be worse than the abuses.[14] Resistance of the establishment notwithstanding, California's initiative process must be cleaned up.

Redefine State/Local Fiscal Relationships

Because Proposition 13 weakened the ability of local governments to collect revenues for local uses, local governments have sought to offset their losses by turning to the state to fund local programs and services, including public education. But tough times have made it difficult for the state to help local governments, given the structural deficit discussed earlier in this volume. We need to come up with a system that allows local governments to raise enough revenues to satisfy their needs.

The easiest way to facilitate revenue at the local level would be by allowing local cities and counties to raise taxes and fees through simple majority votes of the public. In actuality, we've gone in the other direction, considering the passage of Proposition 26, the Supermajority to Pass New Taxes and Fees Act, passed by the voters in 2010. Under the terms of this initiative, local governments must acquire a two-thirds vote from the voters for just about any new tax or fee.

This must change. With each passing year, local governments will have a more difficult time meeting the needs of their citizens with services such as law enforcement, libraries, parks, road maintenance, and most of all, K–12 public education. Without the ability to self-fund, local governments will wither away. We've already seen a few cities declare bankruptcy, while others have all but decimated public safety and other traditional local government services.

Not all local governments have suffered to the same extent. These days, affluent areas either pass taxes by the often-required two-thirds votes or simply turn to privately financed services, whether they're in education, security patrols, or private clubs in place of public parks. The less affluent continue to downsize public services because of shriveling tax bases and the inability to gain two-thirds votes from income-challenged communities.

By establishing a simple majority vote for local government taxation of any kind, the citizens of these entities can take more responsibility for their own well-being. Not all elections will capture majority approval, but at least the system will not be stacked against the general public. Furthermore, once relieved of the pressure to assist local governments, state policymakers will be free to focus on statewide issues. It's a win-win, except for the forces who want to prevent the majority from having its say.

Merge Local Government Units

As part of the new state/local arrangement, local governments need to consolidate wherever possible. Perhaps the best way to facilitate the change would be by the state legislature passing a law that sets minimum sizes for any local government unit, whether a city, school district, or special district dealing with topics such as water, lights, or mosquito abatement. Tremendous savings can occur with consolidation, assuming reasonable geographical boundaries. This is not to say that consolidation is always right; in fact, a school district like the huge Los Angeles Unified School

District might benefit from dividing into smaller, more manageable units. But in most cases, consolidation has merit, even for adjacent small towns with police departments, fire departments, and other services. If people can just get over the idea of "their" local school district or fire department, real efficiencies can take place.

Some might argue that such changes will generate a spike in unemployment among local government employees. If this turns out to be the case, so be it. The fact is that whereas local governments were relatively far apart, today they are virtually on top of each other. This reality of the 21st century should be acknowledged and reflected in the organization of modern local government units. Governments should not be designed as full employment agencies, but rather as institutions to provide needed services for citizens in efficient ways.

Challenges to Widening the Political Bottleneck

Let's not kid ourselves; overcoming these challenges will be a daunting task, but not an impossible task. Yes, most of the proposals discussed in this section will require changes through constitutional amendments and face formidable opposition. And yes, the forces of the status quo are powerful in California, especially because they are consistently able to protect the privileges of the few. Fair enough, but that doesn't mean that change can't prevail, especially if reformers are patient and take these or other proposals to the public one at a time. In all likelihood, such proposals will require several efforts, yet they will be worth the wait if we can get California moving again.

A LITTLE KUMBAYA WOULDN'T HURT

Finally, a thought or two about the people of this state, many of whom have lost their way. California has transformed into such a complicated place over the years that it's become difficult for many of its facets to connect. Large elements of the population have been left behind, others no longer care, and others still are just plain angry. Like an inefficient machine, Californians these days are wasting a lot of political energy. To find our way collectively again, we have to think differently, act differently, and dream differently. In short, we need to embrace a shift in the current framework that no longer works for most of us. Three places to start would be with better training and education, the development of tolerance, and efforts to build political efficacy.

Training and Education

A strong workforce is a bedrock for a successful society. More than most states, California suffers a disconnect between available jobs and the capabilities of those who would take them. We need an education system that teaches students the skills they need for the 21st century workforce. Data tell the story: the United States has fallen well behind dozens of countries in preparing its students,[15] and California has fallen off the education bus altogether. These realities have been noted here and elsewhere. Our best hope of becoming an economic juggernaut once again is by investing in the next generation and those that follow. That includes dramatic fund increases for reduced classroom sizes, better-trained and -paid teachers (with poorly functioning teachers weeded out), and longer school years for openers. We'll need to spend even more in our poorest areas with the greatest numbers of under-achievers who should be incorporated into society rather than pushed out.

Where do we get the resources to improve public education? Some savings can be found through careful reorganization of the more than 1,000 school districts into more rational models of administration. We should eliminate every wasteful dollar from duplication and excessive administrative costs. Beyond that, we must raise the necessary money through taxes, with all elements of society sharing the burden. Yes, this calls for sacrifice, but the burden we bear now will pay off in bounty later with fewer dropouts and more employed people in better-paid jobs. Every day and every school year, we're falling further behind in this effort. The sooner we commit, the sooner California begins its economic recovery from the bottom up.

Tolerance

There's more. In 21st century America, schools are more than centers of education and training. More than ever, they have become critical agents of socialization. This quality is in short supply in what has become one of the most diverse states in the nation. We can't leave to chance the possibility that people from different backgrounds and cultures will automatically accept one another—clearly, that's not the case. But we can use the school as a harmonizing platform to show students of different backgrounds the many values they share in common while appreciating their many differences. This may sound overly simplistic to many, but the fact remains that in our racially and ethnically diverse society, we have become much more adept at separating ourselves from each other than understanding and embracing our differences. Socialization begins early in life, and the best place to bridge differences and build bonds is in the schools.

Some of this should come from the requirement of a second language for all students from the earliest years on. There are at least two significant benefits from such a re-tooling effort. First, in this age of globalization, we can't expect others around the world to work with us in English; we need to know their languages, too, in order to be successful in many jobs. In California, students would benefit particularly from learning Spanish, Vietnamese, or Mandarin Chinese either because of the large numbers with those backgrounds here or because of the business we do elsewhere. Other languages would be welcome as well. The second benefit would accrue from understanding the history and cultural values that accompany the learning of another language. The acquisition of such information would further contribute to breaking down the barriers that have come to divide Californians.

Another way to facilitate understanding of diverse backgrounds could come through statewide implementation of programs like Green Circle. Created in 1957, this program is designed to help students learn how to respect each other irrespective of differences in race, ethnicity, or religion. Such efforts could go a long way toward improving the quality of overall education and reducing behavior problems. They may not help the adults who got us into this mess, but they can become powerful steps toward a better future.

Political Efficacy

Also in the kumbaya tool kit is the need for our citizens to develop a greater sense of political efficacy. Too many Californians now believe that the state's condition is near hopeless, that their voices aren't heard, and that our institutions are no longer responsive to the state's needs. This pervasive alienation is a threat to both the "haves" and "have-nots" as well as in between. For the "have-nots," the larger their numbers grow, the more their dropping out will create a greater drag on the political environment, whether in unemployment, crime, or a growing collective malaise. For the "haves," they will discover increased difficulty in managing society, not to mention the growing need to protect their resources with gated communities, private education, and the other amenities no longer available to the rest of the state. Long term, no one wins with such extremes in play.

As with so many of California's ills, there is no magic potion to cure citizen alienation. Nevertheless, there are steps we can take to help people feel part of the process again. Once more, we turn to the schools, where students can learn the value of political involvement through various education techniques. One program, "Project Citizen," is a portfolio-based curriculum that introduces students to the policymaking process through the identification of public problems, research on their harm, investigation of solutions, and determination of which policymakers can actually solve the problems. The curriculum can work at any level of education from the earliest years in elementary school to university. Elementary students might focus on a problem such as a broken drinking fountain or poor quality cafeteria food, whereas college students might examine something like plagiarism, uneven healthcare, or high school dropouts. In each case, the protocol is the same. The idea is for students to discover a public problem, understand the harm it brings to society, and recommend solutions as well as the appropriate policymakers to address the issues.

Studies show that as students become familiar with the political process, they will embrace it rather than run from it or throw up their hands in disgust. Moreover, the efficacy they develop from these experiences at a young age will continue throughout their lives. With this kind of socialization and political knowledge, they become learned participants instead of disaffected, uninformed observers.

FINDING COMMON PURPOSE AGAIN

Just as California has a rich past, it can have a rich future. The state has a glorious history of innovation, abundant human energy, and incorporation of endless streams of talent into an often-dynamic collage. The entrepreneurialism that appeared with California's first settlers continues to this day in areas ranging from agricultural breakthroughs to high technology. These traits are vintage California, but the state's luster has dulled considerably in recent years.

Too many Californians have left others behind, whether because of businesses outsourcing jobs, citizens fearing immigrants, or unions protecting unfit teachers. Too many narrow interests have sought to protect their own turf to the extent of stomping on others. Too many "haves" have shut the door on "have-nots," whether by refusing to support public schools or rejecting taxes intended to improve elements of the state's infrastructure. In the process of all these changes, Californians have lost sight of California. This must change.

By adopting some of the changes recommended previously, California can return to greatness. By being smarter in the ways we govern, investing more in our infrastructure, and committing additional resources to the state's future, we can make California golden again. But political change will not occur without social and cultural change. That begins with each person acknowledging that the state's future depends upon our willingness to sacrifice more now for a better tomorrow. Whether Californians are up to the task remains to be seen. But one fact is certain: The rest of the nation, and in fact the world, will be impacted by the next chapter of the California experiment.

ENDNOTES

1. Janet Fowler, "Top 9 States with the Most Billionaires," *Financial Edge*, May 10, 2011, http://financialedge.investopedia.com/financial-edge/0511/Top-9-States-With-The-Most-Billionaires-.aspx#axzz1WiuaZwkC.
2. "State of Homelessness in the United States in 2009," National Alliance to End Homelessness, Washington, D.C., January 10, 2011, Chapter 12, p. 9.
3. Peter Schrag, *Paradise Lost: California's Experience, America's Future* (Berkeley, CA: University of California Press, 1998), p. 275.
4. Harmon Zeigler, "Interest Groups in the States," in Virginia Gray, Herbert Jacob, and Kenneth Vines, Eds., *Politics in the American States*, 4th ed. (Boston, MA: Little, Brown Publishers).
5. USC Dornslife/*Los Angeles Times* Poll, July 21, 2011.
6. "Political Accounting," editorial, *San Francisco Chronicle*, August 30, 2011, p. A9.
7. George E. Mowry, *The California Progressives* (Berkeley, CA: The University of California Press, 1951), p. 18.

8. Jed Kolko, David Neumark, and Marisol Cuellar Mejia, "Business Climate Rankings and the California Economy," Public Policy Institute of California, San Francisco, CA, April 2011.

9. "Gov. Pulls Plan to Abolish Panels," *Los Angeles Times*, February 18, 2005, pp. B1, 10.

10. "Louisiana Most Corrupt State in the Nation, Mississippi Second, Illinois Sixth, New Jersey Ninth," *21 Corporate Crime Reporter 40,* October 8, 2007, http://www.corporatecrimereporter.com/corrupt100807.htm.

11. For an excellent review of term limits in California, see Bruce E. Cain and Thad Kousser, "Adapting to Term Limits: Recent Experiences and New Directions," Public Policy Institute of California, San Francisco, CA, 2004.

12. See "Bicameral vs. Unicameral Legislatures," South Dakota Legislative Council, Issue Memorandum 98-03, 1998, and "Hawaii Should Adopt a Unicameral Legislature," *Honolulu Star Bulletin*, January 24, 2010.

13. "Ballot Measure Changes Weighed," *Los Angeles Times*, August 30, 2011, pp. AA1, AA4.

14. "Bills Would Rein in State Initiatives," *Los Angeles Times*, August 27, 2011, pp. A1, A14.

15. Motoko Akiba, Gerald K. LeTendre, and Jay P. Scribner, "Teacher Quality, Opportunity Gap, and National Achievement in 46 Countries," *Educational Researcher*, October 2007, p. 374.

Index

Printed by Publishers' Graphics Kentucky